In Sierra Leone

MICHAEL JACKSON

In Sierra Leone

Duke University Press Durham & London 2004

© 2004 Duke University Press

All rights reserved

Printed in the United States of
America on acid-free paper ∞

Designed by C. H. Westmoreland

Typeset in Carter & Cohn Galliard
by Keystone Typesetting, Inc.

Library of Congress Cataloging-
in-Publication Data

Jackson, Michael.

In Sierra Leone / Michael Jackson.

p. cm.

Includes bibliographical references.

ISBN 0-8223-3301-5 (cloth : alk. paper)

ISBN 0-8223-3313-9 (pbk. : alk. paper)

1. Jackson, Michael, 1940–
2. Anthropologists — Sierra Leone —
Biography. 3. Political anthro-
pology — Sierra Leone. 4. War and
society — Sierra Leone. 5. Marah,
Sewa Bockarie. 6. Kuranko (African
people) — Biography. 7. Sierra
Leone — Social conditions. 8. Sierra
Leone — Politics and government.
I. Title.

GN21.J337A3 2004

301′.092 — dc22

2003019451

To the Memory of

SEWA BOCKARIE ("S. B.") MARAH 1934–2003

and NOAH BOCKARIE MARAH 1942–2003

"that the path not die"

A Klee painting named "Angelus Novus" shows
an angel looking as though he is about to move away
from something he is fixedly contemplating. His eyes are
staring, his mouth is open, his wings are spread. This is
how one pictures the angel of history. His face is turned
toward the past. Where we perceive a chain of events, he
sees one single catastrophe which keeps piling wreckage
upon wreckage and hurls it in front of his feet. The angel
would like to stay, awaken the dead, and make whole what
has been smashed. But a storm is blowing from Paradise;
it has got caught in his wings with such violence that the
angel can no longer close them. This storm irresistibly
propels him into the future to which his back is turned,
while the pile of debris before him grows skyward. This
storm is what we call progress. — Walter Benjamin,
Theses on the Philosophy of History

Contents

Illustrations

Sierra Leone

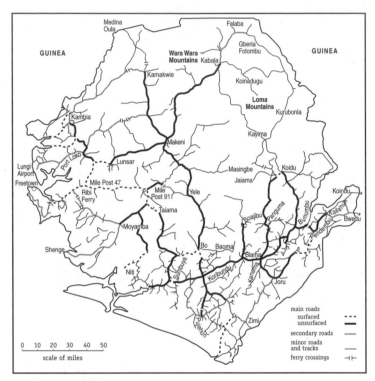

·Roads in Sierra Leone

1 Night Flight to Freetown

In the late 1960s, the English writer Graham Greene, expressing his fondness for the West African country where he had spent time during the Second World War, referred to Sierra Leone as "soupsweet land." When I first went to Sierra Leone in 1969 to do ethnographic fieldwork for my Ph.D., Greene's affectionate comments and famous signature were still in the guest book at Fourah Bay College, where Pauline (my first wife) and I stayed for a while before going north. Before long, the ebullience and piquancy of life in Sierra Leone captivated me, and though the ominous shadows of a corrupt regime and bankrupt economy were increasingly evident in ordinary people's complaints, frustrations, and fears, it was still easy for a stranger like myself, living up-country in a remote town or village, to imagine that life would go on as it always had, despite the hardships. Then, in 1991, fighting in Liberia spilled over into eastern Sierra Leone, fomenting a rebellion that quickly gathered force. In the years that followed, the Revolutionary United Front laid waste to the country whose soul it had purportedly set out to save, killing, raping, and maiming tens of thousands of innocent people. In the West, media images of amputations and atrocities committed on civilians by "child soldiers" toting AK-47s reinforced, in many minds, a view of Africa as a place of incorrigible savagery. After the intervention of, first, a Nigerian-led military force, then the UN, the rebellion was finally crushed. And in January 2002, as Sierra Leone prepared to announce the end of the war, I went back to the "soupsweet land" to find out what fate had befallen the people with whom I had once worked and lived, and to see how their stories might be fitted into the broken mosaic of the decade through which, as the Mande say, God slept.

During the years I had been away, my friend Sewa Bockarie Marah had been urging me to help him write his autobiography. After a political career spanning the four decades since Sierra Leone's independence in 1961, and interrupted by two stints in prison as a political detainee and ten months of exile during the war, S. B. was now one of the president's right-hand men, and had, no doubt, an intriguing story to tell. But was I the best person to assist him in this task? Though I knew something of his illustrious Kuranko heritage and his political constituency in the north, and had long been fascinated by Hannah Arendt's notion of the political as a power relationship between private and public realms,[1] I balked at the prospect of venturing into the vexed and often duplicitous world of Sierra Leone politics. Besides, unlike his younger brother Noah, who had been my close companion and field assistant for many years, and had introduced me to S. B. in 1970 when he was managing the Alitalia agency in Freetown (during a five-year break from politics, following his party's electoral defeat in 1967), S. B. had always been a somewhat remote and enigmatic figure to me. And I did not want to compromise myself by writing hagiography. Yet, as I made ready to leave for Sierra Leone, none of these misgivings seemed to matter.

Perhaps the reasons for this change of heart could be divined in my dreams, or lay in the impasse I had reached in my writing, for in the days before I left Copenhagen, its public squares half-covered with dirty, frozen snow, and the air misty and dank, my mind was crowded with images of renewal.[2] There are times when we need to break with routine, to get away from it all, and start over. But how can such fantasies of a new beginning be reconciled with the reality of the world of which one is already and inescapably a part? And how can the quest for renewal avoid the destructiveness of revolution?[3]

Daybreak was still three hours away when the night flight from Gatwick landed at Lungi, and I followed the other disembarking passengers across the tarmac to the dismal hangar that served as an arrivals hall. "Under Rehabilitation," read the sign on the wall. "Sorry for all Inconvenience and Discomfort."

Under dim fluorescent lights, I waited as baggage was manhandled from a trailer, and everybody jostled around the low tables on which it was dumped. After retrieving my bag, I let myself be pushed along by the crowd to where helicopter tickets to the city were being sold. Then I made my way to the north end of the old airport building where people were waiting for the first helicopter. British soldiers in mufti. Aid workers. NGO personnel. Businessmen from Russia, Eastern Europe, and Lebanon. Returning Sierra Leoneans. A few minutes later it began to rain, unusual for January, and as the first helicopter settled awkwardly onto the tarmac its spotlights rendered the rain visible, like scratch marks on glass.

Since I was scheduled to take the second helicopter I passed the time talking to a young man from Lungi village who worked part-time for the helicopter company, loading and unloading baggage. When I asked Isa how the war had affected his life, he told me that his brother had been abducted by rebels while traveling from Kenema to visit their father in 1996. Though he managed to escape, he came home with a bullet in his knee, which now caused him great pain and prevented him from working. "During the war, everyone was alone," Isa said. "Everyone had to fend for himself. There was no order."

It was still pitch dark and raining heavily when the dilapidated helicopter crossed the broad expanse of the Sierra Leone river, with me a nervous passenger, and followed the coast southward towards Lumley. When we landed, I breathed a sigh of relief, and clambered quickly out. The helicopter's spotlights illuminated the wet sea grass battered by the downdraft from the rotor blades.

I had taken no more than a few steps when a young man with a broad smile walked up to me and introduced himself as S. B.'s nephew and namesake. Small S. B.'s instructions were to drive me directly to my hotel. "Uncle says you are to get some sleep, eat breakfast, and then call him," he said. "Then I will come back and drive you to the house."

After two hours' shallow sleep, I went to the hotel dining room for a breakfast of dry bread and jam, instant coffee, and a plate of sliced papaya and pineapple. Then I phoned S. B. and returned to my room to wait, only to find myself besieged by memories, as unspecific as they were unassuageable — the smell of the woodwork, a curious mingling of varnish and mildew . . . the frangipani and bougainvillea outside my window . . . the long stretch of Lumley beach, its ochre and buff sands scoured by the unceasing tides.

S. B.'s house was in the hills, overlooking the west side of the city and the sea. When I entered the parlor, Sewa rose from the chair in

which he was sitting, heavier than I remembered him, and moving with difficulty, but essentially unchanged. The same odd mixture of charismatic self-confidence and acute sensitivity.

We shook hands, and he asked me about my flight, and whether the hotel accommodation he had arranged was to my liking. Although I said I was happy with the arrangement, I had been mystified when he phoned the night before I left Copenhagen to say he had booked me into a hotel in order that I should have "peace and quiet," for in the past I had always stayed with Sewa and Rose, and peace and quiet had never been an issue.

When I told S. B. I was looking forward to collaborating on his biography, he said that he already had the title for the book. "Within These Four Walls. I have had it in mind for many years. But I am tied up today. We have a crisis in Parliament. One of our senior ministers has resigned." And he abruptly called for small S. B. to come, and for one of the houseboys to bring him a cap. "But don't worry," he said,

as he walked toward the door, adjusting his cap on his head. "We will be going north the day after tomorrow and we will have plenty of time to discuss our business then."

Within minutes of S. B's departure, Rose entered the room. Fuller in the face and figure than when I last saw her, she was still stunningly beautiful. We embraced with tears in our eyes, marveling at how swiftly the years of separation were annulled, as if no time at all had passed since we were last together. I then showed Rose several photos of Heidi, my daughter, and of my wife Francine and our two children building a snowman with Heidi in a churchyard near Sankt Hans Torv on Christmas day. As for Rose's children, they were now, like Heidi, young adults, and all living in London where they had taken refuge from the war.

"But you know," Rose said, "I was expecting that you would be staying here as you always do. I had prepared your room. Then S. B. told me that you would be staying in the Cape Sierra hotel. But this is your home, Mike; you must come and eat here whenever you like."

I asked Rose about S. B's younger brother Noah, with whom I had done my fieldwork during the 1970s and 80s. How could I get in touch with him?

It had already been arranged. Noah was aware I was arriving today and he would come to the house that afternoon.

Of all my reunions, this was the most overwhelming. When Noah walked into the room, I did not recognize him at first because of the glare from the doorway behind him, and because he was wearing glasses. But then he emerged from the shadows, and we fell into each other's arms, clasping each other, tears rolling down our cheeks, and when we sat down together on the sofa and began to talk we continued to touch each other, as though still unable to grasp the transformation that had just occurred. If the sights and smells of Freetown had reawakened memories of a long-eclipsed period of my life, then seeing Noah again was as if a lost part of my soul had been restored to me.

"I cannot find words for what I feel," Noah said, "but seeing you is like being born again."

"It's the same for me," I said. And I had a fleeting memory of some lines I had read the night before in W. G. Sebald's *Austerlitz,* while waiting for my flight at Gatwick, about the compulsion we sometimes feel to go in search of places and people in our past we have all but forgotten, to keep a rendezvous with them, and thereby, perhaps, create some semblance of unity in our own lives.[4]

When I last saw Noah, he had been working as a trade inspector in Koidu. What had happened to him since then?

"I continued to work as a trade inspector," Noah said, "but I was transferred several times. From Koidu I moved to Port Loko. Then to Makeni. Finally Lunsar. I was suffering from glaucoma, and had to have an operation. But the rebels were threatening Lunsar at that time, and the two expatriate doctors had to flee the town within a day of performing the second operation. They had given me medication, and bandaged my eyes, but when the rebels broke into my house and took me captive I had to leave everything behind. They taunted me. They said 'Pappy, here, drink' and thrust a bottle of beer at me. I said I didn't drink. They pushed a cannabis cigarette into my mouth. I told them I didn't smoke. I said: 'Would I eat if I were not hungry?' From Lunsar we walked to Masimera where we stopped for two days. I asked if I could talk to their C.O. They said 'What! A civilian like you wanting to see our C.O.!' One of them lifted his weapon to show what would happen if I went on pushing my luck."

Four days later, Noah said, the rebels abandoned him in a Temne village. His eyes were no longer bandaged, and he was in a lot of pain. In the months that followed he lost the sight of one eye, and now had only limited vision in the other. Unable to return to teaching school — which he was doing when I first met him — and with little hope of finding any other work, he survived in Freetown on his wits, scrounging money to buy rice and food for his family and pay school fees for his kids.

That afternoon small S. B. drove Noah and me downtown, and I saw some of the changes that had come to the city in my years away. The City Hotel, where my wife and I stayed when we first came to Sierra Leone in 1969, had been a casualty of the war, though one of the coconut palms in the forecourt had survived the fire that gutted the building.

It was strange to look up at the windowless concrete space where our

room had been, and to think further back to when Graham Greene killed time here during the war, later describing his character Wilson, at the beginning of *The Heart of the Matter,* as sitting on the balcony with "his bald pink knees thrust against the ironwork . . . his face turned to the sea."

We drove east to Noah's sister's house, so that I could pay my respects to their mother, Aisetta Sanfan. Physically not much more than skin and bone (S. B. and Noah were convinced that their mother was at least a hundred years old), Aisetta was lying on a palliasse on the floor of a back bedroom. I had never expected to see her again, and as I touched her shoulder and greeted her I felt as though I was reaching out across an unbridgeable gulf. Then her eyes flickered open. "How is Heidi?" she whispered, without stirring. "Is she there?" My daughter had been born in Sierra Leone, and Aisetta had cared for her when she was a baby.

"No," I said, "but she promises to be with me next time I come, and she sends her love." When Aisetta closed her eyes it was as though she were closing them on a world of immense sorrow and disappointment.

By the time we returned through the East End, the narrow, potholed streets were clogged with traffic and the air thick with exhaust fumes. Along Kissy Road I saw more of the destruction left by the rebels three years before — the fire-blackened laterite walls of public buildings and churches, concrete facades pockmarked from gunfire. An unbroken stream of people flowed and eddied around the stalled lines of *poda podas*, overladen lorries, broken-down taxis, *omolankeys*, and white Land Cruisers. UNHCR. Save the Children Fund. Child Rescue Mission. Planned Parenthood. Save the Youth. Sight Savers International. I could not but wonder how many people were actually helped by this influx of NGOs and foreign aid, and thinking of Noah's failing eyesight I asked him if he had ever sought help from any of these agencies. His attitude was both stoic and skeptical. Despite all the rhetoric of reconstruction, rehabilitation, and resettlement, he knew the odds against anyone receiving immediate benefit. "The leg that steps forward is soon enough the leg that steps back," he said, citing the Kuranko adage, as if one had no choice but to accept things as they were, and live one day at a time without great expectations or undue hope. "Things change," he added, "but seldom because of anything we say or do."

"Nonetheless," I said, "we must see what we can do for you."

In a small yard, some young men in shorts were playing soccer with a half-inflated football. Whenever we came to a standstill, kids clamored at the window of the car with packets of bubble gum and biscuits, bottle openers, disposable razors, key rings, and pocket calculators. Along every street, women sat at small tables, selling onions, tomato paste, bunches of cassava leaf, magi cubes, bottles of palm oil, bundles of split firewood, groundnuts, charcoal, kola nuts, loaves of bread, and peeled oranges. And in small booths made of lashed poles and corrugated iron, men and women plied their

trades — making furniture, dying cloth, cutting hair, selling enamel-ware, shoes and sandals, stationery, and lottery tickets.

So many people waiting, I thought. Waiting for a transaction or lucky break that would make the difference between having food and going hungry. I found myself reading the slogans emblazoned on the poda podas and lorries around us — Allah Is in Control. God Is Great. Better Days Are Coming. Be Yourself. Respect Education. Never Give Up. Still With My Paddle Nevertheless. Labor and Expect. No Condition Is Permanent. Then, mindful of Noah's long wait for a change in his fortunes, I asked him if he was still *sunike* — the Kuranko word for a person who was neither Muslim nor Christian.

"I have never embraced any moral system," Noah said, "and I hope I never will."

It crossed my mind to ask Noah why some of us need to believe that there is some overarching or implicate order in the world that rewards virtue, punishes evil, and reveals meaning, while others of us accept the arbitrariness of fate, or at least renounce the possibility of divining its hidden workings, and — considering it as foolish to congratulate ourselves when fortune favors us as it is to express outrage or envy when it does not — focus on steadying ourselves in the midst of life's flux, struggling to embrace both the rough and the smooth with equanimity. But I said nothing.

It was almost dusk when I left Noah, and small S. B. drove me back to my hotel. The tide was out, and as we approached the Aberdeen ferry bridge, I asked small S. B. to slow down so that I could look for S. B.'s old house on the edge of the inlet. Another casualty of the war, it stood in ruins near a grove of huge mango trees. Out on the mudflats, women and children were searching for shellfish, and I remembered an evening, long ago, sitting on the balcony and looking at this very scene, when Rose told me that it was from here that the slave ships set sail for the Americas with their human cargoes. At that moment, small S. B. broke into my thoughts, telling me that scores of rebel soldiers were brought to the bridge in January 1999, summarily shot, and their bodies thrown into the bay.

As the bluish twilight settled over the mangroves, the mudflats, and the sinuous channels of water beneath us, I found myself thinking how easily scenes of horror and tranquility succeed each other on the same stage, and recalled Marlowe's words in *Heart of Darkness*, as he and his companions watched the light fading on the sea-reach of the Thames: "And this also has been one of the dark places of the earth."

2 The North

The ostensible reason for our journey north was to launch the Civil Defence Force Wives, Widows, and War Orphans' Development Project in Koinadugu District. But this was also to be S. B.'s triumphal return home after years of war and exile. Following a series of last-minute phone calls to hire a minibus for the musicians and newspaper reporters, borrow some electrical cables and lights, and order supplies of mineral water, S. B. asked me if there was anything in particular I needed for the trip. Though I knew that S. B. would not agree, I asked if Noah could accompany us. There is no room, S. B. said, and quickly changed the subject by asking if I wanted a bodyguard. Much to S. B.'s delight, I declined the offer.

It had been planned that we would leave early that morning, but it was nearly midday before the piles of suitcases, blankets, generators, amplifiers, bags of rice and onions, tins of palmoil, and cartons of enamelware, tomato paste, and dry fish were loaded onto the various vehicles and we finally got away. I was in the backseat of a Toyota 4-Runner, directly behind S. B. and in the company of two of his staunchest allies, while small S.B., who had been under a relentless barrage of orders all morning, was at the wheel. In other vehicles were M.P.s from northern districts, numerous Sierra Leone People's Party stalwarts, and leaders of the Civil Defence Force Wives, Widows and War Orphans' Development Project, which was to be officially launched at the weekend rally in Kabala.

As we passed the forbidding concrete walls of Pademba Road

Prison, S. B. remarked that this was where he had conceived the title of his book. These were the four walls he had spoken of.

It was here, in 1974, following a bomb explosion on the night of 29 July at the house of Minister of Finance C. A. Kamara-Taylor, that thirty-five opposition leaders, including S. B., were incarcerated under the Public Emergency Regulations. Within a month of their arrest, fifteen of these men appeared in the high court in Freetown charged with treason and plotting the overthrow of the government, and in November all were found guilty and sentenced to death. I was living in New Zealand at the time, and got wind of S. B.'s plight when my application for a visa, in which I had named S. B. as a reference, was turned down, and when Noah, who was then teaching at the Wallace Johnson School in Freetown, wrote to say that S. B. was in detention. Enlisting the assistance of Amnesty International, who immediately took up the case, I wrote numerous letters to S. B.'s former employers, urging them to petition the president for S. B.'s release, and addressed several submissions to President Siaka Stevens, asking whether Sewa Bockarie Marah was indeed a prisoner, what charges had been brought against him, and when he would be brought to trial. It was not until the end of the following year that I received a reply from the president's office, the wording of which was as wry as it was cynical *(see overleaf)*.

"Either you are in power or in prison," I remarked to S. B., and my mind again went back to Noah's situation, and to the volatility of life and the unpredictability of fate. Perhaps Noah was right. One could do little but remind oneself that the wheel of fortune turned, and that, as the Kuranko say, the sun that shines on you today will not necessarily shine on you tomorrow.

At the lower end of Pademba Road, in sight of the famous cotton tree whose huge buttressed trunk and vast canopy rose as high as any building in the downtown area, we drove past the Executive Secretariat of the National Committee for Disarmament, Demobilization, and Reintegration, where about thirty young ex-combatants were holding up sticks on which they had fixed paper plates and inscribed demands for money.

"Who are they?" I asked.

"Troublemakers," S. B. muttered.

"The British government is giving them rehabilitation grants," one of S. B.'s friends explained. "But some of us don't like rewarding these people for what they did."

State House
Freetown, Republic of Sierra Leone

31st December, 1975.

Dear Dr. Jackson,

    I thank you for your letter of 18th December.
I do not know where you obtained your information
from but we have no Mr. Marah in detention just now.
To put it in another way, let me answer the questions
which you raised in page 2 of your letter.

    (1) Mr. Marah is not a prisoner in our country

    (2) It is therefore obvious that he has not
           been arrested

    (3) It also follows that he cannot be put
           to trial because he has not been arrested.

In fact our State of Emergency has been lifted so
nobody can now be detained without a charge.

    I thank you for your enquiry and it gives me
great pleasure to be able to answer it at once.

    I am glad to know that you found the atmosphere
in our country to your liking.

    I wish you a happy and prosperous New Year.

               Yours sincerely,

               PRESIDENT

Dr. Michael D. Jackson,
Massey University,
Palmerston North,
New Zealand.

"You think they should be punished?"

"I am one of those who has never forgiven them," S. B. said.

It took us two hours to get clear of the city, and I was already finding the journey unbearably slow, when the muffler, which small S. B. had had repaired the previous day, came loose and had to be wrenched off and wrapped and stowed under our feet in the back of the 4-Runner. Not long afterward, at Mile 67, our vehicle lost compression on the steep hill, and we again came to a standstill. None of the Big Men seemed in the least perturbed. They assembled in the shade by the roadside, resplendent in their long robes, while an enormous platter of rice and meat was brought to them under S. B.'s sister Tina's supervision. Urged to join them, I ate a few handfuls of rice, then wandered down the road to join the other travelers.

I had noticed that not a village or town along the highway had survived the war unscathed. The rebels had forced people to strip the roofing iron from their houses, then tote loads of twenty to twenty-five sheets on their heads for hours on end, and often through the night, whipping any bearer who flagged or fell, or beating him or her with the face of a machete. The plunder was sold to soldiers for eighty cents a sheet. Everywhere were derelict concrete shells, often with saplings and grass growing through the cracked floors, with nearby rows of newly thatched, mud-brick houses, a cassava garden, a grove of raffia palms, and a dark green mango tree with a rickety stool or a table in its shade, and pyramids of tomato paste tins, bottles of orange-red palm oil, and neat mounds of groundnuts, onions, chilies, and okra.

I fell into conversation with Unisa Mansaray, a young electronic journalist recently returned from a BBC training course in London. When the rebels and their junta allies fought their way into Freetown on 6 January 1999, some came to his parents' house where he was staying. They were kids that Unisa had known at school, with old scores to settle, imagined slights, trivial grievances — pretexts really, Unisa said, for the deeper grudge they bore against a government that had betrayed their dreams. When they shouted his name, ordering him to come out of the house, Unisa leaped from the second-floor balcony and fled. But his grandparents and parents, trapped inside the house, were shot and killed. That night, Unisa returned to the house, dug shallow graves in the yard, and buried them. Two days later, during a lull in the gunfire, shelling, and burning that had

The North

engulfed the eastern suburbs, he exhumed the bodies and organized a proper funeral.

Even if our conversation has not been interrupted by a hurried return to the vehicles (the 4-Runner apparently now repaired), I would not have known how to respond to the matter-of-fact way that Unisa recounted his story. I stared out the window at the empty grasslands, thinking of how, for the rebels, their victims were nothing but an expendable source of labor or sexual gratification, or scapegoats for some loss they could not endure, or simply people who happened to get in their way. And for several minutes my mind was crowded with images from other places and other times — of thousands of young Congolese punished with the amputation of their fingers, hands, and arms under King Leopold's brutal regime, of the human cargoes packed into the holds of slave ships, and a group of naked women in a Polish death camp, forced to run past a line of ss officers . . .

It was after dark when we crossed the Mabole river on the southern boundary of Koinadugu district, and S. B. broke into song. *Home, home on the range, where the deer and the buffalo play, where seldom is heard a discouraging word, and the skies are not cloudy or gray.* I sang along with him, for the granite inselbergs that loomed as solid shadows in the soft rain made me feel as though I too were coming home.

At Fadugu, the road was thronged with people. Women were singing and clapping, and welcoming banners were held high above the heads of the crowd. In the headlights of a police Land Rover I made out the stenciled words: "We the People of Kasunko chiefdom heartily welcome the Hon. S. B. Marah, Leader of the House and Chairman of the SLPP (North) and entourage to Fadugu." As policemen and soldiers cleared a space in front of the 4-Runner, the great man was hoisted onto a litter, and carried shoulder high toward the covered market. It made me aware of how spurious it was to try to distinguish between chieftaincy and political power in S. B.'s case. Indeed, in Kuranko, one is commonly assimilated to the other, political office being known as the white man's chieftaincy (*mansaiye*).

With the crowd closing in his wake, I followed as best I could, accompanied by Abdul Bangura, a man my own age and one of S. B.'s oldest friends. "He is a powerful man," Abdul observed. "He has the ability to accommodate people. He is always there for his people, listening to their needs, accessible to everyone, showing his concern."

"He must be special," I said, "or else you would not have stood by him all these years."

"That is it," Abdul said. "That is exactly right." And then he explained that it was because Fadugu had been an ECOMOG (Economic Community of West African States Monitoring Group) checkpoint during the war that it had suffered so atrociously at the hands of the rebels. Unable to defeat the Nigerians, the rebels vented their spleen on ordinary civilians. "S. B. has not been here since 1996," Abdul said. "Today is the first time in five years that people have had a reason to celebrate anything."

Following Islamic and Christian prayers, the speeches began with a local SLPP organizer apologizing for our late arrival (we had been expected at 2:30!) by saying that the Honorable S. B. Marah had many responsibilities. He then listed some of the problems people now faced in the aftermath of the war—houses destroyed, crops unplanted, rice in short supply, medicines unavailable, roads in disrepair. . . . But with President Kabbah at the helm, he added, and S. B. Marah at his side, Koinadugu would again enjoy peace, stability, and development.

S. B. thanked the people for the warmth of their reception, and their assurances of support for the SLPP in the forthcoming election. "In fact Fadugu is my second home," he said, pausing for the young interpreter to shout his Krio-to-Limba translation into the crowd of people who had crammed into the open-sided building. "I was a schoolteacher here before I became a politician," S.B. went on. "But tragically this is no longer the Fadugu I used to know. I cry in my heart when I see the devastation visited on this place by the RUF. Though I apologize for not arriving earlier this afternoon, I am glad to have been spared the sight of all the destruction here. For I am, as Mr. Sankoh just said, your brother, your son, your nephew, your grandson. And when you are related, you suffer whatever your kinsmen suffer. As for the RUF, God knows who they are, but God will see they get the fate that they deserve."

S. B. then introduced the various members of his entourage, myself included. "This is an old friend," he said. "A man who has told the world about our life here. Who has been steadfast and true, and has now come back to see the peace."

After leaving Fadugu we drove the remaining thirty miles to Kabala with the police Land Rover going ahead of us, its headlights on full beam and its siren wailing *ware ware ware ware ware*. Every few miles, soldiers sprang to life and ran out from sandbagged checkpoints to hastily lift barriers and salute their passing superiors. Then we plunged once more into the dark and deserted landscape of elephant grass, palms, and rocks, illuminated momentarily by the flashing blue lights of the police vehicle.

I could recognize no landmark, and even as we drove through the rain-eroded lanes of Kabala where I had once lived, wending our way toward the house in which we would lodge, I remained disoriented.

S. B., however, was in his element. Exuding confidence and imperturbability, and accepting declarations of welcome and praise from every quarter, he installed himself on a chair halfway along the broad veranda of the house, other dignitaries ranged on either side of him — the man his faithful friend Abdul Raman Kamara called "Supremo." Lights were quickly strung under the eaves, and the generator started up, revealing the huge crowd that was now filling the forecourt. Beyond, in the darkness, I could see bobbing lanterns as more people made their way in single file toward us. Xylophonists and drummers were playing, women were dancing in tight circles, and soldiers were shouting at kids to make room. In the midst of all this singing and commotion, S. B. sat like a magnificent stone.

Abdul Bangura, who was standing with me at the far end of the veranda, was overwhelmed. "You know," he said, "I want to die before S. B. He's our savior. We don't want anything to hurt him. You can't imagine. Except we sit down together, I can't explain . . . what he has done for me, what he is doing for our country. If I die, I know he'll take care of my family. But if he dies who will take care of the country?"

"That is extraordinary loyalty," I said.

"It's not that I would like to die right now, you understand," Abdul went on. "It's just to make the comparison."

"I understand what you are saying," I said.

After plates of rice and meat sauce had been brought out from the house and the Big Men had eaten, S. B. descended from the veranda to dance. As the anthem of *ferensola* (the Kuranko-speaking area as a whole, and by extension Koinadugu district) filled the night, he moved through the crowd, swaying and shuffling, his arms held high and face suffused with pleasure. And one after another, women draped their headscarves around his shoulders, urging him on. "Ma'l koinyna," sang the *jelimusu* who had traveled north with us, her amplified voice shrill and triumphant above the jangle of her sons' electric guitars. "Ma be kan kelan, yandi yandi yandi; ma'l koenya na ra fanka le la." We are one voice, yandi yandi yandi; our business has come to power. And this music, that I had not heard for twenty years, flooded through me like an intoxicant, so that I too descended from the veranda and lost myself in the body of the crowd.

The music and dancing were still going on when I begged tiredness and went inside. Soldiers stood in the shadows, with automatic weapons, standing guard over the various rooms. My own room was unfurnished except for a bed. After scribbling a few notes in my journal, I blew out the candle on the window ledge, and it was as if the dark immensity of the granite massif behind the house suddenly entombed me. Drifting off to sleep, my thoughts were a jumble of images of the day and blurred recollections of Copenhagen. It was hard to believe that only three days had passed since saying goodbye to my wife and children. And then a single image from earlier in the evening swam into focus — of torches and lanterns moving shakily but steadily through the darkness, like fireflies, I thought, or the souls of the dead.

3 Place of Refuge

From first light, praise-singers and bards were arriving at the house to greet S. B. The *finabas* stood before him, shouting their breathless phrases, stabbing the air with their forefingers, the veins standing out in their necks. S. B. listened without emotion as they named the greatest of the Marah clan, extolling their power, recalling their magnanimity and courage, and emphasizing S. B.'s place in this heroic genealogy. "You might be older than the Marah," one praise-singer declaimed, "but it is under a cotton tree planted by the Marah that you were raised. Mansa Morowa, Fayira, Faramata Morowa, Kaima, Manti Kamara Kulifa, Tina Kaima, Tina Kome, S. B. Marah—all were born into a ruling house. Chieftaincy was with them from the beginning, and chieftaincy will remain with them until the end."[1] Still dressed in his bathrobe and bleary-eyed, S. B. made no comment as he doled out banknotes from his black briefcase, paying the *jelis* their due. In his studied indifference, I thought, he resembled the more astute of his chiefly forebears, for was it not true that many a great man had allowed himself to be stirred to rash deeds by the flattery of praise-singers?

As the praise-singers came and went, flautists, drummers, and xylophonists played in the forecourt for groups of CDF wives and widows, many of whom had walked from villages two or three days distant to pay their respects, pledge their loyalty, and celebrate the launch of their association. Some of the women had babies asleep on their backs. All were dressed alike in a patterned green cloth. And watching them dance, pressed up against each other in tight circles,

shuffling their sandaled feet from side to side, inching forward, it was impossible to reconcile their untroubled faces and exultant singing with the atrocities they had witnessed and the losses they had endured. The Kabala police chief made no bones about it. "It is a miracle we are still here," he said. "When the RUF first invaded Kabala on November 7, 1994, we would have been shot had we not fled. We took refuge in the Wara Wara hills." And I followed his gesture toward Albitaiya—the immense, rain-eroded rock face that overshadowed us.

"We slept up there," he added, "until it was safe to return. Albitaiya saved us."

This was not the first time that Albitaiya had served as a place of refuge, and my thoughts went back to the oral traditions I'd spent so many years collecting in an attempt to chronicle the turbulent history of S. B.'s forebears, who had ruled over the central and eastern chiefdoms of the ferensola since the early seventeenth century when they arrived in the west Guinea highlands, seeking refuge from Islamic jihads on the upper Niger.

In the mid-nineteenth century, the chiefdom of Barawa was ruled by S. B.'s great-grandfather Bol' Tamba Marah, a tireless warrior who made frequent incursions into the Kissi country to the east in search of slaves. He was also a feared magician, who could conjure thunder and lightning at will, even in the dry season, and thereby strike fear into the hearts of his enemies. But such power can protect as well as destroy, and some time in the 1870s, mindful of the rise to power in the upper Niger of a Mandinka warlord called Almami Samori Turé, the Kuranko rulers of Diang, Kalian, Morfindugu, Neya, Mongo, and SaNieni elected to put their lands under the protection of Bol' Tamba. "This is what we can do in the name of Allah and Mohammed," declared Marama Sandi of Diang. "Let us take this country and give it to Bol' Tamba so that we may live without fear." So they placed their countries in the hands of Bol' Tamba, saying that he should keep ferensola in his heart. It was then that Bol' Tamba said that if he was to safeguard their collective lands and livelihoods, it was only proper that one of the other chiefs mount the lookout for marauding birds (an allusion to the elevated platform erected in the middle of an upland rice farm, where children keep watch over the ripening grain and scare birds away with slingshots). And so, Maran Lai Bokari, whose country Morfindugu lay to the east, became Bol' Tamba's lookout.

Although Samori would soon declare a jihad against the pagan Yalunka and Kuranko,[2] and in the 1880s leave a trail of death and destruction through the Kuranko heartland, oral tradition tells us that before this happened Samori heard of Bol' Tamba's reputation and sought an alliance with him. "Let us meet," he said, "and swear an oath that neither of us should threaten the other."

On his way to meet Samori, tragedy overwhelmed Bol' Tamba from an unexpected quarter.

According to Kuranko traditions, the people of Barawa were betrayed by their Sa Nieni neighbors, who informed the Kono to the south that Bol' Tamba had left the country unprotected. Seeking plunder, Kono warriors under Senkerifa traveled north through Sa-Nieni, and sacked and burned almost every village in Barawa. Even today, people remember the names of the fifteen destroyed towns that were never rebuilt.

Bol' Tamba was at a town called Kamaia when he heard that the lands under his protection had been invaded and laid waste. "Then accept *my* dead body now," he said. And he entered the house where he had lodged that night, and without using either knife or gun, took his own life.

When Samori heard of Bol' Tamba's suicide, he said, "Ah, you have done a courageous thing. But before killing yourself you should have come to me and told me that war had entered your country." Samori then dispatched mounted warriors to drive the Kono from Barawa.

For all its dramatic poignancy, the story of Bol' Tamba's suicide may be apocryphal, or arise from a confusion with Marin Tamba, who ruled Barawa in the mid-eighteenth century, and was also known as Sewa. It is also possible that this Sewa was confused with the Yalunka chief Sewa, who, with his family and several elders, killed himself rather than submit to Islam or be enslaved by the sofas besieging his capital, Falaba, in 1884.[3] In any event, whether because of the loss of their lord and protector or the destruction of their homes, villages, and granaries, the people of Barawa trekked north as refugees. For a while they found refuge in Morfindugu, but the locals feared domination by the exiles, who dispersed again, some seeking distant kin, before settling around the Wara Wara hills, of which Albitaiya is the highest point. Here, however, they quickly came into conflict with the local Limba. After an incident in which Aisetta Karifa was driven from Albitaiya when he went there to cut grass for thatching, the Barawa refugees took up arms and made Albitaiya their own. The cotton trees they planted for protection around the new settlement are still there today.

It was from Albitaiya, which means "Under the protection of Allah," that S. B's father's father, Manti Kamara Kulifa, went out to wage war against Samori's sofas.

Though his given name was Yira, he had earned the nickname *Kulifa* (leopard slayer) as a boy when he single-handedly fought off the attack of a leopard which, he was later told, was most likely an enemy who had assumed animal form. As it turned out, the shape-shifting facility of an enemy would prove less daunting than the fickleness of a woman.

In time of war it was the prerogative of a principal warrior to take his wives with him on his campaigns. So Kulifa took his first wife, Kumba (who hailed from the Sankaran country that Samori now dominated), and left his younger wives, Sirasie and Tina, to look after the children. Moving constantly from one strange place to another, and under threat of attack, Kumba yearned to return home and asked her husband if she might stay with her parents while the war lasted. Manti Kamara Kulifa refused to let her go. One evening, on the pretext of collecting firewood in the bush, she ran away.

Her husband set out after her the next day despite warnings from his men on the dangers of penetrating sofa-held country.

At Kumba's village, the girl's parents begged him to leave their

Place of Refuge

daughter in their care. Kulifa said he would wait three days: this would be time enough for them to remind Kumba of her duty.

At midnight on the third day, alarmed by rumors of sofa spies, Kulifa went into the bush beyond the village to reimmunize himself against swords and sorcery. Under the feeble light of a waning moon, he sprinkled herbs and gunpowder in two calabashes of water, then stripped naked and sat between them. The water began to stir and simmer and, without his aid, stream across his body from one vessel to another.

He was never to know that a sofa spy, having overheard Kumba talking carelessly about her husband, bribed her to confide the secret place and time that Manti Kamara Kulifa was without his sword and war gown. Before the magical immunization could take effect he was seized by the sofas. The following day he was taken to Worekoro. There, with wrists bound and legs shackled, he was led out of the town to an outcrop of granite surrounded by bleached bones. The sofa leader ordered Kulifa's head shaved in case his hair was imbued with the power to deflect sword blades, and he was executed.

Manti Kamara Kulifa's younger brother Sewa inherited the young widow Tina. Tina's youngest son, Kome, was only two years old when his father was killed. His elder brother, Kaima, became like a father to him. Indeed, for as long as he lived he would call him daddy. Tina Kome grew up hearing repeatedly the story of his father's betrayal. Nor was Kulifa the only brother Fa Sewa lost in the war, and he nursed two grievances — that the white men had supplied the sofas with arms, and that the deceitfulness of women was more ruinous than war. In years to come, even though three wives would desert him, Tina's youngest son Kome would vow never to pursue an errant wife, and would warn his sons to divine well the character of a woman before marrying her.

At the Kabala sports field thousands of people were gathered, some sitting under bough-shades, some standing in the sun with banners held high. One read: "CDF of Sierra Leone ex-combatants wives war widows and orphans development project Koinadugu District welcomes Hon. S. B. Marah and entourage to Koinadugu District. We say one People one country." Another bore the stenciled letters:

"Folosaba Dembelia Chiefdom Koinadugu Project. Motto: togetherness peace is wealth."

As their names were called over the PA system, various groups detached themselves from the crowd and danced before the assembled Big Men, all of whom were ensconced at a long table under the covered stand. Male dancers in raffia skirts and coxcombs leapt through hoops, blowing whistles. Kuranko hunters and *tamaboros* (hunters who had fought the RUF) brazenly addressed my camera, wearing country-cloth leggings, tunics, and tufted buffalo caps.

Place of Refuge

And war widows in green-and-white print dresses patiently bided their time.

When the speeches began I drifted toward the edge of the crowd, feeling the same boredom with official occasions I'd felt as a school-boy, when visiting dignitaries droned on about civic virtues before presenting prizes and certificates to those of us who were destined, presumably, to exemplify them. Yet I caught the drift of what was being said—the pledges of support for the SLPP, the expressions of gratitude to the UN peacekeepers, the calls for national reconciliation

and regional development, the tributes paid to those who had lost their lives in the war — Nigerian and Guinean soldiers from ECOMOG, Civil Defence Force fighters, the army and police . . .

It was then S. B.'s turn to address the crowd.

"I am really happy to be back in Kabala," he began. "I have not been here since 26 May 1997, when the Junta seized power . . .

"This reception is truly impressive. I thank you for it. It makes me proud of my constituents. But, you know, I have heard people say that Kabala is not my constituency. Yet as far as I know, I am the leader of the whole of Koinadugu!" As the crowd clapped in affirmation, S. B. continued in the same vein. "In fact, I don't belong to any one constituency. Everywhere is the same for me. All people are the same to me. If you interviewed people in this crowd you would find that one out of ten is a relative of mine. A brother, a sister, an aunt, an uncle, a grandchild, a cousin. Even among the Limba I have relatives. I am connected everywhere. And you know what they say about Limbas, how they love beautiful women. When they want to marry they look for Kuranko girls because they are more beautiful!"

When the laughter and clapping had subsided, S. B. went on to speak of the devastation wrought by the war, and to contrast the present state of the district to the way it was when his party was previously in power. "During the last elections," S. B. said, "my opponent came here and told you he was a Kuranko man. That was a lie. In fact it is an insult to us Kurankos. Moreover, Karefa-Smart said he would bring you a shipload of rice! Where is that rice today? Because of these deceptions many of you did not vote for me. No problem. I am convinced you have learned your lesson and will vote solidly for me and the SLPP in the forthcoming elections. People in the south are proud of me, and Koinadugu should be proud of me as well. I have been in Parliament for more than forty years, and you have never heard it said that S. B. Marah is corrupt. I don't eat people's money. I am content with what I have."[4]

S. B. then returned to the subject of the war. "I am proud to say that the CDF began here in Koinadugu with the tamaboros," he said. "We drove the rebels from our country. It was only unfortunate that the rebels were in complicity with some of our children here, and caught the Kabala CDF napping. But on January 18 the government will formally declare the war over. Perhaps at that time, it might be appropriate for the CDF to change its name, because when we think of CDF we think about the RUF — the devils . . ."

Place of Refuge

S. B. then brought his remarks to a close by observing that the government had waived some school fees and was subsidizing others, as well as supplying books and equipment to schools. "And the SLPP has promised," he added, "to upgrade roads, and provide agricultural equipment and potable water for Koinadugu. For all these reasons, Koinadugu should be solidly for the government of Alhaji Dr. Ahmad Tejan Kabbah [the president of Sierra Leone]."

As a libation was poured to inaugurate the CDF Wives Development Project, I got talking with the young man standing beside me. His name was Leba Keita. Leba had run a small photographic studio on Kissy Road, Freetown, until the RUF destroyed it in January 1999. Knowing that he had also been targeted, Leba fled the city. Traveling at night, and leaving the road whenever he approached a town or village, he walked to Kabala where his wife had already taken refuge. In Kabala, there were fears of another RUF attack. "You must become invisible," friends told Leba, "like salt in the sauce." So he continued on to Guinea, where he spent the next four years in refugee camps.

"I returned to Kabala seven months ago," Leba said. "I found my house still standing. But I have nothing. My wife gardens, and she sells vegetables at the market so we can buy rice. I do a little voluntary teaching. But my dream is to own a camera again. To start my business up again." (Leba had asked me if I could help him get a camera.)

At that moment, my name was called.

Somewhat bewildered, I pushed through the crowd toward the covered stand, where S. B. rose to his feet, picked up the microphone, and announced that in recognition of my services to the Kuranko people I was to be invested with the title of honorary paramount chief and given the name Denka Marah, in memory of the father of the late Paramount Chief Balansama Marah III of Sengbe. Before I could take stock of the situation, I was surrounded by chiefs, and a rust-colored country-cloth gown was pulled over my head. Capped with a matching hat, I was then enjoined to dance, which I did so with a mixture of elation, gratitude, and embarrassment.

Thankfully, the ceremony was quickly over and I could again lose myself in the crowd.

That afternoon I talked to dozens of people, and their stories were all the same. They had lost everything in the war, or were owed money, or did not have the wherewithal to live.

Patrick Koroma was a self-effacing man in his forties, with a

thin, graying mustache. He bore little resemblance to his father, Keti Ferenke Koroma, with whom I spent so much time during the years of my fieldwork. Renowned throughout ferensola for his skills as a storyteller, Keti Ferenke died in 1993. I asked Patrick if his father's stories were still told. Patrick was ashamed to say he did not know. He had attended a mission school (it had been established after my time) and so missed out on hearing his father's stories or committing them to memory.

"I will send you the book I made of his stories," I said. "Perhaps you can read them to your children." And I wondered what experiences of the war might now be recounted in the long rainy season nights, when people gathered to tell stories.

As Patrick drifted away, a young man showed me a typewritten petition that he and his workmates had prepared. They had been laid off from the Ministry of Works in July 1993, and though some had received back pay, the war had prevented others receiving theirs. Could I intercede with S. B. on their behalf, then deliver their letter to the Ministry of Works in Freetown?

A lance corporal in the army told me he had enlisted when he left school. He had seen action in the war, and recently been retrained by the British. But he received only sixty dollars a month, no rice, no accommodation. It was scarcely enough for him to live on, and his family was obliged to live elsewhere.

Given such discontent, which had precipitated coups in the past, how, I wondered, could the vicious circle of division, dissent, and armed revolt ever be broken?

That evening, after eating, Abdul Bangura opened his heart to me. "I wouldn't tell this to anyone here," he said, "because I have my pride. But I can see that you are interested in how things are here, and you should know. We in Sierra Leone have been turned into beggars. But for S. B., I would have nothing. I have four sons, and am struggling to get them through school. But if I am not to die of shame I must have my own means."

Abdul had had a diamond mining concession in Kono, but the rebels drove him into the bush where he survived with a few friends for three months, living on beans. They were afraid to light fires, or remain for long in the same place. When ECOMOG soldiers liberated the area, Abdul and his companions were at first suspected of being rebels. Abdul managed to get to Freetown, only to witness the horrors of 6 January 1999. He described five hundred people trapped under the bridge at Congo Cross. Most were killed. The bodies could not be buried for days. Vultures picked at the rotting flesh. You held a handkerchief over your nose, but could not stop breathing in the stench of death. There were people who were forced to drink boiling palm wine, Abdul said. To eat their own feces. To dance as their children were shot in front of them. "Grey-haired men like me were killed because we looked like the president. Civilians were killed because they voted for the government."

"You may forgive but you cannot forget," Abdul said. "The rebels are still among us. Even though the country has decided on peace, retaliation will happen secretly for years to come. This is a small country. The rebels might move to other areas, but sooner or later they will be found. And the special court will bring them to justice."

What can we do with the past, I wrote in my journal that night. How can we outlive it? And what of the stories we tell? So partial, so fugitive. Did Bol' Tamba kill himself or not? Did the people of Sa-Nieni betray their neighbors and kinsmen to the north, as Barawa traditions attest, or do we accept the story told in SaNieni, that they had come under attack from the Limbas to the west, and when their capital, Yifin, fell, a corridor was opened up through which the Kono swept into Barawa?

We tell stories in order to come to terms with what has befallen us. Through stories we create the illusion that we are more than creatures of circumstance. That we have a hand in our own fate. There is, perhaps, nothing worse than finding oneself passive and powerless in the face of overwhelming events. In sharing one's story with a stranger there is, perhaps, the possibility that one's fortunes will change, or that, at the very least, one will feel a little less alone.

The night was filled with the sounds of drumming and singing, and when I finished writing in my journal I thought of returning to the courtyard and joining in the dance. But I was exhausted. I needed to sleep. Yet, as I lay in the darkness, I could not help seeing myself dancing that afternoon, like a fragile puppet, my hands held aloft not through my own will or strength, but because they were attached with strings to the hands of the chiefs who were dangling and jerking me about in a parody of power, like something from a Jean Rouch film. And as I recalled how men had come up to me, shaking my hands, calling me chief, powerful chief, and encouraging me to take one of the young widows to my bed, I saw myself as a slave now to S. B.' s will, his hireling.

4 In Kabala

It was Sunday morning. Now that the meetings, rallies, and festivities were over, the women who had walked so far to celebrate the launch of the CDF Development Project — a project that would hopefully bring medicines, nurses, and teachers to their towns, sponsor classes in *gara* (dyeing), masonry, horticulture, dressmaking, and carpentry, and help reconstruct clinics, schools, and mosques — now came to our compound to sing and dance for the last time before returning home. As S. B. doled out money to the departing visitors he turned to me and said he was trying to guess what messages these women would take back to their villages from the ferensola meeting. "I like to imagine those places," he said, "where the women walk about with headloads, what they will say, what they will think . . ."

As for me, I would like to have joined the women. To have visited Firawa again, after so many years away, despite its destruction at the hands of rebels and renegade soldiers (sobels) in 1999. And when I said goodbye to Patrick Koroma, who was heading home to Kondembaia, I felt like going with him.

Patrick said that this had been the first time he'd visited Kabala in five years. When the rebels attacked Kondembaia for the third time in April 1998, only the church, the mosque, the school, and one house were left unburned. "Even now, we are living on our farm," Patrick said. "My two children no longer attend school. I have no means of rebuilding our house in town. It is a place of sadness, anyway." And he told me that the immense cotton tree in the center of the town, where Keti Ferenke and I had sat and talked so often, was the same tree in whose shade the rebels had hacked the limbs off fifteen villagers.

The war seemed to dominate everything that day, like the great, rain-darkened, granite flanks of the inselberg that loomed over the town. And it was in a somber mood that I set out that morning to see what had survived of the Kabala I remembered.

With S. B.'s permission, small S. B. accompanied me. We sauntered along dusty lanes that had once been thoroughfares, past rows of derelict houses, and through unfamiliar neighborhoods. So many refugees had poured into Kabala during the war that the town had expanded almost beyond recognition. But we were soon trudging up the rutted road toward the traffic circle, and then past the mosque into the main street. Opposite the market there was a poster advertising a Nigerian movie, *Okuzu Massacre* (The Robbers Revenge). "On the 19th of July my entire family and 22 others were killed. Who is responsible? The Governor, the Igwe, the Robbers, or the Gods?"

"What do you think?" I asked small S. B.

"You can rent a video if you want," he said. And sure enough, a few doors away we found the Kaku Video Centre, with *Evil Forest* (The Lord Vindicates) for rent. And *Jungle Rats*: "A war of betrayal and deceit. The fight to the finish."

"I would have thought," I said, "that people were sick and tired of this kind of violence."

"Sometimes you have to remember," small S. B. said. As we headed along the road toward the Catholic school, he told me his story.

In Kabala

He had come to Kabala from Freetown to spend some time with his mother, Tina. Tina was S. B.'s sister, and wife of the Diang chief, Sheku Magba Koroma II, who lived in Kondembaia. Both Tina and her husband were in Kabala at the time, though not staying in the same house. "At about four in the afternoon of 7 November 1994," small S. B. said, "we heard gunfire. People were running about in a panic, saying that the rebels had entered the town. I was with my cousin Sheku. We went to my dad and said, 'People are saying that the rebels are here.' My father said, 'No, it is the tamaboros.' But the rebels had entered the town on foot, without vehicles, using cross-country paths rather than roads. By nightfall, many houses were on fire, and my father was asking us, 'What shall we do, what shall we do?' Sheku and I wanted to get away from the house, but there were rebels moving down the street, so we stayed inside and locked the door. About eight o'clock the rebels banged on the door. They shouted, 'If you don't open up we'll set fire to the house and you'll burn.' I quickly threw my father's staff under the bed. Then they smashed the door. The rebels saw my father's briefcase. It was filled with money and gold dust. They shouted, 'Whose is this?' I said I didn't know who it belonged to. I told them that we had taken shelter in the house when the shooting began. The rebels said, 'If you had nothing to hide, why did you run away?'"

As the rebels moved on down the street, small S. B. and Sheku found themselves face to face with two young men their own age, armed with AK-47s. The one who gave orders was called Kujé. His sidekick was called Abu. "Fortunately," small S. B. said, "they believed my story, and did not suspect that the old Pa was my father, let alone a chief. Had they known the truth they would have killed him. But I think they were afraid of us. Only two of them against the two of us. They were thinking we might overpower them and take their weapons.

"Kujé said, 'Now we'll kill you,' and he shot Sheku in the stomach. As Sheku died, I pleaded with them. 'Don't kill me,' I said. 'I'm going to come with you. I want to come with you.'

"They ordered me to pack a bag, and to make up a headload of food. Then we headed off the way the rebels had come, along the path to Kamadugu Sukurela. We spent that night in Kamadugu Sukurela, which the rebels had already burned and looted on their way to Kabala. I was one of many captives. One of the girls was Fanta Konteh, who was Miss Koinadugu. Next day we went on to Singbian. We arrived there at nightfall. The town crier was in the process of announcing that the RUF had entered Kabala. He was blind. He did not realize that these same rebels had just entered his village. 'So you're telling everyone that we are evil?' the rebels said. And they shot him dead. Next morning we left for Dalako, near Lake Sonfon. We reached there at about four in the afternoon.

"When the rebels said they wanted food, I told them that there was a cassava garden behind the house, and that I would prepare cassava for them. They trusted me now. I had been helping them talk to the other captives, especially the girls, who were afraid for their lives. So they let me go to the garden alone. It was then that I made my escape. I had dreamed about it the night before. And because I believe that dreams foretell real events, I had already decided to escape that day. I made my way to Yara where I met the town chief and some hunters. They were very happy to see me and to hear that my father was alive. One of the hunters then escorted me back to Kondembaia."

"Three years passed," small S. B. said, "before the captured girls emerged from the bush. They told me that the rebels claimed to have shot me when I tried to escape. Everyone believed I was dead, like my cousin Sheku."

I left small S. B. near the turnoff to the Catholic school, and walked on alone toward One-Mile (an intersection a mile out of town), passing the Kabala Secondary School where Guinean soldiers held off a ferocious RUF attack in 1994, and which was now the headquarters of the UNAMSIL (United Nations Mission in Sierra Leone) Bangladeshi contingent. Though I could not remember who had occupied the ruined houses on the corner, all with jagged holes from mortar fire in their rusting tin roofs, I soon began to make out familiar landmarks. The granite boulders near the culvert, the swamp, the mango trees at the junction. As I approached the place where my wife and I had lived thirty-two years before, my pulse quickened, as if I were entering a place of terrible uncertainty or peril. In the shade of the trees, an elderly woman was standing beside a roadside stall. I asked her whether she knew of Pa Kamara, who used to live in the house under the trees. She said that Pa Kamara was dead. She was his widow. She had been away in Freetown for several years because of the war. She had only just returned. I found it difficult to reconcile my memory of the buxom young woman who became such a close friend of my wife with the haunted, perplexed person who stood in front of me. When I told her who I was, and that Pauline had passed away, she must have felt something similar. For how does one cross such a gap in time, when memory works not to heal our wounds but to open them?

After asking Mrs. Kamara if I could take a look at our old house, which was behind her own, and half-hidden by the mango trees, I felt unsure of myself. But as I approached the house, I was astonished to find that the shutters were still yellow and blue, the barred windows dark green, and the exterior walls still showing traces of the pale blue paint that covered them in 1969 when the house was new. Though the earth around the well in the backyard had been eroded by the rains, and the roofing iron was rusty, and the rafters collapsed as a result of termites or decay, the place was unbearably familiar. Inside, the rooms were smoke-stained and gloomy, but our old table was still standing in the backroom that we had used as our kitchen, in exactly the same place it had been in our time. I pointed out to Mrs. Kamara, who had followed me into the house with her blind daughter, that one could still discern smudges of red oxide on the cement floor from when Pa Kamara painted it while we were away in Freetown for the birth of our baby.

By the time I left the house and said goodbye to Mrs. Kamara, I was fighting back tears. I had not felt this way for a long time. And as I walked away down the back road, I stopped to look back, like Orpheus impatient to see his Eurydice, thinking I might glimpse Pauline in her red shot-silk dress, hugging the porch post, and smiling.

In Sierra Leone 36

Yet, for all the intensity of my emotions, I was conscious that I was grieving a ruination wreaked by time, and not by human hands, and was angry at myself that I should be so upset about changes one can do nothing about. Why should I mourn the ineluctable and natural order of things? And given that I had survived my loss, how could I allow its memory to eclipse my awareness of what people had suffered here?

Standing on the road, near the grasslands that Pauline and I used to watch burning at night in the dry season, I thought of the events that small S. B. had recounted to me only an hour before, and of the widows who had traveled so far to launch the CDF Development Project. What destroys us, I thought, is not loss in itself, but the lack of what one needs to go on. And from my shirt pocket I extracted the scrap of paper Leba Keita had given me, when he asked if I could help him buy a camera.

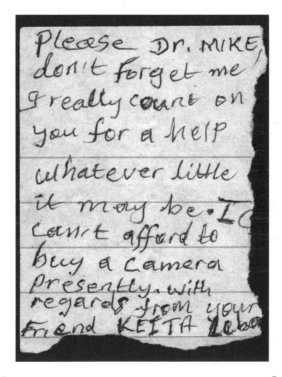

In Kabala

That evening, as if it had been a sudden squall, my anguish left me, and I sat with S. B. and the other Big Men on the porch, eating the meal which had been prepared for us, and talking about the events of the last few days. But my mind kept wandering, and as the light began to fade I went to my room to write up the notes I had been furtively scribbling in my notebook all day.

One remark of small S. B.'s about the RUF — among whom there were many renegade soldiers — particularly intrigued me. The rebels, he had said, were all young men. Many were only boys. They smoked a lot of cannabis, which made them "wild." And their leader, whose name was Mohammed, and hailed from Makeni, wore a red beret, with a red bandana around his neck. His companions praised him constantly. And he did not carry a gun, only a knife, and was at all times surrounded by his bodyguards.

What fascinated me was this odd mix of bravado and brittleness. Surely small S. B. was right when he suggested that the rebels shot Sheku because they felt threatened by the pair of them, that they killed Sheku in order to break S. B.'s spirit and to reduce the danger of taking two friends prisoner together. Perhaps, too, I thought, they felt vulnerable — so far from their homes (they had come from Kailahun in the south), afraid of the tamaboros, who possessed magical medicines to ward off bullets or kill their enemies, and the powers of shape-shifting and witchcraft — their way of dealing with *their* terror.

Unless one has been caught up in a war and experienced the terror that comes of knowing that thousands of heavily armed individuals are bent on one's annihilation, it is hard to realize that most violence is not primarily motivated by evil, greed, lust, ideology, or aggression. Strange as it may seem, most violence is defensive. It is motivated by the fear that if one does not kill one will be killed. Either by the enemy or by one's own superiors. Against this constant anxiety, and the acute sense of fear and vulnerability that accompanies it, one conjures an illusion of power — torching buildings, shooting unarmed civilians, firing rocket grenades, smoking cannabis, shouting orders, chanting slogans, seeing oneself as Rambo, taunting, torturing, and abusing the individuals one has taken captive. But all this display of might — this weaponry, these medicines and amulets, this noise, these incantations, both political and magical, these Hollywood images, these drug-induced fugues, these rituals of brotherhood and solidarity—simply reveal the depth of one's own impotence and fear. This is Hannah Arendt's great insight—that while military power consolidates itself in numbers, and in coordinated, automatic forms of mass movement, terrorism seeks power in implements, and is driven not by might but by its absence.[1] And so it is that in the auto-da-fé, with explosions and bomb blasts, fire, noise, and mayhem, that the terrorist, like a child, finds his apotheosis, achieving the recognition, presence, voice, and potency he has been denied in the real world.

Like any other animal, human beings will fight to the death when threatened or cornered, but as a species we are perhaps alone in imagining that our survival depends on such elusive properties as recognition, love, identity, honor, prestige, and wealth. Only we will feel that our very existence is endangered when our name is taken in vain, our pride is hurt, our nation threatened, our reputation impugned, our voice ignored, our loyalty betrayed. No other animal will fight tooth and nail, not only to see that such symbolic losses are made good, but that those who have allegedly taken these things from us are themselves subject to all the torment, degradation, and loss that we have suffered at their hands. This is why violators seldom admit to guilt. For they believe they were fully justified in their excesses; they were only taking back what was rightfully theirs, preserving their civilization, defending their rights, upholding their honor, and, of course, obeying orders from above.

It is not easy—seeing images of bewildered refugees on a Kosovo road, or of a column of men, women, and children, some with hands held above their heads, others clutching small suitcases, herded along a smoke-darkened Warsaw street to oblivion, or of villagers in Sierra Leone with their limbs amputated by axes—to believe that in the eyes of their tormentors they are part of a single, monstrous entity bent on *their* annihilation. When I asked Leba why the RUF mutilated and killed so many innocent people, he thought for a moment and said, "They used to say the government was not paying any attention to them." And when I asked Patrick the same question he recalled one man from Kondembaia who had had both his hands cut off. "The rebels wrote a note to the president, saying, 'We rebels did this,' and they stuffed the note in the man's shirt pocket and told him to go to the president. 'You used those hands to vote for him,' they said. 'Now he is bringing in all these ECOMOG soldiers to fight against us. Encouraging the CDF to kill us. Go to the president and ask him to give you another hand.'"

5 The Beef

For two days, a young steer had been tethered by a short rope to a mango tree at the edge of the compound. It was a gift to S. B., to be taken to Freetown, along with several goats. Constrained by the rope, the steer was unable to stretch its neck to the ground; all it could do was occasionally nose or lick the dew from the long grass that was within its reach. When it defecated, it held its tail horizontal, its spine as straight as a spirit level, and the tuft of hair by its penis twitched when it finished urinating. So forlorn did this animal seem that I became convinced that it knew its impending fate.

On the morning that we packed the vehicles, preparing to leave Kabala, it became obvious that there was not enough room in the back of the pickup for the steer. As the Big Men discussed their quandary, I sat some distance away, listening to an elderly man recount the history of Mande to a young newspaper reporter — passing from a description of Sundiata, who ruled the empire in the mid-fourteenth century, to an account of the first clans, the origins of the xylophone, and the beginning of praise-singing. Old Musa's spectacle frames were tied upside-down to his cap, because this was the only way the one remaining lens could cover his one good eye. Earlier in the day, he had asked if I could send him some new glasses from Freetown — just as Leba had asked for a camera, and the musicians had begged me to help them buy new guitars and amplifiers.

When I noticed that the Big Men and soldiers were gathering by the mango tree, I went down into the courtyard to talk with Leba, who said he had come to say goodbye. "They are killing the beef," he observed. And as we watched from a distance, saying nothing, the steer was forced to the ground and its throat cut. The carcass was then cut into portions, and the head, neck, forequarters, rump, underbelly, entrails, hide, heart, and liver set out in separate piles on some banana leaves. Nearby, ten vultures stood their ground, occasionally flapping their ungainly wings and craning their necks toward the kill.

Suddenly a young man standing next to Leba muttered something about how short life was. When I asked him what he meant, he said: "The way they slaughter these cows for these ministers. If we the young men wanted some of that beef, those Big Men would fight us, juju-way. They'd say, 'If any young man looks at the meat, let him beware.' So they make you afraid to go there. That is why we young people should not open our eyes too much on the meat. The Big Men could make us impotent.[1] Or they could shoot us with their fetish guns."

"In Kuranko, we fear meat," Leba explained. "When eating with our elders, you must not take the meat from the plate. They can share it or give it to you, but you must not take it. The elders might feel challenged. They will say, 'Ah, this small boy is not afraid!' If one of them has the power of witchcraft, the meat may stick in your throat, until someone comes and hits you, to dislodge it."

Leba's remarks reminded me of the rumors of leopard societies that, in days gone by, committed ritual murders so that Big Men might augment their power by eating the vital organs of children.[2] The logic ran as follows: Children, women, and cattle were wealth. A man's capacity to father children, to marry many times, and to acquire cattle were signs of power. And status and stature were intimately linked. It was not for nothing that one of S. B.'s praise names in the north was *simba* (elephant) — an allusion to his physical bulk as much as his commanding presence, his social standing, and his political power. Still, it amused me that so many Big Men were immobilized by their own obesity — sluggish, unwell, and impotent. Was this why they were so preoccupied with the virility and appetite of young men? If so, the young men, denied meat and obliged to do the Big Men's bidding, seemed to find little consolation in the fact that what they lacked in status they made up for in strength and vitality.

When we drove off, I noticed that the vultures were clumsily quarreling around the spot where the steer had been butchered, and picking at the blood-blackened earth.

The sun was hot. The summit of Albitaiya was lost in the haze of the harmattan. In the backseat of the 4-Runner I felt cramped and uncomfortable. Underfoot were several bags of meat, including the steer's severed head. Copies of the Noble Qu'ran in English, which Fasili had mysteriously acquired in Kabala, kept falling on my head. And our police escort again filled the landscape with wailing sirens as we drove through smoke from burning elephant grass, and over the rice and clothing that villagers had spread on the roadside to dry.

At Fadugu the police Land Rover left us, and as if released from an obligation to behave itself, the 4-Runner began to lose compression and suffer from brake failure. Yet even as we labored up the last hill toward Makeni, S. B. was pressing his nephew to overtake slower-moving poda podas, and urging us on. "Kam on bo, le we go now," he said, as if his impatience and will power would be instantly trans-mitted to the vehicle and it would obey. By the time we crawled the last few yards into a roadside repair shop, I realized it had taken us five hours to travel seventy miles. The hood of the 4-Runner was quickly propped open, and the engine exposed to the scrutiny of a dozen or so grease monkeys, while the Big Men issued advice, diag-noses, and orders from the makeshift seats that had been brought out for them. "This car don make beaucoup problem for we," S. B. ob-served. "Le we make haste," Fasili urged helpfully. Watching the Big Men as they sat unmoving and unmoved in front of a rusty, wheel-less vehicle that had been chocked up with driveshafts and a wooden mortar, I had a flashback to Gatwick airport, when I had found myself with several hours to kill before my flight. The departure lounge had been almost deserted, though not far from where I was sitting a young businessman was talking on his mobile phone. As I listened to his conversation with diminishing interest, a woman started vacuuming the walkway between us. As she drew near, I lifted my feet so she could reach under the seat. But when she moved on to where the man in the suit was talking on his mobile phone, he ig-nored her completely. It wasn't as if he couldn't see her; he simply did not want to acknowledge her. Nor, it appeared, did she expect any-thing of him. When he showed no sign of moving either his feet or his bag, the woman left the space around him as it was — littered with candy wrappers and used telephone cards. Trivial in itself, this inci-dent left me troubled. Not only did I want to know why certain

The Beef

people, as a matter of principle, will make absolutely no concession to those they consider their inferiors; it made me ask myself why I felt so acutely uncomfortable with status distinctions, and sought wherever possible to avoid or nullify them. Recollecting this incident at Gatwick also reminded me of how awkward I sometimes felt at the hotel. Where most people would readily accept being waited on — for after all, this is what waiters are paid to do — I felt embarrassed by the deferential or obsequious rigmarole, and could not abide having someone pour water into my glass, place a napkin over my lap, or call me sir. No one could be less suited for high office than myself. Indeed, so assiduous was my need to avoid the trappings of authority and privilege that I instinctively sought the margins and the shadows — the world of the underdog or the young.

I wandered away across the tamped, grease-and-oil-stained earth, past the decaying mud-brick building that served as an office, the lean-tos under which old car seats, cylinder blocks, radiators, differentials, mufflers, and cannibalized engine parts had been stacked, to where I could sit alone, collect my thoughts, and scribble some notes. Then I strolled up the road to buy a bread roll and a tin of sardines with which to make a sandwich.

When I returned to the vehicle, small S. B. explained that the brake fluid line to the rear wheels had been burned through by the broken muffler and needed to be replaced. The air filter also required cleaning. As one of the grease monkeys was dispatched into town to find a spare brake fluid line, food was brought for the Big Men — for the third time that day. But eating did not interrupt their critical commentary on the mechanics' efforts. "Watin make you no fixam yet?" the Alhaji asked testily. "Le we go now," S. B. added, with a weariness that appeared to preclude any response. Dr. K. said nothing. He was too busy ordering one of the mechanic's boys to uncap two bottles of Heineken beer for him as he tugged rubbery strands of meat from a boiled goat's head. "Kam eat," he said to me. When I explained I did not eat meat he was incredulous. "Where do you get your protein?" he asked. "Where do you get your strength?"

"We Africans have tough stomachs," Fasili observed.

"It's not stomach," I said. "It's heart. I don't eat meat for health reasons."

When he had finished eating, Dr. K. removed his gray safari shirt, and summoned a small boy to scratch his back. He was like a hippo, as dour as he was massive. And while he picked his teeth with a sliver of wood, the boy started to massage his enormous shoulders.

S. B. was being earbashed by two local men who had lost their local businesses in the war.

Makeni, I knew, had been an RUF stronghold. Even now there were billboards at the traffic circles in the center of the town with photos of the RUF leader Foday Sankoh and RUF political slogans.

Perhaps this was why S. B. showed so little sympathy for their plight. "No one went into exile here," he asserted. "You have only yourselves to blame for what happened here."

"We had nowhere to go," one of the Makeni men replied.

And then, as if to elicit my understanding, the second man described how well the RUF were organized. "They would send small boys to spy on prominent people," he said. "The kids would disguise themselves as cigarette-sellers or petty traders. They would carry messages. We never knew who they were. They would get information about a place before they attacked it."

"You know," S. B. said, half-smiling, "one time the RUF entered a mosque and asked, 'Anyone here believe in God?' 'No, we don't,' everyone said. Even the imam. 'No, no,' he said, 'I do not believe!'"

The Makeni men both laughed.

"But seriously," S. B. said, "the SLPP expects people to work for the country. Government is composed of people. You should not fear to speak the truth to your government. The government does not want to hurt you. As long as you are on the right side, you have nothing to fear."

As S. B. was talking, a truck had pulled in at the roadside. Intrigued by the slogan emblazoned on its side — "Fear Not the World but the People" — I walked over to the truck to see what it carried, and was dismayed to find that twenty-five steers were crammed together on the back, their horns roped to wooden beams that were in turn lashed to a metal frame covering the vehicle's tray. The animals were unable to move. The flank of one had been so badly lacerated by the jolting of the truck over degraded roads that its hipbone was exposed. Like sardines in a can, they had been packed top to tail, in rows of five, to maximize space. Their muzzles were dry, foam flecked their mouths, their eyes were closed with pain and exhaustion, and their heads had been forced up over the rumps of the animals in front. From time to time an unbearable moan was released from the herd, and I was reminded instantly of the bobby calves I used to hear baying mournfully in the night when I was a child, as they waited out the hours of darkness in a cramped railway wagon on a siding in my hometown before going on to the slaughterhouse the next day.

The driver and his partner tilted the cab of the truck forward and began inspecting the engine, while a couple of other young men clambered up onto the back of the truck and walked over the steers, checking the lashings.

"You should have brought your camera, Mr. Mike." It was small S. B., who had sidled up to me unseen.

"I was thinking," I said, "that this is how Africans were once packed in the slave ships, head to foot, to save space."

But where I saw slaves, or imagined myself, small S. B. saw only cows. And I did not feel inclined to share with him my ruminations on when, and under what circumstances, we might extend human rights to animals, or, for that matter, deny these rights to our fellow human beings, treating them as if they were mere chattels or beasts. Yet it was suddenly very clear to me that my own notion of rights reflected the egalitarian ethos of the country in which I was raised. In tribal societies such as Kuranko, one's worth was ostensibly relative to one's patrimony, rank, and title, which is why, I guess, the Big Men always wore their status on their sleeves—honorable, doctor, paramount chief.[3] In such a society, one's due was generally reckoned in terms of birth, not worth. A chief was due a retinue, and tithes, not to mention praise and honor. A father was owed his children's respect. And a wife was duty bound to honor her husband, and obey him without question. For the Kuranko, this calculus of social distinction was both categorical and unambiguous. People were superior to animals, firstborn were superior to second-born, men were superior to women, adults were superior to children, the patriline was superior to the matriline, rulers were superior to commoners, and commoners were superior to praise-singers, blacksmiths, and leather-workers. At the bottom of the social scale, finabas—the bards and custodians of chiefly traditions—were superior to no one, except perhaps slaves. In practice, however, the worth of a person was far less fixed than this schema would suggest.[4] When Keti Ferenke explained this to me many years ago, he began by punning on the word *kina,* which, depending on a subtle inflection, could mean either beehive or elder. His argument was that someone who is nominally elder could lose the right to be considered superior if he behaved unjustly or idiotically. A person might be designated an elder, a status superior, he said, but if he acted like a child he *was* a child. Superiority, he noted, derived not only from being born first, or from being big and powerful; it also stemmed from the way one behaved.

For Keti Ferenke, whose pride in his own intellectual acumen was, at least in my company, undisguised, a person's true worth was defined by his or her social gumption, or *nous*, though other innate traits, such as temperament, bearing, and moral courage might also elevate a person beyond his given social position. Consider the myth of Saramba, for instance, a warrior chief of great renown, whose jealous half-brothers decided to waylay and murder him. When Saramba's humble finaba, Musa Kule, got wind of the plot, he devised a plan to save his master's life. After persuading the ruler to exchange clothes with him, Musa Kule rode the chief's horse ahead along the road where the ambush had been laid. As a result, Musa Kule was killed instead of the chief. In recognition of his sacrifice Saramba declared that from that day henceforth his descendants and Musa Kule's should be considered equals, because the moral qualities of the lowborn fina had effectively eclipsed the status superiority of his master.

Subtle reciprocities are disclosed here. The relationship between respect given and recognition returned, for example. Or the implicit understanding that a chief will give his protection to those who submit to his authority and place themselves in his hands. But what if a chief or political leader turns into a tyrant—seizing people's property, taking advantage of his subjects, repaying tribute with obloquy? What if a husband abuses his dutiful and obedient wife? And should the young have regard for the ancestral order of things when it is evoked only to bolster the powers and prerogatives of an elite that is indifferent to their needs, contemptuous of their aspirations, and blind to their talents? "The Big Men fear that the young will steal from them," a middle-aged man called Biru once told me. "And the young are often jealous of what the Big Men have."

For many young people in Sierra Leone, their patience with autocracy, traditional or modern, had worn thin. For them, their due was determined by need, and this was not delimited by their inferior station in life but by what they imagined might be theirs as citizens of the world. These questions, born of my Kuranko research, were, I realized, not unrelated to the R U F rebellion, but at that moment, as if to derail my train of thought, small S. B. said that the 4-Runner had been repaired and we could go on our way.

As I walked back to the vehicle I found the boss mechanic negotiating with S. B. for a little extra money. The mechanic's son was at his father's side. He was about the same age as my own son. As the father spoke to S. B. he cradled his son's head in his hand. Then he ran his hand over the boy's shoulders and back, pressing him to his side. And all the while, the boy was beaming with happiness.

6 Within These Four Walls

I visited S. B. the day after our return from Kabala, but the trip had exhausted him, and he felt lethargic and had no appetite. It was because of diabetes and high blood pressure, he explained, and a prostate problem. So I asked small S. B. to drive me back to Cape Sierra, where I spent the day walking on the beach, swimming lengths in the hotel pool, and reading at random from Paul Auster's *True Tales of American Life*. True though these stories were — in the sense that they set down exactly what an individual remembered about a critical moment in his or her life — it was clear that what made an event both memorable and narratable was the extent to which it disclosed synchronicities, coincidences, or insights that transfigured the humdrum reality of everyday existence. Despite the fickleness of fate and the contingency of events, most people seek evidence of a hidden hand, an implicit order, a latent design. Yet most lives, I suspect, lack natural symmetry or narrative form, and seldom attain sudden significance in a moment of epiphany or denouement. Certainly this was the case with the terrible stories I had heard in the north. People bore witness to the events that had befallen them. Oddly detached, and matter-of-fact in tone, they simply detailed a chain of events, an unbearable sequence of sheer happening (the phrase is Hannah Arendt's) with little emotion or elaboration. Indeed, when I later read comparable stories on an Internet site, I came upon only one in which a person described his feelings as the ax fell. "Oh, I felt so bad. I felt as if I am finishing the world. My eyes were dark. My blood was pumping as if they had opened a tank, a water tank to run. Oh, I fell down. I could not see my way . . . One after another. You go next. When they finished with you, when they cut your two hands, you run. They say, 'Move! If you don't move, we'll fire on you.' Fifty on that particular day."[1]

In the testimonies I heard, no meaning was arrived at, no closure was sought, no moral questions were posed, let alone answered, no injustice was redressed, no wounds were healed, no consolation was provided, unless it lay in the hope everyone expressed, after they had recounted their stories, that I would be able to help them recover, in some small way, what they had lost.

When I asked S. B. what kind of book he had in mind, what kind of audience, he said he trusted me to do justice to his story. He gave me carte blanche. "In that case," I said, "let's begin wherever you want, and go on in whatever way you feel is right. I will try not to interrupt with questions or suggestions until you have finished."

We went out onto the veranda, and after setting up my tape recorder, we sat side by side, looking out over the city — the downtown buildings smudged by the harmattan.

"I had slept soundly that night," S. B. began, "but when I woke I had no idea where I was. Then I realized I was in Pademba Road Prison. I had been taken there at about four o'clock the previous afternoon. They had made me remove my shoes, my tie, my watch, and my ring before taking me to the cells. There was a latrine bucket there that had not been emptied. The warden told me that the buckets were emptied in the morning. 'Sorry, but you'll have to live with it.'

"Early the previous morning, I had been at my office when three men, two from CID and one from the Internal Security Unit, came and said that Assistant Commissioner Frank Jalloh wanted to see me. I said, 'OK, I'll come outside.' As I went toward my car, the ISU man said, 'Come this way Mr. Marah, unless you want me to rough you up.' I could not understand what was happening. They ordered me to get in a VW car. I sat in the back with one of the CID men. The other one drove, with the ISU man beside him with a gun. As we were getting out of the car at CID headquarters near the Cotton Tree, a vehicle drove up and orders were given for me to be taken to my house at 29 Main Motor Road.

"That week, we had been preparing to go up-country for two months. My wife Rose had her annual leave from the Income Tax Department where she was staff superintendent, and school was closing for the holidays on Friday. We'd planned to leave the following day. My mother was also staying with us. She was on her way to Mecca, and I'd been arranging her passport and health certificates. So when I turned up at the house with the CID, my wife, my mother, and my children were frightened. Especially Aisetta, who was only four, and used to being with me all the time. Every day, when I got home from work, she would be at the gate to greet me. I would drive her up to Hill Station so we could spend some time together, just the two of us, before dinner. The CID men said they were searching for a speech. 'What speech?' I asked. They said they were also looking for arms, dynamite, and ammunition. They hunted high and low, and turned the house upside down. In the course of their search they found my gun, and asked if I had a license for it. I said, 'Yes, of course,' and I told them I also owned a revolver, which I kept at my office.

"So we returned to my office. You can imagine the crowd that had gathered there. S. B. Marah in police custody! They took my pistol and we went back to CID headquarters. They kept me there all day, before announcing that I was to be taken to Pademba Road Prison and detained with the others. I told them that I still had the keys to my office, and that my car was still parked in the street outside. Could I make a phone call? Rose was at the office with my elder sister, Ai. Rose was in tears. She asked me what she should tell Aisetta, what she should do. I told her that I left her in the hands of God. I was very close to them. Aisetta was very dear to me. She would not go to sleep at night unless she was holding my hand. Rose said, 'OK, your elder sister is here.' And so I spoke to Ai, who told me, 'Sewa, there is only one thing I have to say to you. You have to be a man. Remember you are a Kuranko, and that you have to be a man. Do you promise?' I said, 'Yes, I promise, and that is what I will do.'

"At the prison I was given two blankets—one to lie on, and a thinner one to cover me. My corduroy jacket, that they had allowed me to keep, served as my pillow. As I said, that first night I slept well. In the morning they took me out of my cell for a bath. I asked for soap. They gave me some soda-soap. This was to be my only bath for thirteen months.

"Ten days passed before I left my cell again. This time I was taken

51 *Within These Four Walls*

to CID headquarters to make a statement. One of the police officers there was an old friend of mine from Fadugu, Sorie Conteh. He often came to my house, because I had represented Fadugu in Parliament. So I told him to hurry to my house and get me my brown suit, a pair of bathing trunks, my toothbrush, and some toothpaste. When he returned, I changed into the clothes, which I would not have been allowed to carry into the prison.

"An officer called Newlove was then assigned to take my statement.

"The first allegation was that I had given money to a certain Unfa Mansaray, to pay for transportation to and from a house in Murray-town where a plot was being made against the government. The second allegation was that a man called Suma had visited my office one day and overheard me and Paramount Chief Bai Makari N'Silk plotting against the government. In my statement I pointed out that the money I'd given Mansaray was not for transportation at all, but for some paint he sold me. He wanted Le 5,000 for it, but I gave him Le 4,000. A day or so later, he came by the house and asked if I could help him get back downtown. I remember the day well. It was a Sunday, and Aisetta and I were weeding the flower garden at the time. I sent Aisetta to my room to fetch the Le 1,000 I'd left on my bedside table after paying for the paint. This was the only money I gave him for 'transport.' In the case of Suma, I did not recognize him when he came to my office. But Chief N'Silk, who was sitting in the lounge at the time, reminded me that Suma had been a student of mine when I was teaching at Kitchon. I remembered him then, and asked him what he was doing and where he was living. He said he had been at the Wilberforce Barracks for a while. I said, 'I didn't know you were there, but I am pleased you have dropped by to greet me.' He said, 'Yes sir, now I know where you live, I will visit you sometime.' That was it. There was nothing else.

"As Newlove took down my statement, I could see that he was in tears. Rose, who had returned with Officer Conteh to bring me my suit and the other things I'd asked for, was also in tears. Clearly this was a plot. An innocent man was being charged with treason. Why else would this police officer be crying?

"When it was time for me to go, I also shed tears. Rose told me that for the last ten days, Aisetta had kept asking her, 'Who is going to hold me now, Mummy, so I can go to sleep?' Rose did not know what to say. 'Where is Papa?' Aisetta asked. Rose told me she did not know how to answer Aisetta's questions.

"I was then returned to Pademba Road.

"A few days later, at about seven in the morning, they opened my cell door and said, 'You are going out.' So I picked up my corduroy jacket and my toothbrush. But the officer said, 'Put them down, you will be coming back.' All the detainees were assembled and taken to the main gate. About ten open lorries were parked there. There were benches on each side of each lorry, but we the detainees had to sit on the floor. Each of us had a CID and ISU man on either side of him — the CID man holding you by your trousers, the ISU man holding a gun. As we drove away from the prison, Bishop Bangura's wife recognized Fred Carew from the veranda of one of the houses opposite the prison gate. She and Fred attended the same church, and she was in tears. As we drove toward New England, my first reaction was that they were taking us to the president's house at Kiama road. But we passed there. My second thought was that they were taking us to the stadium for more justice. When we turned west toward Congo Cross, I said to myself, 'We must be going to Lumley Beach so we can wash.' But at Congo Cross roundabout we turned up Signal Hill road toward Wilberforce. It was then that I realized that we were going toward my house. I said, 'Please, I don't want to see my children. When we pass the house, please tell me.' As we approached the house, I looked out. I saw the kids playing by the side of the house. You can't imagine how I felt.

"We drove on to Bottom Mango where some of the suspects were taken down from the vehicle. I saw my houseboy Sori there and asked Newlove if I could be permitted to talk to him. He said, 'Yes.' I said, 'Sori, I have been detained, and I don't know when I am going to be released. I therefore beg you, I appeal to you, not to leave my family. Stay with them.' Then, while I waited, the other detainees were taken into the PZ employees' compound, next to the Wilberforce Barracks, to make their statements. This was where the plans were allegedly made to assassinate the vice presidents. Unfa Mansaray had been a cook at this compound. After about thirty minutes there, we were driven to the house of Vice President C. A. Kamara-Taylor at Spur Road, which the plotters had tried to blow up with dynamite. All this time a CID man was holding me by my trousers, and an ISU man stood guard over me with a revolver. The CID chap was a Mende. He said, 'Brother, after all this you will know all the facts.' I then felt, wrongly as it turned out, that my detention might soon be over.

"Next day I was driven to my house. Again I asked the police officers not to let my children see me. I had to demonstrate how I had given the Le 1,000 to Mansaray. While we were at the house I asked Mr. Walter Nicol, the officer in charge — who subsequently became inspector general of police, and is now chairman of the National Electoral Commission . . . I begged him to let me write some checks for my family. He said OK, and I left the checks with Rose. We now returned to my office. People were in tears. I heard that the girls from Barclays Bank were all crying. Seeing me dressed so badly, my hair shabby, my office closed. I opened my office, and once more demonstrated what had happened the day Suma came to see me, how I had been inside my office, and come out to find him and the chief in the lounge. I was then taken back to Pademba Road. It was that night, I remember, locked in my cell, that in my wild thinking I went back over my life, from my childhood up to the day I was arrested, and I thought, 'Someday I will put this down on paper, perhaps write my autobiography, or something about my life.' And that is when I thought of you, of doing the book with you, because I knew I would need a writer."

After S. B. left for Parliament, I went downstairs to talk with Rose. She spent every morning in the kitchen — an unfurnished concrete room, with a large charcoal brazier placed near the back door so that smoke could escape outside. She had only occasional help. The two girls she'd had working for her until recently had left on account of S. B.'s irascibility. As she replaced the heavy lid on the huge country pot in which the rice was simmering, I asked her if she remembered the time S. B. was detained in Pademba Road Prison. "Mike," she said, "I can remember every detail. The CID coming to the house that day and ransacking every room, looking for incriminating evidence. He could have escaped arrest. Someone at the president's office let him know that his name was on a list of people to be detained, but he took no notice of it. He could see no possible reason why they would arrest him. Ever since the SLPP lost the election in 1967 and David Lansana declared martial law, S. B. had kept himself well away from politics. I remember the day Ibrahim Taki and Mustapha approached S. B. at home, trying to persuade him to return to politics — though not, I think, to get involved in any coup. He refused. He even brandished his revolver at Mustapha to show how adamant he was. Then, in July 1974, there was this plot to dynamite the houses of the two vice presidents. The plan was to blow them up at the same time, at three o'clock one morning. S. B. was indicted, like Dr. Forna and Ibrahim Taqi and the others, because the CID and ISU tortured their so-called witnesses until they named the people they wanted to be named. But the truth is that S. B.'s political rival Kawusu Conteh was the one who wanted him out of the way, not the president. It was Kawusu who said that S. B. attended the meetings at which the coup was planned. And it was Kawusu who wanted to remove Kamara-Taylor and S. I. Koroma from power, so that he could become vice president. In any event, the plot failed. The man who was hired to blow up S. I. Koroma's house did nothing. The other one got drunk, and by the time he sobered up and set off his charges, it was too late. Anyway, the vice president wasn't even at home, though he claimed he was. The CID arrested Unfa Mansaray, who was a cook at the PZ compound house where the plotters met. When they questioned him about S. B., he said S. B. knew nothing of the plot, but they beat him mercilessly until he confessed that S. B. once gave him money for transport. This evidence would, of course, have been demolished in court, except there was no court hearing. Mansaray ended up in Pademba Road along with the others. Apparently, Mustapha sent a letter to the president saying that S. B. had had nothing to do with the plot, but the president did not read the letter, thinking it was a plea from Mustapha for clemency."

"How did you manage," I asked, "while S. B. was in detention?"

"S. B.'s mother stayed with me. I continued to draw S. B.'s Alitalia salary from Tony Yazbeck. The Yazbeck family paid our rent, our phone and electricity bills, and helped us with money for school fees. And like you, Tony petitioned the president for S. B.'s release. But for all those thirteen months he was in prison I did not see him or hear from him once."

Rose went on to speak of the perils of African politics with a kind of resigned and bemused helplessness. One of her sisters was married to a businessman from Ivory Coast, she said. They met in the United States where she was studying for her B.A. in French. When S. B.'s brother-in-law once expressed an interest in going into politics, S. B. warned him against it. "But then, S.B is a politician," Rose added. "His life is not his own. It belongs to the people."

7 The Executions

In one of his theses on the philosophy of history, Walter Benjamin observes that "to articulate the past historically does not mean to recognize it 'the way it really was' . . . *It means to seize hold of a memory as it flashes up at a moment of danger.*"[1] I remembered this line as S. B. continued his story, and as I realized, sitting beside him on the veranda, how painful many of his recollections were. At times his voice was scarcely more than a whisper, and he leaned forward against the rail of the balcony as if to protect his face from being seen. He first described the layout of the detainees' wing. The two rows of thirty-six cells. Each row two-tiered. His own cell on the lower level, with one small barred window above the steel door, about seven feet above the floor. The cell was lit night and day by a single bulb that made the walls appear yellowish. By standing at the back wall, S. B. was able to see through the window above the door, and so observe the movement of people along the concrete catwalk that ran between the lower and upper tiers. Food consisted of one pound of cooked rice per day, with some thin soup. No pepper or salt. No fish or meat. The toilet bucket was removed once a day by an ordinary prisoner. "But there was never much in it," S. B. said, "because we ate and drank so little.

"As a political detainee, I was never allowed out of my cell. And I was not allowed to wash. In the first few months we were given half a gallon of water each day, but one day, when several of the detainees were taken to the high court, it was discovered that Dr. Forna had used some of his drinking water to wash his jacket during the weekend so that he would look presentable in the courtroom. As punishment, they took away our water supplies, and gave us a communal bucket, which was placed outside the cells. If you wanted a drink you had to bang on the door, and a prison officer would come and dip your cup into this bucket. It was a plastic cup. You could do this no more than twice a day. Every day he was taken to court, Dr. Forna was handcuffed. I would see him go and come back. I had known him years before as a brilliant scholar at Bo School (a high school established by the British in 1906 for the sons of Protectorate chiefs — its motto, "manners maketh the man"; its aim, to create a loyal rural elite). I had known him when he was a medical officer at Wilberforce Hospital. And I had known him when he was minister of finance and acting prime minister, being driven in a motorcade, with motorbikes going ahead of him. Now I saw him going to court in handcuffs, as later I would see him going to the gallows . . ."

When S. B. paused, I asked him how he passed the long hours alone in his cell, how he kept his sanity.

"I would close my eyes," he said, "and clench my fists, and pretend I was running from my office, along Siaka Stevens Street, passing Barclays Bank." As he spoke, he mimed this old routine of running on the spot, imagining himself jogging through the city. "The law courts now, passing the cotton tree, Pademba Road, the petrol station, the bridge, Hill Cut Road, Hill Station junction, Bottom Mango, Main Motor Road, home. I would remember every detail of the route. At every place I passed, I would say aloud where I was. I am approaching my house now, I am getting close to home, I am coming to the compound, I am saying to Rose, 'How are you? How are the children?' That was my exercise. Running in my mind's eye. Daydreaming. Another thing I used to do was sing quietly to myself. Kuranko songs. Making up the words. 'Go tell them all around the Loma Mountains that I am here and that I am well. Tell my mother to pray for me. Tell them that I remember what my father used to say to us — A man must endure hardship. Today I am passing through such hard times, but I am sure I will conquer. Tell the people around the Loma Mountains that I will not give up, I will not relent. I will not disappoint them. When I am released from this place I will fight for them, to see that they are recognized.'"

'What was the worst thing you had to endure?"

"Not being with my family, not seeing my children. At Christmas, at midnight, I called out to them, 'Merry Christmas Rose, Merry Christmas Fatmata, Merry Christmas Abu, Merry Christmas Aisetta, Merry Christmas Aisha . . .'

"One day," S. B. said, "I asked for the doctor. I told him it was not healthy that we should all be drinking from the same bucket. One of us might have TB. We could contract the disease and contaminate our families when we went home. But my pleas fell on deaf ears. In fact, none of our questions were ever answered. None of our requests were allowed. We lived like slaves. We were not even permitted to speak, except to say good morning to the prisoners in the cells next to our own. One morning I greeted a fellow prisoner whose name was Alhaji Salam. He was a very soft-spoken man, and I was not sure he had heard me. So I raised my voice: 'Alhaji Salam, Alhaji Salam.' An officer came to my cell, opened the door, and took away my blankets. He said I was making too much noise. I said, 'Sir, I was only saying good morning to my neighbor. I wasn't sure he could hear me. That's why I kept repeating his name. I am sorry.' The officer ignored me. He took away my blankets for two weeks, and I had to sleep on the bare floor. He said I had broken a rule, and that was my punishment.

"I was a very poor sleeper in prison. I pleaded with the medical officer to give me Valium or something to help me sleep. I found it difficult to get my family out of my mind, even for a moment, especially at night. My mind would wander, thinking of them, how they were in the house. But the medical officer told me that if I took Valium it would get into my system and when I left prison I would not be able to sleep without it. I told him that if I could only sleep in prison I would gladly face sleeplessness when I returned home. 'While I am here, I said, I want to forget about my family. It is terrible at night, thinking about them all the time, and not being able to sleep.'

"There were many deaths during the time I spent in Pademba Road. Many people died during an epidemic. Their stools were bloody, and they died within days. I remember a young Fula chap, very handsome, brought down from Kono, who died this way. And then there were the Mammy Yoko murderers. They were only boys, about eighteen or twenty. Two of them I knew very well. One was the son of Mr. Sheku Jabi and my cousin Fatmata. I remember when he was born. The other, Sila, was another cousin's daughter's son. They were tried and condemned to death. They were in the cell above mine. When I learned that they were to be executed next day, I could not sleep. Imagine someone you know well, who you have known as a baby, going to the gallows. I cried that night. The third boy, who I did not know personally, managed to communicate a message to Bedor Bangura, one of the detainees in our group. 'When you are released,' this boy said to Bedor, 'please tell my parents to forgive me for all the pain I have caused them. Let them pray for me. And tell them that I did not kill Kabiya.'

"Bedor never left Pademba Road Prison alive. So the message was never delivered. And since I did not know the parents of this boy, who was hanged that night, I could not deliver the message either. Had I known them, I would have done so.

"I remember another man, too, a soldier from Murraytown Barracks. He had gone mad, and was kept in chains. At night you could hear him singing Poro songs in his cell. The prison officers would order prisoners to flog him. They said that flogging was the best medicine. Then he was tried and condemned to death. I saw the medical officer arrive the night of the execution. I had known him in Kabala, though I forget his name . . .

"The chap in the cell next to mine at that time was Alhaji Lamine Sidique. We used to joke around.[2] 'Cousin,' he would say, 'I've got over three hundred bedbugs here in my cell.' 'Well, you're a Fula man,' I'd say, 'these are your cows!' It was fun, but it wasn't fun. Life wasn't easy. One day, Lamine told me that he was going to ask the prison director for pen and paper so that he could write to Siaka Stevens. 'I have been here for a year,' he said. 'I have done nothing wrong. I am going to ask him why I should be detained.' At that very moment, his cell door was opened and he was taken away. A prison officer then told the rest of us that further charges of treason were to be laid. This was to frighten us. We became very uneasy. But next morning we learned that Lamine had been released. I was very happy for him. I thought, 'Perhaps now he is free he can use his influence to get the rest of us released.'

"The following day, an old man called J. J. Davis, an ex-serviceman, told me that he had overheard some prison officers saying that some of the detainees would be released. And he started planning a celebration at Brookfields Hotel. 'Even if we are released,' I said, 'I do not want to go anywhere except home, to be with my family, to see my wife and kids. Anyway,' I said, 'if we all went to Brookfields wouldn't the CID arrest us again, and accuse us of plotting against the government? We would have to meet in the open.'

"Ten minutes later we learned that Pa Davis was dead. It was incredible. My temper rose up and I banged the iron door with my fist. How could he have died in that short space of time? I was distraught. I did not sleep that night.

"I had been in prison for a year when one night my ulcer burst. I pleaded with the prison warder to open the door so I could breathe fresh air. I was finding it hard to breathe. He said he did not have the keys with him and that I would have to wait until morning, when he could see the director. That night I thought I was going to die. But in the morning the doctor came and directed that I be taken to the infirmary. I had not seen sunlight for twelve months, and when I was taken out through the main gate of the prison the sun blinded me, which is why I now have to use reading glasses. In the infirmary there were two condemned prisoners. They were in chains. They wore black, with C for 'condemned' written on them. One day a prisoner, whose father was actually a prison officer, told me that I should be extremely careful of these men. If they happened to kill again, the government would set them free. You can imagine how I felt. I could not sleep properly after this, fearing that these men might strangle me to win their freedom. Even though I knew that this was surely impossible, I also knew that anything could happen to a person in prison. So I slept during the day.

"One morning, while I was still in the infirmary, a friend of mine whom I had known outside prison (he used to come to my Alitalia office with iced water, and do the football pools with me) came to me with news that all the detainees who had been tried and found guilty were to be executed that night. My friend's name was Renner. When he told me this news I implored him not to tell anyone else. I did not want the others to know. But they were in my thoughts all day. Dr. Forna. Ibrahim Taqi. All of them. I was thinking of them all.

"I will never forget that night. The main power supply was disconnected, and a generator turned on. I tried to sleep by persuading the nurse to give me a double dose of Valium. I was scared. You can't imagine how I felt. It was terrible. I did not want to be conscious of what was going on. But the pills did not work, and every hour, from one in the morning, I watched from my bed as the medical officer went to the execution cell and then returned. I saw corpses. Eight were executed that night, at hourly intervals. The last was my friend N'Silk, paramount chief of Makarigbanti. I had known him for years. He was a schoolteacher like myself. At one time he was captain of the

Protectorate football team. He went to Parliament as APC (All People's Congress Party), but later went over to SLPP. I'm sure Siaka Stevens never forgave him. When he was found guilty of treason, he was not spared. He was a friend of mine. His children called me uncle. I hate to remember that night. The deaths of Paramount Chief N'Silk, of Dr. Mohamed Forna, of Ibrahim Taqi. It is something terrible, an execution. I would hate to sign the death warrant of any man. This part of politics I find abhorrent.

"After that I did not know what would happen. Though I played no part in the coup attempt, anything could have happened. I was very worried.

"One morning, not long after the executions . . . it was a Thursday . . . I heard my name being shouted: 'S. B. Marah, S. B. Marah, you've been released!'

"People in prison believe you'll be so excited when you hear news of your release that you will forget to say goodbye. But I took time to go along the cells, saying goodbye to some of the prisoners I had gotten to know. I was then taken to the main office, where my shoes were handed over to me, and my ring. My watch I did not get.

I stood outside the prison and picked up a taxi. I went straight-away to Tony Yazbeck's house. I had not had a bath for thirteen months. I was shabby, with unkempt hair, and a beard, though my jacket was clean because I had not worn it all the time I was in prison. Tony was not at home, and his children did not recognize me. I said, 'I am Marah, S. B. Marah, your daddy's friend.' They were about to go to town, so they gave me a lift to my house at 29 Main Motor Road. I went straight to Rose. She hugged me. I think she knew I was going to be released. Then the children came. I had dark glasses on. Rose said, 'Look Aisetta, it's Papa.' Aisetta thought I might be Father Christmas! She did not remember me. When I left her she had been four years four months old. She said to me, 'Take off your glasses.' She was still afraid. Abu was very small. He did not know who I was either. And there were other children that I did not know. They belonged to a family who lived nearby. Their house had had its roof blown off in a storm. Rose had allowed them to use our garage as a place to stay.

"Rose then prepared my bath, a warm bath. She gave me a good scrub, brought me a towel, got me a new shirt and trousers. I was now united with my family again.

"In prison I had been told that I should go and see the president the day after my release; he wanted to see me. But Siaka Stevens had been involved in a road accident on the afternoon of the day I was released, so it was not possible to see him at that time. A few weeks later, Tony Yazbeck gave me and my family air tickets to Abidjan, Beirut, and London. Rose wanted to visit her elder sister in Ivory Coast. And I needed a medical checkup in England. We stayed in London for a month, where I saw my *agba* 'mentor' Sir Albert Margai, I also saw S. I. Koroma, who was then vice president. I first knew him when he was at Bo school, though we were never close. I never followed anyone. I was always my own man. S. I. Koroma told me: 'I do not have anything against you. I don't know whether or not the Old Man has something against you, but in my opinion we should not molest people like you.' I told him that I had been arrested and detained. Nothing more. I did not know why. But this was the price one has to pay in politics."

Though moved by S. B.'s equanimity as he recounted his story, I also felt troubled. For his remarks had brought home to me the paradox of power — which, for all its promises of a brave new world, invariably attracts envy and resentment. For this reason, whoever attains high office must perforce divide his energies between nurturing this illusion of a better future and defending his hold on power. "The trick in politics," S. B. once told me, "is to promise people the earth; I learned this from old Pa Wurie [one of S. B.'s political mentors]. 'What the African likes is promises,' he used to say. 'Even if you don't have the means to keep your promise. Give people excuses, or make some new promise, and they'll forget about the first thing you promised them.' Pa Wurie didn't go along with the idea of a bird in the hand being worth more than two in the bush!"

I didn't agree that one could fool all of the people all of the time, and was reminded of what Max Gluckman so perceptively called the frailty in authority, born of this gap between the expectations we have of rulers, secular or divine, and the flaws and failings we all too readily see in them.[3] This is why dissent and rebellion are endemic to political life. When a country is impoverished, like Sierra Leone, a leader may, through no fault of his own, fail in reconciling high expectations with grim reality, and end up bearing the brunt of people's disappointment. Perhaps this is why politicians sometimes give up on the idea of the general good, and focus on feathering their own nests — throwing occasional sops to their faithful followers, consolidating their power base, silencing dissent. In the 1967 general elections, Albert Margai's Sierra Leone People's Party was narrowly defeated by the APC.[4] As his successor Siaka Stevens was being sworn in at State House on 21 March , a young army officer and aide-de-camp to the governor general, Lieutenant Samuel Hinga Norman, stopped the ceremony, on orders from his Force Commander, Brigadier David Lansana, whose justification was that the results of the chiefs' elections had not been taken into account. Martial law was declared, and two days later Siaka Stevens and several of his ministers were driven in a military Land Rover to Pademba Road Prison. By the time a countercoup reinstated Siaka Stevens in April 1968, the new incumbent had doubtless had ample time to decide what he must do to remain in power, and how he should deal with his opponents. Understandably distrustful of the army, he created a paramilitary unit comprising many recruits from Guinea, called the State Security Department (SSD), also known as Siaka Stevens's Dogs.

These, then, were some of the background events and experiences against which Siaka Stevens's shadow state began to emerge — with its insidious control of the nation's diamond wealth by a ruling elite, the deployment of spies and thugs to intimidate enemies, and finally the stage-managed dynamiting of C. A. Kamara-Taylor's house, followed by the trumped-up charges, the litany of lies, the confessions under duress, and the abuse of high court protocols that in the early hours of 19 July 1975 culminated in the judicial murder of S. B.'s colleagues and friends.

A few months after hearing S. B.'s account of his detention, I read Aminatta Forna's *The Devil That Danced on the Water,* in which she speaks of her search for the truth about her father's life and death.[5] In his final hours, Dr. Mohamed Forna "used the paper and pen supplied to him for his mercy plea to compose an account of his life from boyhood to his death," Aminatta writes, and she goes on to describe, on the basis of an eyewitness report, his walk to the gallows, and how, on the morning after the executions, her father's body, "and those of the seven other men who had been hanged, were displayed in open coffins before the crowds outside Pademba Road Prison." That night, she concludes, the bodies were loaded into military trucks and driven out to Rukupa Cemetery on the road to Hastings, where they were doused with acid and dumped in a mass grave.

8   Fina Kamara's Story

I spent a lot of time mulling over what S. B. had told me about his thirteen months in solitary confinement, surrounded by death, and the "wild thinking" that drew him back to his beginnings. It seemed to me that this urge to retrace one's steps into the past arises neither from nostalgia nor from a need to tell one's story to the world. It is a way of cheating death. An instinct for life in the face of oblivion. For to recollect the innocence of childhood or the vigor of youth in a moment of peril is to retrieve a sense of life's infinite possibility, to conjure a period in our life when the world seemed ours for the taking, and we thought we would never die. It is, in essence, to recapture a sense of our capacity to act and initiate something new, for, as Hannah Arendt notes, action is synonymous with our capacity to bring new life into the world.[1] Mortality is thus countermanded by natality, and it is this unquenchable desire for renewal, this refusal to go gently into that good night, that explains why we go back, stumbling through the darkness, in search of the light that flooded and filled our first conscious years. The days of wine and roses. When our lives stretched before us like a field of dreams. But if our imagination springs to our rescue in such dark times, holding out the promise of rebirth, how do we fare when we are released from darkness, and are returned to our everyday lives? How do we address the injustices we have endured, the life we have wasted, the pain we have so needlessly suffered?

This question was much on my mind the day I went to see Fina Kamara in the Murraytown Amputee Camp.

Exactly three years before I had read a story in the *Guardian Weekly* titled "Machete Terror Stalks Sierra Leone."[2] It concerned a rebel attack on Kondembaia in April 1998 — the same attack Patrick Koroma had described to me in Kabala — and its focus was the ordeal of a young Kuranko woman and her six-year-old daughter.

Fina Kamara's husband was small S. B.'s maternal uncle, so we had little difficulty in locating her at the amputee camp. After parking the 4-Runner and asking some kids if they knew where the people from Kondembaia were living, small S. B. led the way through a labyrinth of alleys to the center of the camp. Though many of the refugees were living in makeshift dwellings, made of white- and blue-striped UN plastic tarps pulled over lashed poles, Fina had a room in a disused barracks.

I recognized her at once from the photo that had appeared in the *Guardian*, and after small S. B. had introduced me, I told Fina of the fieldwork I used to do in Kondembaia, and the recordings I had made of Keti Ferenke's stories. I then showed her the clipping from the *Guardian* that I had brought with me. She looked at it without emotion or interest before passing it on to the other refugees who, out of curiosity, were crowding around. No one commented.

When I asked Fina if she would mind if I tape-recorded her story, she raised no objection, but wanted to know if she should speak in Krio or Kuranko. I suggested she speak in Kuranko.

"We were hiding in the bush for three months," she began. "We were afraid the RUF might come at any time and attack the town. But then we received messages from Freetown and from ECOMOG to come out of the bush and return to town. So we came out of the bush.

"One day we went to our farm to plant groundnuts. We returned to town that afternoon. Suddenly, we heard gunshots. Because there were ECOMOG soldiers in Kondembaia, we were used to hearing gunfire, but this time we were confused.

"The RUF came suddenly. They shot many people. They stacked the bodies under the cotton tree. Then they grabbed us. Their leader said they were going to kill us, too. But then they sent their boys to bring a knife. My daughter Damba was six. They took her from me and cut off her hand. After that they cut off all our hands. One man

Fina Kamara's Story

died because of the bleeding. We ran. We fell to the ground. After some time we got up. Damba said, 'Mummy, I am thirsty.' By now all the houses were on fire. We went behind one of the houses. One of the RUF boys came and said, 'What are you doing there?' I said, 'I want to give water to my daughter.' I gave Damba some water. Then I sat down and tied her on my back. We began running again, but they stopped us in the backyard of one of the houses. One RUF girl said, 'You move one step and I will shoot you.' I had to go back. But there was a place behind the houses. We went down there. After a while I felt hungry. I found a mango but could not eat because my blood was all over it. A little while later I overheard the RUF saying it was time for them to leave. When they had gone, I found my son, and tied Damba on my back again and went to the bush. From there I came out on the road and sat down. I met my husband and uncle there. Everyone was crying. I told them to stop crying. We went to our farm, and in the morning we set off for Kabala. We did not reach Kabala that day because of the pain. It took us two days. People in Kabala said we were lucky; the Red Cross was there. After treating us they brought us by helicopter to Freetown here. We were taken to Connaught Hospital. They treated us there. Then we were taken to Waterloo. When the RUF invaded Freetown, we had to flee from Waterloo. We fled to the stadium. From there we were brought to this camp. If you ask me, this is all I know. We were ordinary people, we were farmers, we had nothing to do with the government. Whenever I think about this, and about the time they cut off my hand, and my daughter's hand, only six years of age, I feel so bad. Our children are here now. They are not going to school. Every morning we are given bulgur. Not enough for us. We are really suffering here. We only hope this war will come to an end and that we will be taken back to our own places. If we go back home, we have our own people there who will help us."

Though I asked Fina some questions, I was oppressed by my inability to respond to her story with anything other than sympathetic words. Even giving her what money I had felt like an empty gesture. So as I retraced my steps to the vehicle with small S. B., down the fetid alleyways, past other amputees, I felt like a thief, or voyeur.

As we drove back toward the city, across the bridge, I saw that the tide was in. It made me think how, in the ordinary course of events, change occurs gradually, almost imperceptibly, allowing us time to adjust, to acclimatize, even to ignore it. So we age. Things wear out and decay. The tide ebbs or flows. But when an accident happens, our whole world is changed utterly in a split second. Time is intensified, compressed, giving us no time to think, to take stock, to prepare. It overwhelms us, and we are instantly sundered from our lives, from all that we have been, and plunged into nothingness. The shock is absolute.

Yet now Fina Kamara seemed to exist outside time, in torpor and nothingness. Killing time. An endless waiting that had claimed her soul.

Three and a half years had passed since Fina Kamara's world fell apart, and she was still struggling to grasp how this could have happened. The rebels came and went within an hour. In this short time they murdered fifty people and mutilated another ten or fifteen. They also set fire to every building in Kondembaia, except the mosque, which they used as a kitchen, and the school, the church, and a house where they stashed their belongings. Though Fina had spoken of the RUF, many of the rebels were in fact young junta soldiers, avenging their ouster from power a few weeks earlier when the Nigerian-led ECOMOG reinstated the elected government of Ahmad Tejan Kabbah. Unable to defeat the ECOMOG soldiers or the Civil Defense militias, they took their revenge on the defenseless people who had allegedly voted for the government, or sheltered and supported the tamaboros. Of all this, Fina Kamara knew nothing. "We are ordinary people," she had told me. "All we do is go to our farms."

When I asked her if she thought she would ever learn to live with what had happened, she said, "I will never forget."

"Would it make any difference to you, if the people that did these dreadful things were punished?"

"I no longer waste my anger on them. But I will never forget what they did. When they burned my house, how can I forget that? When I look at my hand, how can I ever forget? I feel the pain constantly. Even now, talking to you, I feel it. At times, I can feel my fingers, even though they are not there."

When I saw Noah the following day, I told him of my visit to the amputee camp, and of Fina Kamara's description of the phantom pain she felt in her hand, the embodied memory of all she had suffered. But I was perplexed, I told Noah, by the way that Fina had explained her feelings toward those who had visited this suffering on her, and on her village.

Noah was ready for this conversation. He had come to see me at

S. B.'s house the day before, only to be turned away at the gate. The soldiers and security guards had refused him entry, though they knew he was S. B.'s brother. Even now, the humiliation and insult rankled. "You see," he said, "how I am shut out. How I have no one inside who can help me. How I have to look outside for help."

I told Noah that when I had asked Fina Kamara what she might do to redress the damage that had been done to her and her daughter she said, "There is nothing I can do." And when I asked her what she thought about reconciliation, she used the phrase *m'bara hake to an ye,* which small S. B. translated as "I can forgive, but I cannot forget." What exactly did she mean by this?

"It's what you might say," Noah said, "when someone offends or hurts you, and you are powerless to retaliate. If, for instance, someone takes something from you without justification. Or insults and humiliates you for no good reason. Say a hawk came out of the blue and seized one of your chickens. What can you do? You can't get it back. The hawk has flown away. You have no means of hunting it down, or killing it. All you can do is accept, and go on with your life. But you don't really forgive, you don't really forget. You simply accept that there's nothing you can do to change what has happened. Look at me. I have no way of taking revenge on the rebels who took away my livelihood, but at least I can rid myself of them. I can shut them out of my mind. I can expel them from my life."

Noah's words were reminiscent of a passage in Hannah Arendt's *The Human Condition.*[3] Forgiveness implies neither loving those that hate you, nor absolving them from their crime, nor even understanding them ("they know not what they do"); rather, it is a form of redemption, in which one reclaims one's own life, tearing it free from the oppressor's grasp, and releasing oneself from those thoughts of revenge and those memories of one's loss that might otherwise keep one in thrall to one's persecutor forever.

"If I say *i hake a to nye,*" Noah continued, "I am freeing myself from the effects of your hatred. I am refusing to hate back. But this doesn't mean that justice will not be done. Most of us here feel that God sees everything, and that God will mete out punishment in his own good time. That's why we say, *Altala si n'hake bo a ro,* God will take out my anger on him. Or I might say, *m'bara n'te to Al'ma,* I have left it up to God. Same as they say in Krio, *I don lef mi yone to God.* I think this is what Fina Kamara meant. She was not saying that she forgives the RUF, but that she is leaving it up to God to see that justice is done. Because how can you ever be reconciled to someone who has killed your father or cut off your hand? *Reconciliation, forgiveness, forgetting* . . . these are all relative terms. In Sierra Leone right now, we are letting sleeping dogs lie. You understand? We are fed up with the war. Fed up with atrocities. If we talk about the war, it is not because we are plotting revenge or want to prolong the suffering. We simply do not want it to happen again."

Writing up my notes that evening at the Cape Sierra Hotel, I kept being drawn back to this issue of reconciliation and revenge. Though Fina Kamara and Noah had found it expedient to give up all thought of payback, this did not mean they rejected the possibility of retaliation or the principle of *lex talionis*. They were simply realists, acutely aware of what they could and could not do. But payback is an open and vexed question in Sierra Leone. For who will see that justice is done? How can apologies atone for the material and social losses people have suffered? Who will pay for reparations? And will the trial of war criminals in special courts set up at both national and village levels simply rub salt into old wounds, arouse bitter memories, cause resentment and enmity, and set in motion another cycle of violence?[4]

This issue of power and powerlessness came to the fore in September 2002 when the people of the Murraytown Amputees Camp declared that they would not testify before the Truth and Reconciliation Commission. While those who had perpetrated atrocities were being promised reintegration allowances of $150, they the victims had been offered nothing, and they called on the government for better shelter, free education and health care for their children, a monthly stipend of rice, and their own reintegration allowances. Not only were the amputees protesting their plight and their social invisibility, they were, albeit obliquely, reminding us that powerlessness attracts, at most, a politics of pity, seldom a politics of justice. And this suggested, in turn, that the rebels still wielded power, at least in the minds of many Sierra Leoneans, for why else should the government offer such generous resettlement packages to rebels and ex-combatants, unless, like the gifts that villagers give to strangers, they were attempts to appease, buy off, or control a force that was still feared, and a problem that peace declarations and the rhetoric of reconciliation could not resolve?

Clearly, both one's point of view and one's tactics reflect one's hold on power, and I wondered about S. B.'s unforgiving comments about the RUF. That he gave them no quarter was not because his anger was stronger than Fina Kamara's, but simply because he was in a stronger position. When I asked him for his opinion of the truth and reconciliation process, he said: "I come from a warrior family. My ancestors went to war. So with this war now, I wanted to fight to the finish. I wanted the fight to go on to the end, until the RUF were defeated. The president knows my views. He knows I was against the Loma peace accord. This was a useless war. The perpetrators must be brought to justice, and not forgiven. They destroyed us. In fact everything I worked for for over thirty years they destroyed. So I do not forgive or forget."

One year later, I raised this issue again with S. B., asking for his opinion of the special court that was now under construction in Jomo Kenyatta Road. "It's all right," he said, "but what is done is done, what is past is past. Perhaps there is some point in deterrence and punishment, but whatever the punishment it won't pay off the crimes that Foday Sankoh has committed against property and humanity." S. B. was similarly resigned when speaking of his detention in 1973. When I asked him what he felt as he recounted his experiences in Pademba Road Prison, and the execution of his peers, he said, "It is painful, but it has happened, it has happened. That is the price one has to pay if you go into politics. It is the kind of thing you have to expect." But for S. B. the RUF atrocities were something else. Something beyond the pale, something outside the bounds of what was human, and could not be forgiven.

Though S. B., Fina Kamara, and Noah were as different as any human beings could be, I had been struck by their sound sense of what, in any given situation, was possible and what was impossible — of where the limits of their freedom lay. All too often in the West, ideas like truth and freedom are discussed in total abstraction. We are encouraged in the belief that there is nothing we cannot do if we put our minds to it. That there is no corner of the universe that is intrinsically beyond our understanding and control. No limit to our power to manipulate genes, to prolong life, to alleviate suffering. I had left Europe at a time when the media were still registering the political fallout of the World Trade Center disaster of 9/11. A millenarian discourse about ridding the world of terrorism, poverty, illiteracy, and disease. This rhetoric also pervaded Freetown. Poda podas were called Better Days Are Coming, Human Right, and O Life at Last. A fishing boat on Lumley Beach had been named Democracy. People were wearing t-shirts saying "Forgive and Reconcile for National Development." And everywhere there were vehicles and offices belonging to NGOs and UN agencies, with *reconstruction, rehabilitation, reconciliation,* and *resettlement* the recurring words. One could not help but be affected by the ostensible spirit of renewal. But how realistic was it all? The aid programs. The disarmament process one read about in the daily papers. The Truth and Reconciliation Commission that was being set up. Isn't this language of reconciliation a little like the language of human rights — a jargon of the North imposed on the South, and as such, simply the new face of the old self-extolling theme of the white man's burden? At every city traffic circle there were banners that read "Di Wor Don Don, Now Wi Di Pwel Di Gun Dem." But as one of the Kondembaia men I met at the amputee camp said to me, "For us the war is still not over."

What struck me forcefully about Fina Kamara's story was not only her sober sense of what she could and could not do, but the absence of any dwelling on the self. Unlike S. B., who recounted his experience as a unique biography, most Kuranko relate a story of shared, critical events. Fina was well aware that those who suffered in Kondembaia had not been singled out by the rebels. If they were victims, it was simply because the rebels classified everyone who was not for them as being against them, and because they happened to be in the wrong place at the wrong time. All were equal in the eyes of the rebels, and their suffering was therefore shared. This was made plain in the way Fina related her story. Only at the moment her forearm was severed, or when she attempted to eat the bloody mango, was her narrative consciousness centered entirely on herself, for in pain one is seldom aware of much else. At other times, however, she spoke of herself as part of the village, as one among many, and recounted events as they happened to "us." Perhaps this explains why, although people had suffered humiliation, bereavement, mutilation, and grievous loss, few spoke of unhinged minds, broken spirits, or troubled souls. Rather, suffering was seen as something shared, and healing was sought not through therapy but in things. Not through words, but deeds. Fees to send children to school. Cement and roofing iron to rebuild houses. Grain. Micro-credit. Food. Medicines. It may well be that a diagnostic label like post traumatic stress disorder is empirically justified, but it is imperative that we acknowledge that psychic wounds and national reconciliation are, for many Sierra Leoneans, not the burning issue. Rather it is the material means that are needed to sustain life, and ensure a future for one's children.

Another reason why people are not fixated on themselves may be their wariness about tempting fate. How often have I heard the phrase, "Don't even think about it" — as if by entertaining a possibility one increases the likelihood of it occurring. Perhaps this is why Noah said he preferred to empty his mind of what had happened, in the hope that it would not happen again. The thought being father to the deed. This magical manipulation of one's thoughts and feelings may also explain the silence of one Kuranko man whose son and daughter had been abducted by the RUF. The son managed to escape during a battle to dislodge the Sierra Leone army from the town of Makeni, and return home to Freetown and his family. But his father told him that he did not want to hear anything of what happened. It made him feel bad. As for the boy, apart from saying he hated the RUF, and would never forgive them for what they had put him through, he craved only that his ignominy not become public knowledge. During the disarmament period, his father urged him to go and find his weapon and hand it in to the authorities, but his son said, "No, I want no record of the fact that I carried arms; I will not do it, even if I am paid millions of leones." As for the daughter, she was sexually abused and traumatized (her father's words). When she finally came home, she refused to return to school. Like her brother, she felt deeply ashamed of what had befallen her. Her father had to "talk and talk and talk to her" before she enrolled in a vocational school in Freetown, and took a dressmaking course for a year. Her father told her, "You are not the only one this happened to. It happened to thousands. So you should return to school." Now, he told me, she is doing well at school and going on with her life.

There was a full moon, and I lay on my bed for some time, gazing out the window into the milky blueness of the tropical night, and imagining that I could hear, beyond the noise of the hotel generator, the sound of the sea pounding its fists on the beach. Perhaps it was because I was missing my own children that my thoughts turned to Fina Kamara, and the question as to when she would see her daughter again. An aid agency (she did not know which one) had taken Damba to the United States for advanced medical treatment, leaving Fina with no way of communicating with her, and no idea when

Damba would return to Freetown. I had no way of knowing how this unidentified agency had justified such a prolonged separation of mother and daughter. Perhaps the overriding consideration had been rescuing Damba from the brutality of war, and giving her a prosthetic limb, rather than the bond between her and her mother. In her despair, Fina had no option but to look to God. Yet, in our complacency, have we not arrogated the power of God to ourselves, and as a consequence placed people like Fina in the invidious position of having to look to us for what we may not have the means to give?[5]

9 Tina Kome Marah

For someone who set such store by the Kuranko virtues of self-containment and impassivity, S. B. was a curiously emotional, and sometimes volatile, man. One morning he suggested I accompany him to his parliamentary office at Tower Hill, to meet some of his colleagues and observe him at work. It was the first time we had been alone together, undistracted by the perpetual comings and goings in the house, and our conversation turned to the past. Driving slowly down Hill Cut Road in his air-conditioned Mercedes, with its personalized SB1 license plate, S. B. surprised me by recalling Pauline's death in 1983, and the long letter I had written him at the time, explaining what had happened. "When I read your letter," S. B. said, "I could hear Pauline's voice in my head, telling me how cool it was in the Loma mountains. Her death was such a blow to me. That's why I found it so difficult to talk to Heidi when I called her from Canberra." Two years ago, S. B. had been in Australia on government business and phoned Heidi in Sydney. "When she picked up the telephone I could hardly speak to her. I had not talked to her when her mother died. So I was all in tears. I could hardly get a word out. I imagined her mother. I imagined how proud Pauline would have been to see her. As I tried to tell her all these things, Heidi was consoling me, so I finally told her I was calling from Canberra, and would call her again to tell her when I would be in Sydney, so we could meet."

I admitted that Heidi had been a bit mystified by his call, and remarked how the past sometimes rises up like a wave and overwhelms us when we least expect it. At that moment, as though in corroboration, the massive walls of Pademba Road Prison slipped by, with the UNAMSIL road blocks and troop carriers, and the Sierra Leonean guards with red berets and automatic rifles standing outside the gates, and as if on cue S. B. recalled an incident from the period just after his release from the prison in 1975. "It was Aisetta's first day at school. She was crying and shouting, not wanting to say goodbye to Rose and me, and we left her there reluctantly. In the space of an hour I heard gunfire from the area around the law courts. People were saying there was a coup. There was total confusion. Cars were running into one another. People rushing about. I left my Alitalia office, picked up Rose at her office in the Ministerial Building, and dashed to pick up Aisetta from school before driving home to Murraytown. We didn't let Aisetta return to school for several days after that. It was the same during the war years. We never knew what was about to happen. We lived with constant uncertainty and false alarms. One day we heard intense gunfire in the direction of Pademba Road Prison. Fearing a coup, I phoned the president, only to learn that a nervous prison guard had accidentally discharged his weapon, and that others had done the same, probably to release the tension. Some weeks later, after the ECOMOG troops had returned to Nigeria, there was another outbreak of small arms' fire." On this occasion, S. B. and Rose drove to Lumley Beach, where they waited several hours for news of what was going on. But when they saw that cars were passing up and down the beach road and everything seemed normal, they shamefacedly returned home where they later learned that the gunfire had actually been a tire blowout that had drawn return fire from the security police. Recalling how easily he had lost his sang-froid under such absurd circumstances, S. B. laughed. "These were the sort of things that happened," he said. "We were often scared, very scared."

The following morning, remembering his father, there was, however, no shame in the strong emotions that were stirred in him. Hesitant, his voice almost a whisper, he said, "I think one of the greatest . . . things I have lost . . . in my life, or someone I have lost . . . is my father. I love him so much that even now . . . when I think of him. . . . I shed tears." Focused on the tape recorder, which I had placed on a chair between us, I had little time to reflect on S. B.'s words, but later that day, walking into the city, I concluded that the reverence S. B. felt for his father reflected more than the Kuranko view that a man's worth is measured against the status and deeds of his forebears; it stemmed from S. B.'s profound regret that Tina Kome had not lived to see how admirably his son had followed in his footsteps and honored his lineage. S. B.'s elder brother, Kulifa, on whom the responsibilities for the family would ordinary have fallen after Tina Kome's death, had gone first to Liberia, then the United States, many years ago, leaving S. B., the second son, to assume this filial role. Perhaps this had increased S. B.'s resolve to fulfill his father's expectations — to engage with the modern world and improve the lot of his countrymen. By entering politics, staying the course for forty years, S. B. had earned the respect of his party, his people, and his president. No other current parliamentarian had been in office at the time of Sierra Leone's independence. Perhaps no one else had known the president as a friend and ally for so long. And no one had greater influence and seniority in the governing SLPP party. Who would not forgive S. B. for feeling proud of having done his duty by his predecessors, despite adversity and loss, and for mourning the fact that Tina Kome had not lived to bear witness to his son's achievements?

Of Tina Kome, I already knew a great deal from Noah, and for many years I had chronicled the ways in which this remarkable man experienced and reflected on a lifetime that coincided almost exactly with the historical epoch of colonial rule. Born in Albitaiya, the mountain refuge to which his people fled after the Kono war, he was only two years old when his father Manti Kamara Kulifa was betrayed to the sofas and executed. Thus, before he was even conscious of his birthright, separation and loss had cast their shadows over his life. The same violent impress of history marked his youth. About the time of his initiation, a European expedition, consisting of policemen, army engineers, interpreters, servants, hammock boys, and bearers, passed through Kuranko country on its way to the headwaters of the Niger.[1] Using plane tables, meridian and circummeridian observations of the stars, trigonometrical plotting and lunar distances, the surveyors established the precise location of the Niger's source. Later that year (1896), the French and British agreed on the international boundary that would henceforth divide their colonial domains, effectively cutting Kuranko country in two. Though his elder brother, Tina Kaima, turned his back on these changes, Tina Kome saw them as presaging a future that he would be foolish to ignore. Around the turn of the century, having married for the first time, he made several journeys to Freetown, which people called

Saralon, traveling for safety in caravans of about two hundred people, for there was a constant danger in those days of being captured and enslaved. The caravans would travel from Kabala to Bafodia, Bafodia to Kamakwie, Kamakwie to Batkanu, Batkanu to Gbinti, Gbinti to Port Loko, then cross the Rokel by canoe before continuing south to the coast. The northerners carried beeswax, kola nuts, soda, song-birds, and leopard skins to sell to the white men, and purchased beads, salt, tobacco, soap, and Manchester cotton to take back home. Sometime during this same period Tina Kome embraced Islam. Given that the Kuranko had first settled the mountainous region of the west Guinea highlands in the early seventeenth century as refu-gees from Islamic jihads, and that the Mara had been staunch pagans for so many generations, Tina Kome's conversion seems, at first sight, strange. But in his eyes, the times were changing. And in any event, he had become, so Noah told me, an unwilling slave to bamboo wine, and Islam's rule of abstinence offered him salvation.

In 1904 the British made Kabala their administrative headquarters, and G. H. Warren was appointed district commissioner. Tina Kome and Tina Kaima were, at this time, farming together near the village of Belikoroia, some five miles from Kabala. Late in the dry season of 1906 their only sister Tina Dondon married a man from Sengbe and went to live in Koinadugu town. No one expected the marriage to last. The husband was an old man, indifferent to women and partial to bamboo wine. Before the rains were over that same year, Tina Dondon left her husband and ran away with her lover.

The old man's sons went to Kabala and filed a lawsuit against Tina Dondon's brothers for refund of bridewealth. For two days receipts were laboriously recalled and counted — the gifts the husband's fam-ily had given to Tina Dondon's family on this or that occasion: the mats, salt, palm oil, kola, soap, and rice during her initiation, the necklaces and trinkets when she married, the five days' hoeing done for her mother Tina, the *lapa* and head-ties that had also been given to her, the lengths of country cloth and bunches of tobacco that Fa Sewa had received . . .

The brothers pleaded for time to make the repayment, but the hus-band's people were in no mood for lenience. "It is the custom to refund on the same day of the accounting," they reportedly said. "We never wanted this divorce. It creates bad feeling all round. Your sister always seemed happy. But what is done is done. We cannot change it."

Tina Kome and Tina Kaima sought help from friends and distant kin, but the main rice crop had not been harvested and they were unable to amass even half the amount required. They considered going to fetch their errant sister from Lengekoro, where she had gone with her lover, and demand that she return to her husband, but Fa Sewa, mindful of his brother's tragic misadventure, advised against it.

The in-laws descended on Belikoroia like scavenging birds. They thronged into the house and brought out everything they could lay their hands on. Hoes, machetes, boxes of clothing, sandals, hearth-stones, mats, baskets, rice, pots, mortars and pestles, and even a bunch of bananas were piled up outside. As the women chased hens around the yard, trapping them against the fence, the men entered the plundered house and hoed up the clay floor, hacked at the walls with their machetes, tore the thatch from the roof, and made up bundles of poles to carry away. Enraged and humiliated, Tina Kome pulled off his gown and threw it down for the scavengers to claim. Fa Sewa was spared the spectacle, but Tina saw it all. The brothers were left with nothing but their trousers, their mother with only a single *lapa* (cotton dress cloth). They returned to live with their mother and Fa Sewa, and over the following months worked from daylight to dark on neighbors' farms, repaying kindnesses and earning the right to call on help to make their own farms. Their mother wore herself out pounding rice for neighbors in return for a small pannier of grain, some groundnuts, and red peppers. Her three hearthstones, made of clay from an anthill, had been taken, but she refused to replace them: for cooking she made do with a hearth of river stones and a chipped country pot.

That same year the outside world imposed its own changes. Having discovered why the people of Barawa were living in and around Kabala, District Commissioner Warren ordered their return home. He had toured the country, he told Chief Belikoro, and found it exceedingly rich in palm kernels. Kuranko would remember Warensi for the cases of champagne he took with him, the tent he preferred to a house, and the elephant cow he shot and wounded near the insel-berg of Senekonke. In his intelligence diary for 14 September 1907, Warren noted, "I have told the people that if they don't return there I shall have to hand over the chiefdom to some other chief." Tina Kaima returned to a country he had never known. His grandfather and namesake had founded the village of Kurekoro when returning exhausted from a border skirmish. Famished and thirsty, he and some other warriors had rested in the shade of a kure tree. After eating ripe fruit and drinking cool water from a nearby stream, the replenished Kaima had declared that they would return there to farm and to build a town that would be called Kurekoro — "under the kure tree." His grandson, however, decided against returning there, and he and other men of the ruling lineage founded a new settlement under a steep hill, where two streams flowed into a third. They called it Firawa — "place in the bush" — after one of the old towns. Tina Kome did not join the returnees. Earlier that year, a British recruitment officer with the West African Frontier Force had visited Belikoro in Kabala and demanded a levy of Kuranko men. On 17 April 1907, Tina Kome, along with thirty-five others, enlisted at the Wilberforce Barracks in Freetown and was assigned the name Bokarie Kabala. Many of his kinsmen and peers took the view that Tina Kome had thrown his life away to become a child of the white men. As he saw it, perhaps, his life had already been thrown to the winds and he had nothing to lose.

When war broke out in June 1914, the Sierra Leone battalion of the West African Frontier Force was made ready to embark for the German colony of Neu Kamerun.[2] Two companies of the Sierra Leone battalion and eight hundred carriers left Freetown on the first of September. The troopship was overcrowded. Cockroaches gnawed the soles of men's feet as they slept. Soldiers chewed lime and red peppers to suppress seasickness. In the hot and fetid atmosphere, food became moldy. On 27 September, after a furious naval bombardment, Duala was taken, and the troops disembarked. Tina Kome first saw action at Yabasi, a railroad town on the Wuri river, north of Duala. Advancing through head-high elephant grass and raked by constant bursts of machine-gun fire, the initial assault failed, though the town was taken the next day. The Sierra Leoneans then held it against a German counteroffensive for more than a month — torrential rain, mud, trenches, and barbed wire entanglements anticipating the nightmare of the Western Front. After a further eight months in the field, marching barefoot through abandoned banana, cocoa, rubber, and oil-palm plantations, slogging along mountain trails turned into quagmires by the rains, enduring sickness, chigger-infection, and heavy casualties, the Sierra Leoneans were finally pulled back to Duala. Following a stint of garrison duty, they returned to the front and a succession of desperate skirmishes at Mbo, Mborokoh, Kayraybi, Mborowah, Sha, Bakan, Bamu, and Fakuundeh (the spellings are Tina Kome's own), in the course of which the Germans retreated, first to Yaounde in the south, then to the Spanish enclave of Rio Muni. As British and French diplomats busied themselves with partitioning another piece of Africa, the troops that had so courageously served imperial interests were shipped back to Freetown, where they arrived in April 1916, almost two years after they had left. This was not, however, the end of Tina Kome's war, as he would note many years later, on 22 December 1946, in the course of writing a letter to the district commissioner of the Northern Province, submitting his name as a candidate for the Barawa chieftaincy. In this letter he describes how, in 1917, four companies of Sierra Leonean troops were dispatched to Nigeria, after a French outpost at Zinder was attacked by Tuaregs under the urging of Sanusi chiefs from Tripolitania.[3] The Sanusi were calling for a jihad in Niger and Nigeria, and the British believed that German advisers were fomenting the rebellion. As it turned out, the Tuareg rebellion was suppressed without the Sierra Leoneans being called on, but during their four months in Nigeria they were not entirely inactive. "When the emir of Zaria refused to pay taxes," Tina Kome writes, "we were sent to arrest him and bring him to Lokojah. During the Cameroon war," he continues, "I was appointed Company Sergeant Major, and subsequently awarded some medals as follows: 1914 Star, British War Medal, Victory Medal, Long Service and Good Conduct Medal, and again awarded the Jubilee Medal, and again I received a Coronation Medal from His Majesty King George VI together with a compliment from the Colonial Secretary." During the war he also taught himself to read and write. Proud of his war service, and having proven himself the equal of any of his warrior forebears, it is difficult to know whether Tina Kome ever questioned the new world order he had so loyally served, and which, after the war, continued to determine his destiny. In the light of the hut tax wars in Sierra Leone, what did he think when he was ordered to arrest the Nigerian emir? Was he ever aware of the thousands of Senegalese conscripts who went to their deaths on the Western Front in a war that could provide no possible amelioration of their own situation in West Africa? And did he ever reflect on the bitter irony that he had risked his life transferring the Cameroons from one colonial power to another? When I put this question to S. B. he said, "Well, as colonials we were brought up to think the British way, and to give our support to England. I remember when we were small boys, we were told that

Japanese things were no good. We believed this, we repeated it. And during the war we were shown posters of shade lamps made from human skin, and they told us that if Hitler won the war all black men would be forced to work at night, and our skin made into shoes. This sort of thing. It was propaganda. But that's the way we were brought up. My father too. So he must have gone along with that sort of thing, that idea that we were all British. It's only now that we have grown up and are ourselves a nation, proud of our own nationality, that we see things differently."

Whatever his views, Tina Kome returned to a town whose name he had carried as his own for ten years, to find that his mother and stepfather had died the year he went away to war.

He also returned to an imperiled birthright. A series of ordinances enacted between 1901 and 1905 (and later, in the 1930s) dramatically reduced the powers of chiefs, and even permitted the replacement of rulers who would not accept colonial decrees. At the same time, a series of amalgamations effectively undermined the autonomy of many chiefdoms, among them Barawa, which was absorbed into the expanded chiefdom of SaNieni.

"We have passed through three ages," an old man once told me in Kabala. "The world began in Mande (the great fourteenth-century empire to which all Mande-speaking Africans, including Kuranko, trace their origins). We then left Mande and came to this country. Then began the age of the white man's rule. Yesterday and today are not the same, but whatever sun shines, that is the sun in which you must dry yourself."

During his years in the army, Tina Kome had befriended a man called Sara Kule, and it was on a visit to Sara Kule's home town in 1922 or 1923 that Tina Kome met the woman who would become his beloved wife Aisetta Sanfan. Sara Kule was married to Aisetta's elder sister, and Tina Kome asked his friend if he and his wife would help facilitate his marriage to the younger woman — her mother's last-born child. He was told that he should meet Ali Mansaray, Aisetta's father, at Mapema. Ali, who was also known as Baba Mapema (father Mapema), was a renowned mori-man, or alpha. Many years before, he had used his mystical powers to help a warrior called Bimba Horo, who hailed from Sirekoro (under the Monkey-bread tree) in the Port Loko district, assume the chieftaincy in Pendembu. In gratitude, Bimba Horo offered his daughter Bahai in marriage to Ali.

81

Tina Kome Marah

Tina Kome traveled from Freetown to Mapema with another army friend — Amara Kargbo — and declared his intentions to Ali. But Ali's answer was a firm no. "I am not ready to give my daughter in marriage to a man living so far away," he said. Tina Kome's friend responded: "Well, the Mandingo Mansarays and the Kuranko Kargbos are one [i.e., the clans had a common historical origin] so this woman is my sister. For my sake give her in marriage to my friend." He then added that Tina Kome was from a ruling house. When Ali asked, "From where?" Tina Kome answered, "From Barawa." Ali said, "I know that place, I have visited it on horseback." He then invited Tina Kome to lodge in Mapema, and shortly after gave him permission to marry his youngest daughter.

Aisetta Sanfan went to live with her husband at the Wilberforce Barracks in Freetown. "There was no electric light, no motorcars, in those days," she once told her twin daughters. "Only chiggers. We used to rub liquid carbolic on our feet to avoid infection." She also remembered selling fried seedcakes to the soldiers, and the visit to Sierra Leone of the son of a prominent person — perhaps the Prince of Wales — who refused to stay overnight in Freetown because it was too dirty, and so returned to his ship to sleep. It was in Freetown, too, that she bore her first child, Kulifa Bockarie, named, as tradition demanded, after her husband's father. Her second child, also named according to custom, took the name of her mother, Bahai Sisay, though the Loko Bahai was changed to the Mandingo Aisetta.

For as long as he lived, Tina Kome was regarded with ambivalence by many of his countrymen. One year, when the British were short of district officers, Sergeant Major — for this was how everyone, including his wives, now addressed Tina Kome — was appointed acting district officer. S. B., then a small boy, remembers him doing the rounds of the Bonthe district, collecting taxes. People would call him a black district commissioner, recognizing his power, but not sure if it was compatible with chieftaincy. "His children are white men," some said, meaning that they were receiving an English education. "His wives are not Kuranko. If we follow this man our children will never succeed." When Tina Kome made his bid for the Barawa chieftaincy in 1946, following the death of Pore Bolo, the then–district commissioner, Victor Ffennell-Smith, and the Sengbe paramount chief, Denka Marah, both advocated his election. But the junior Balansama line of the ruling family, which had held power in Barawa since the end of the eighteenth century, resented the return of chieftaincy to the senior Morowa line. When the votes went against him, Tina Kome rebuked them all. "Ah, you Barawa," he said, "I've worked for you and helped you, and you do not know it. Tomorrow, however, you will."

The promise of that tomorrow was almost fulfilled when S. B. stood for the paramount chieftaincy of SaNieni in 1964, only to be narrowly defeated by his cousin, Bala Kali Koroma, who is still chief. But perhaps there is consolation to be found in S. B.'s brother Abdul's success in winning back the Barawa chieftaincy for the Moroma line in 2000.

"My father was an honest man," S. B. said. "Very friendly. Very fair. He wanted his children to succeed in life. I felt crushed when he died.

"I had last seen him in December 1953, during my Christmas break from Fourah Bay College. I had gone to Samaia village in Nieni chiefdom, where I met him late one afternoon, just as he was packing his bags and getting ready to leave. We were really pleased to see each other. And he was proud of me, because I had walked over eighty miles to meet him in that village. We came back to Sumbaria together, where we spent the night and he told me about a house he had in Koidu town. When he was a court messenger in Sefadu he built this house as a sort of farmhouse in which to lodge his strangers [guests], because there was not enough room in the court messenger's barracks. One day a Sergeant Morlai was brought before him. He had been arrested for smuggling kola nuts across the border to Guinea. My father and Sergeant Morlai had been soldiers together in the Wilberforce Barracks, and Morlai was very dear to him. They called each other *soko*, which means uncle in Susu. So when this sergeant was brought before my father, and he realized who it was, he ordered him released, and sent him to that farmhouse he had built. In fact, it was the first house ever built in Koidu, and though my father did not know at the time that this was diamond land, the nearby swamp where my mother farmed is today the number one diamond field. My father said that my half-brothers Junisa and Kulifa, who had been living in this house, had been told that it belonged to Sergeant Morlai, and that they owed him rent for it. When they failed to pay this rent, Sergeant Morlai seized their belongings. Dad wanted me to go to Sefadu and plead with Sergeant Morlai to give my brothers back their belongings. He said, 'As far as I am concerned I did not sell the house to Sergeant Morlai. But I did not take care of it either, and Morlai has made several improvements to the house over the years. The house is as much his as mine, but he should give back your brothers' things.'

"After going to Sefadu and delivering my father's message to Sergeant Morlai, I got on the train for Freetown. I remember it was a Saturday, and I had boarded the train with some other students from Kono who were also going back to college, which was due to reopen that Wednesday. But when we reached Kangahun—which means 'place of refusal,' because the people there once refused to submit to defeat during an intertribal war—I saw two teachers at the station, Bennett and Thomas, whom I knew. They taught in Kabala. I was happy to see them. I was laughing. They asked me where I was going. I told them I was going to Freetown; college was due to start again on Wednesday. They asked if I was not going to Kabala. I said no. They stood aside, then they turned to me and said, 'Pa is dead.' I said, 'Which Pa?' They said, 'Your father.' I can remember giving a big smile. Then suddenly I said to myself, 'The wide world is open.' I just felt I was left on my own now. Because in Africa, your father is your guide. He decides your marriage, gives advice, you listen to him. But now there was no one to tell me what to do. And I started weeping.

"Next morning, at five A.M., I went to Fourah Bay College to obtain permission from Dr. Porter, the dean of students, to attend my father's burial. I picked up a lorry to go to Makeni. The driver Pa Yamba was very kind to me. He gave me the front seat, and did not ask for the ten shillings which was the fare to go from Freetown to Makeni via Lunsar. Next morning I reached Kabala, where I met my sisters and relatives. Everyone was crying. I went on to Firawa the next day. It was a two-day journey. I spent the first night in Kamadugu Sukurela. Even there, people were crying. Finally I got to Firawa. I can remember my twin sisters. They were only about twelve at the time. They were in tears. I held them. Two days later, I told my mother I would take the twins with me when I left. I did not want to leave them behind. They had never been to school. If they remained in the bush they would marry there, make farms. I wanted them to have a better life. So I brought them with me to Kabala, and then to Makeni where I left one of the twins with our cousin Mrs. Sadi Mens. I sent the other to our cousin Fatmata Kabbah in Lunsar. They both did well. They married well, and had children, some of whom now live in England and the United States, and care for their mothers. They regard me as a father. As for me, they are my political pillars."

It was from Tina and Dondon that S. B. subsequently heard the story of his father's death.

"He had fallen ill at Yifin, where he had gone for a council meeting (he was an elder of Nieni chiefdom). He immediately told his cousin Mori Dako Dabu to send for Aisetta Sanfan, my mother, who was in Firawa. But his cousin said, 'If you send for your wife to come now, the whole of Barawa will follow her.' My father told his cousin that when a man is ill only his wife will know how to nurse him back to health. So that day passed. Next day, his illness was worse, so Dako went to the paramount chief, Kali Koroma, and said, 'Your nephew is seriously ill.' They decided to take him back to Firawa. They left that night. They put him in a hammock and left at around eleven P.M. It was a two-day journey. They spent the first night at Bambako. The next day they went on. But by then my mother had got news that Dad was not well, and had decided to come with Abdul and my twin sisters Tina and Dondon. When they came, Daddy was still alive. My mother said to him, 'Sergeant Major, what is it? Look at your twins, crying.' Then he opened his eyes and said, 'The chief.' Mother asked him, 'What chief? Are you referring to Kali Koroma?' He said, 'No,' and pointed his hands to the skies. He meant almighty God. He closed his eyes. That meant, 'I leave my twins in the hands of God.' Because they were very close. For years, for years, he moved with them from place to place. They would do his cooking. They were very close.

"Though Dako realized that my father was dead, he did not want to say so. He asked that a pillow be put under my father's head, and told Abdul to straighten his head on the pillow. But it kept falling to one side. So in the end, when it was clear to everyone that he was dead, they laid him on the roadside and cut sticks and made a litter on which they placed the corpse and took him back to Firawa.

"Three years after my father's death I became a member of Parliament. I wish he could have lived to see that day, and to see me now, leader of government business in the House of Parliament. Whenever I think of him — and I think of him constantly — I thank him for having given me the little education I possess today. I know I would have stopped at nothing to get a good education, but nevertheless I appreciate what my father did for us as a family. I admired him. He was my mentor. Even today I still hear his voice saying, 'Carry on, be a man, be a Kuranko.' These words are always in my ears. Not to be afraid. Setting us on the right path. May his soul rest in perfect peace."

Tina Kome Marah

10 Early Days

Although, for S. B., any man worth his salt upheld and exemplified ancestral values, this did not preclude the importance of changing with the times. Still, as his father had discovered long ago, the balance between tradition and modernity was hard to strike. While the old condemned you for breaking with the past, the young condemned you for failing to share the benefits of modernity with them. It was like the split between serving the public weal and feathering one's own nest. Or between duty and desire.

I saw this clearly when S. B. spoke of Aisetta Sanfan's death in 2002. "That July the general and presidential elections were over, and it was my job to interview nominees for ministerial and junior ministerial appointments. As I dressed that morning I was looking forward to the interviews. But then the telephone rang. It was the Honorable Alhaji Ali Sheriff on the line. He said, '*korto*, anything can happen in this world. One must take courage. It is with a heavy heart and sympathy that I have to tell you that your mother passed away this morning.' I was shocked and stunned, because I had not seen her for some time. In fact, it was painful for me to visit her. I would always leave her in tears, not knowing if I would see her again. Now I thought of the years she had nursed and cared for me, right up to the time I became a man.

"But I was in a dilemma. That morning I had these interviews beginning at eleven o'clock. My mother had passed away in Kissy, and I was at PK Lodge [on the other side of Freetown]. I thought to myself, I've got my national duty to perform. The nation is waiting. The world is waiting for the new government to be set up. And the nominees and their families are anxious to know who will be selected. I then reached the conclusion that just as my mother had performed her duty very well, bringing me into this world, caring for me, I should now follow her example. She loved me, she got me off to school, got me educated, blessed me, and my duty was one of the duties for which she brought me into this world. So I said, 'Honorable Sheriff, I would like you to take her to the funeral home, while I go to parliament to do my duty.' At parliament I informed my colleagues of the sad accident that had taken place. Well, as always happens, people think of the moment, and so it was in this case. Everybody was with me, and they appreciated the fact that I had the courage to leave my mother in the mortuary while I went to do my job. I then did the interviews, and we buried her that Friday. My children and nieces from abroad, and a few relatives, wanted me to take the corpse to Kabala, but I told them that I wanted my mother to go home to her people, where she belonged. I had decided to send her to Kande Sayo of Kalangba, her nephew, because he had requested her to be with him, so that one of his wives could keep vigil over her. I had agreed to his request. My mother had served her husband and his people well. It was now time for her to return home, to her origin, to her people, just like a hunter returning home from the bush. But as fate would have it, this was not possible, because the president said that if I took her to Kabala or Kalangba he would go with me. I knew what that meant. If he traveled with me, most of my parliamentary colleagues, many civil servants, and most government ministers would come too. So I decided to bury her in Freetown.

"It rained heavily that day. But many people were there to pay their last respects. The president himself, parliamentarians, permanent secretaries, people form all walks of life, including Lebanese businessmen and several ambassadors."

S. B. went on to describe how he clung to his mother, crying bitterly, when the time came to take her body to the cemetery. From PK Lodge the cortege moved through the city with a police siren clearing the way, and people along the roadsides were telling one another, "That's S. B. Marah's mother, that's S. B. Marah's mother." His face hidden behind his hand, his voice fallen to a hoarse whisper,

S. B. then recalled his last glimpse of his mother as she was lowered into her grave. "May God bless her for all she did for us after the death of our father fifty years ago. May her soul rest in peace."

That evening in my hotel room, as I transcribed S. B.'s account, I felt for the first time that he and I were far less different than I had once thought. As a politician, S. B.'s public persona mattered a great deal to him; as a writer, I was suspicious of appearances, and fascinated by the private life beneath the public image. This is what Rose may have implied when she said that S. B.'s life was not his own; it belonged to the people. She was bemoaning the fact that his priorities were political, not familial. But it would be false to polarise the outward and inward aspects of a person, seeing the former as mere facade and the latter as truth. In the tradition of the European enlightenment, I had for many years believed that truth lay deep within the soul of the individual. Revealing it demanded techniques of demystification, and it was the intellectual's task to tear away the masks, penetrate psychic defenses, see through people's rationalisations and illusions, and find the skeletons in the closet. But Lévi-Strauss's notion that "true reality is never the most obvious of realities, and that its nature is already apparent in the care with which it takes to evade our detection"[1] was one I could no longer accept, if only because I had discovered that social life depends less on individuals realizing or baring their own inner selves than on their capacity to create and embrace truths that bound them together in a common cause, and for the common weal. We habitually speak of sameness and difference, assigning different moral values to these terms (the racist loathing everything that does not conform to his own self-image, the anthropologist having a field day with otherness), but to consummate one's existence in relation to others may have less to do with identity than with our capacity for being open to the world, and taking people at face value.

I think that was the moment when I ceased hoping that S. B. might make me privy to his secrets, or divulge details of the seamier side of Sierra Leonean politics, accepting the manner in which he had chosen to tell his story, not as a search for self-knowledge but as a search to find a place in the world that brought honor to his lineage and transformed his country for the better. Seduced by the future, many Westerners readily dismiss the past, as indifferent to their parentage as they are intoxicated by the new. For them it is hard to grasp the profound sense of duty to one's forebears and family that characterizes African life. In this respect, S. B. was, as the Mande say, like that species of persevering vine that sprouts anew whenever it is cut; or the exemplary son, who travels further than anyone else the path his father started on.

In 1925 Tina Kome was elevated to the rank of sergeant major in the Court Messengers Force, and sent to build the barracks at Panguma (Kenema District). From there he was transferred, first to Sefadu (Kono District), then Moyamba, where he was again promoted—to staff sergeant major. S. B. was born in Koidu on 19 August 1934, the third child of Tina Kome's second wife, Aisetta Sanfan Mansaray. But his earliest memories, he told me, were of Moyamba. "I remember the day war broke out. We saw, or heard the sound of, a plane passing overhead. And as a small boy, I remember the governor's special train coming to Moyamba, and the governor awarding my father a medal. In prison," he continued, "I also found myself thinking about my boyhood friends in Bonthe, where we went to live in 1939. Tambasa Kendu. Tamba Sonofu. Tamba Momodu, otherwise known as Changeover. Ansumana Sahr Jabba. And my younger [half-] brother, Kulifa, who is now dead. One day at school he got beaten up. I went and head-butted this bully. He sat down and fainted. I was scared. The teachers gathered around. But they respected the Marahs after that. We stuck up for ourselves. One of my classmates was Francis Caulker. Little did I know that his elder sister's daughter would one day become my wife, Rose.

"In Moyamba my father was on friendly terms with the district commissioner, and my elder brother, Kulifa, and I used to go to the D.C.'s house and retrieve tennis balls. At the end of the day's play, the D.C. would give us a penny—which was a lot of money for us. My father was also a close friend of Siaka Stevens's father. He was a short man. He had a shop, and some Limba chaps working for him. He used to supply the prisons, I think. Anyway, my father and Siaka Stevens's father and Sergeant Braima Koroma used to eat together every day, taking it in turns to go to one another's house. They were at my father's house one day when something happened that I will never forget. I had often watched my mother breaking eggs into a bowl, and wanted to try it myself. So I picked up an egg and broke it. When she saw what I had done, my mother took me to my father. I hadn't meant to steal the egg, but it looked as if this was indeed what I had tried to do. Siaka Stevens's father said to my father [whom he called Kau]: 'Kau, this boy must not become a thief. We will have to take him to prison. And believe me, they took me to prison that night.' I know my father didn't want to, because it had been such a trivial matter, but his friend said, 'The boy must not continue this way, you must put him behind bars.' So I spent that night in prison. When Siaka Stevens detained me in 1974 I said to myself, 'Your father has already sent me to prison!' Three years later I told this to his face. I told him that I bore him no grudge for having detained me, and that the law had to take its course. Then I thanked him for my release. When the 1977 elections came round, and the Kurankos wanted me in government, Siaka Stevens said he would send a helicopter to bring me from Kabala and Freetown. When I told him I didn't want to fly, he sent his car from State House. He wanted to make me a minister in his government. This was when I told him the story of how his father had sent me to jail. Today I see it as no bad thing. For it made me afraid of stealing. All my life, I have never taken anything that did not belong to me. In all the years I have been in politics — and I would say this proudly, on the floor of Parliament — I have done nothing corrupt. So I told Siaka Stevens, 'Your father put me in jail the first time, and you put me in jail the second time.' And I explained why I called him Pa, even though he was, strictly speaking, my brother. 'Now that our fathers are dead,' I said, 'I will call you Father.'

"After Moyamba we moved to Bonthe. In those days, court messengers had considerable power. They were second only to the district commissioners, who were our colonial masters. So people regarded the Sergeant Major as the most powerful man in the district. My father always told us, 'You are Kurankos.' He did not want us to speak any other language. He used to say, 'If you don't speak Kuranko my kith and kin will laugh at me.' And he was right. But this did not stop me learning Temne, Susu, and Mende. I learned them all, all the languages of our country. And this has stood me in good stead, because wherever I go I can speak the local language fluently."

Tina Kome retired in 1942, after the death of his beloved brother, Tina Kaima, whom he had always called Daddy. For many years, Kaima had worked as speaker under the Barawa chiefs, Belikoro, Teneba Sewa, and Pore Bolo, so Tina Kome now decided that the time had come for him to return to his native soil and take charge. S. B. remained in Bonthe to finish his school year, then joined his father at Kurekoro. But he did not stay long, because his elder brother Kulifa wanted him to continue his schooling in Freetown.

"These were the war years," S. B. explained, "and it was not easy to get to Freetown. You needed a permit from the district office. But I got my permit, showing that my purpose in going to Freetown was to join my elder brother Kulifa and attend school. I remember arriving by train at Waterloo, where you had to show your permit. I did not know where I had put it. I was scared. I kept searching for it, until I finally found it and gave it to the officer. In Freetown there was no one to meet me. But I told a Mende woman — I cannot remember her name — that my brother lived in Waterloo Street. She said she lived at Upper Waterloo Street, and that I could spend the night at her place. She would help me find my brother in the morning. This she did. I had a bag of rice that I had brought with me — the only thing I could really bring from home. So I lived with Kulifa and attended the Government Model School from 1944, though I had to repeat Standard Six.

"One recess period, we were playing at the back of the school, running and shouting, when one of our teachers, Mr. Vincent, came and said, 'Stop shouting! I said stop! Am I talking to a pack of Kurankos?' I raised my hand and said, 'But I am a Kuranko, sir.' I don't know what might have crossed his mind; he didn't say anything. But several years later, in 1957, when I was a member of Parliament, I saw him again. I was in my car, and asked my driver to stop. I got out of the car and said, 'Good afternoon Mr. Vincent.' He took off his hat and said, 'Good afternoon, sir.' He was a bit nervous and uncertain as to who I was, because I had a flag on my car, which was a symbol of authority. We were new to politics at the time, these were the sort of things we admired. I said, 'Do you remember me sir? Do you remember me, Mr. Vincent?' He looked at me, and said no. I said, 'I'm the little boy who told you at the back of the Model School compound that he was a Kuranko. You were shouting at us to stop making so much noise.' He said, 'Oh yes, yes, yes, yes,' but I could see that he did not remember the incident at all. Then I put my hand in my pocket and gave him a pound note. That was it. That was the last time I ever saw Mr. Vincent.

"When Kulifa went to Liberia for a while, I lived with my aunt at Smart Farm. My uncle was a charcoal burner, and I often went there in the weekends to help with the burning and sorting and bagging of the charcoal. Life was not easy. We lived on dried cassava when there was no rice. But I made many good friends at the Government Model School. Francis Conteh, who became minister of mines in the

APC government. Nasiru Tejan-Cole, who rose to the rank of DPP. Stanley Walters, who became a permanent secretary, and has always been my friend, through rain and shine. Though now a pensioner, he was recently appointed director of SaPost. So I paddled along until I went to St. Edward's Secondary School, where one of my best friends was Francis Tucker, who I had also known in Bonthe. His two brothers became priests, and his father had wanted Francis to become a priest as well. I always tease him that he ended up instead in the two worst professions — law and politics!

"After finishing secondary school, I returned home to see my father. The district commissioner of the Northern Province at that time was Victor Ffennell-Smith. My mother's uncle worked for him as a cook. Because Mama and Papa were in Firawa, I stayed with this uncle in Kabala and got to know him very well. Then one day my father sent word that I should go to Tekaw, near Makeni, and see my uncle R. S. Marah. My uncle introduced me to Mr. Dave McBurnay, who was a New Zealander, like yourself. He was planning to establish an animal husbandry project in Musaia, and said that he would send me to New Zealand to study. But not long afterward he was killed in a road accident and I ended up in Musaia with another white man — a West Indian by the name of E. S. Capstick. While I was there, District Commissioner Ffennell-Smith said he wanted to build schools in Koinadugu District, and needed some boys to study at Njala Teachers College. After teacher training, we would return home to teach our kith and kin. He suggested that I go to Njala.

"Among the others who went with me were C. M. S. Carew, A. B. M. Kamara, who became minister of transport and communications, Sieh Mansaray, who became paramount chief in Kabala, and Almami Kalla Kamara of Makeni, my best friend, and Thomas Bobo Mansaray, who both died not long after we graduated. At Njala I studied hard, and the principal, Mr. Ted Evans, a Welshman, remarked that I was the best all-round student he had known in his time there. I was also very popular among my classmates, partly because of the dances I organized. I told the principal that we didn't really want to go off campus in the weekends, especially those of us from the north. We didn't want to get involved with other men's wives. So could we organize Saturday night dances? He agreed, and so we borrowed drums from the Mendes and created our own entertainment. We even had a flautist, called Besema. And this provided the music we wanted for our comfort.

"When I had completed my teacher training I went to see my dad in Firawa, to tell him I had passed my exams. As usual, my father said he had high hopes for me. He knew I would do well in life. My mother's eldest sister's son, N'koro Momodu Kabbah, whom we called our eldest brother, used to say that a man can always tell his child's destiny. And so, because my father said I would do well, I am not surprised that I have. And I shall continue to do so, because I always think of my father, who is very dear to me.

"My first posting as a teacher was Kitchon. The headmaster was I. S. Kahn. I worked with him through 1951. The students liked me. I organized football matches and concerts. Taught well. I also taught at Magaboi. Many of my students went on to do well in life. Dr. Abass Bundu, who became foreign minister and secretary of ECOWAS (Economic Community of West African States), was one of my students. Wusu Munu, who became permanent secretary, and is now an APC member of Parliament. Musa Suma, who became managing director of the Sierra Leone Police Marketing Board. His mother placed him in my care. She told me: 'Teacher, this is my son, please accept him as your son, so that he will be educated.' I accepted, and promised by the grace of Allah that her child would know book. Once in London, many years later, Musa Suma invited me to lunch and afterward gave me five hundred pounds. The money could not have come at a better time. And then there was Thaimu Bangura, who was at one time minister of finance, and a founder and leader of the PDP (People's Democratic Party). Alhaji Ali Janneh, who also became a minister in Parliament, and is now one of the officials who arranges pilgrimages to Mecca. All of them still insist on calling me teacher. In fact I was so liked that when I was transferred to Kabala, many of my students, including the school band, accompanied me on the boat to Rokupr, singing my praises and imploring me not to go. They sang in Susu: 'Teacher Marah, aria tongo wona ka yire, take the praise and let's go!'

"I did not stay in Kabala long. I was transferred to Falaba, as headmaster, then to Fadugu, before taking leave at the end of 1953 to attend an intensive teachers' training course at Fourah Bay College.

"At Fourah Bay College I was captain of the football team, and made many friends, including some from Nigeria, Ghana, the Cameroons, and the Gambia. In fact, the friends I made during these years as a teacher, and at Njala and Fourah Bay, have helped me quite a lot in my political career. Canvassing during elections. Helping me

Early Days

when I needed help. I have always tried to avoid making enemies, because my father told me, 'Why make an enemy of one man when you can make friends with many?' Even today, if someone wants to pick a quarrel with me, I give him way. I wish him luck.

"The Nigerians at Fourah Bay were very keen about their African dress. They didn't like this coat and tie, this colonial thing. I did not like that coat and tie business either, partly because I could only afford one coat! The issue was debated one Sunday. I was one of two student representatives from the teachers' training department, and I took a strong stand against the wearing of coat and tie. But during the interval, our chairman said that from the inception of Fourah Bay College it had been the custom to wear a coat and tie. It had been like this from Bishop Crowther's time. And the question of abolishing this custom had never been raised before. He did not want to be remembered as the person who had overseen the changing of a tradition his forebears had not seen the necessity of changing. 'But I leave it up to you,' he said. 'Posterity will judge us.' His argument completely changed my attitude, and I voted for keeping the coat and tie. I was booed because I had earlier stood as a pillar against it. Even today I do not know if I did the right thing or not, though I like to think I made the right choice.

"From Fourah Bay College I returned to Fadugu for a year. I was now beginning to think of becoming a lawyer, and studying in the U.K. I had saved a little money as a teacher, but I needed more funds. I went to see my uncle, Pa Sheka Mansaray, who was speaker to our grand-uncle, the late Paramount Chief Kande Baba in Pendumbu. I appealed to him, but he could not help me. So I went to appeal to my cousin-in-law, the Reverend J. S. Mens, who was very sympathetic to my request. The Reverend Mens told me that my uncle had not been able to help me because he had given his money to Paramount Chief Almami Dura for safekeeping. I went to Binkolo to see Chief Dura and ask for the money, but the chief said I should come back and see him the following day. I hardly slept that night. I was very happy, very excited. I thought I had struck a deal, and would soon be on my way to England to study law. Next morning I went back to see the chief, and thanked him for receiving me the previous day. Again he asked me to wait another day. This went on for a week, so I made up my mind to go and see my elder brother in Tongo Field where he was diamond mining, in the hope that he would help me. I ran into him at the lorry park, and he told me he was on his way to Freetown. I was happy, because I had not seen him for some time. We traveled to Kenema together, and stayed the night there. Next morning we came on to Freetown. He stayed with our cousin, S. B. Daramy, who was then the first Sierra Leonean financial secretary, while I stayed with another cousin, the late Alhaji Mamadi Kabba, who was living at Magazine Court. For the next week my brother went around buying musical instruments, and ignoring my request. It was futile.

"I had promised a friend of mine, Fam Bulleh, who was on my staff at Fadugu, that I would spend some of the holidays with him. So I went down to Zimmi and stayed a week with him. I then traveled north, via Kenema, Blama, and Bo to Makeni where I stayed with my friend, the late Almami Kalla Kamara. Kalla told me he was going into politics, and that Chief Dura and others were supporting him. This inspired me. I said, 'Well, I had better change my mind. Since I do not have the money to study law, I'll go into politics and represent my people.' The following day I went on to Kabala and discussed my plans with my brother-in-law, the town chief Almami Amadu Koroma, whom we also called Kassi. No sooner had I announced my intentions than he wanted to begin canvassing support.

"My first cousin, Kande Sayo, who is now chief in Guama, was at that time an inspector in the Sierra Leone police force. He knew I wanted to study law. Two months into my canvassing, he sent me a letter saying he had some funds for me, funds he had reserved for me to study law in England. Quite honestly, at first I thought it was a ploy to dissuade me from entering politics, so I sent word to him that I would continue with my bid for political office; if I was not success-ful, then I would study law. But I have always been grateful to him. He has provided all kinds of things for me, such as furniture, and recently a Mercedes car. We are brothers. We love each other very much. His mother Bonporo was my mother's elder sister. Indeed, Bonporo raised my mother, who always looked up to her as a mother rather than a sister."

That afternoon, small S. B. drove me back to my hotel and I worked for a couple of hours transcribing this latest portion of S. B.'s story. "So many names," I thought. Names of persons. Names of places. And so much movement to and fro that it struck me at times that this was not so much a story being told than the signposting of a road — a

road once traveled in the company of an itinerant father, and then in search of a mentor, a patron, a lucky break. It put me in mind of Noah's son Kaima. He was the same age as my daughter, Heidi, and I had known him from the time he took his first steps. But his schooling had been disrupted by the war, and years of penury and displacement, and he was now living in Freetown, dejected and unsure of his future.

It had been his dream to study abroad, he told me. To pursue his interests in political science, civic administration, and literature. He had managed, despite the anarchy and upheaval he had lived through, to complete his A-levels and qualify for university study, but without money he could not enroll.

A few days after I had talked to Kasima, Noah told me that he wanted his son to reap the reward of his own suffering. As if, as Nietzsche put it, "the value of a thing sometimes lies not in what one attains with it, but in what one pays for it — what it *costs* us."[2] I promised to pay Kaima's fees, in recognition so to speak of the credit Noah and Kaima had accumulated through so many years of hardship and indigence. In a way, I suppose, I was doing what the New Zealander had been about to do for S. B., before he met his death in a road accident so many years ago. The promise made a difference. Kaima smiled for the first time. He stood straighter. But I felt oppressed by this mingling of loss and need that I encountered every day, the dashed expectations that so readily lead to recrimination and resentment. "In Africa," S. B. once remarked, "if you do well, people close to you will hate you." "Life is struggle," a friend of S. B.'s told me one morning. "It makes no difference if you're rich or poor. Life is always a struggle. You may have the name and authority like S. B. but how can you satisfy all the demands of the people, all the things that different people will expect of you?" And so I found it poignant that just as S. B.'s elder brother Kulifa had once spurned his younger brother's plea for assistance, so S. B. had, in turn — at least in the eyes of his younger brothers — disappointed them. And I remembered, then, the one time I saw his elder brother Kulifa. It was in Freetown in 1984. S. B. was away in Zimbabwe at an ILO conference, and had given Rose strict instructions not to admit his older brother to the compound. I watched him one afternoon through the half-open louver windows of my room. He was standing on the other side of the high, glass-studded wall, wearing a dark blue suit, and shouting Rose's name. He stayed for several hours, finally taking off his jacket and sitting on the root of one of the mango trees. "I feel sorry for him," Rose said, "but he is not in his right mind, and S. B. doesn't trust him with the children."

11 Independence

Almost everything S. B. said and did bespoke the values his father had instilled in him. Yet these manly injunctions to withstand hardship without complaint and keep one's own counsel were not Tina Kome's alone, but derived from initiation, when every Kuranko boy learns to bear pain without flinching, to respect the words of his elders without demur, and to overcome his fear of the spirits of the wild and of death. As the old medicine master Saran Salia Sano once told me, "Even when they are cutting the foreskin you must not flinch. You must stand stock-still. You must not make a sound from the mouth. Better to die than to wince or blink or cry out."

This control of one's emotions, and of one's speech, was undoubtedly connected to the value the Kuranko place on keeping secrets and promises, and of choosing one's words wisely. To nurse malicious thoughts is to risk malicious acts, and to speak of the devil is to conjure him. Perhaps this was why S. B.'s story was so conspicuously devoid of any ill will, grudges, or snide comments. "S. B. is known in Kuranko-land for his dislike of backbiting," Noah told me one day. "If you start speaking ill of somebody behind his back, S. B. will shout at you. The only problem is that he wants everyone to think as he does."

For S. B., however, what mattered was having convictions, and living up to them. This was what he had long admired about Nelson Mandela, whom he first heard of when a friend came back to Sierra Leone after a scholarship year in New Zealand and played S. B. a record of Peter O'Toole reciting Mandela's speech from the dock. "At the end of this speech," S. B. said, "Mandela told the judge that he was prepared to die. That really urged me. It made me want to know more about this man. It was the same with Anwar Sadat. The day he went to Israel I felt I was on the plane with him. The man had guts. He was willing to risk his life for peace. I followed his trip on the radio, day after day."

S. B. was equally impressed by Sekou Touré. "I admired the way he won independence for his people," he said. "Unlike other African leaders, who negotiated with their colonial masters and made all sorts of compromises, with him it was either yes or no. And when he said no, he was totally on his own. The currency was taken away, telephones were cut, even furniture removed. He was left with nothing. Schools had to be held outdoors, under the trees. But he made his people realize that they had to work out their destiny for themselves. He was a no-nonsense man. I liked his style of leadership. It's the kind of leadership Africa needs at this stage."

One morning, an old political colleague visited S. B., and our conversation turned to President Tejan Kabbah's deference to Anglo-American opinion, his overreliance on British military assistance in the event of political trouble at home. "To make a Kuranko sauce you need a Kuranko stirring spoon," said S. B.'s friend. "That is why we need an African politician," S.B responded. This was not disloyalty, he explained, merely a difference of opinion. "The president was a lawyer and diplomat. I am not a diplomat. I am not hypocritical. I'm a man of action. I don't like all this mark time business."

If S. B. sometimes railed against Western customs, treating *democracy* as if it was a euphemism for bad faith, red tape, and diplomatic evasiveness, this was not because he put himself above the law, ready to waive constitutional procedures, or ignore the views of others. It simply reflected his impatience with indecisiveness, and his aristocratic heritage. It was his pride in this heritage that led him, as an eleven-year-old boy, to stand up to Mr. Vincent's disparaging conflation of Kuranko and savages. To be a Kuranko was, as his father had told him, the only conceivable way of being a man. But when S. B. invoked Kuranko-ness, it was not some form of tribalism that he had in mind, but the values he held dear — not only forthrightness, stoicism, hard work, and self-reliance, but also honesty, generosity, and fidelity to one's principles. Pertinently, it was S. B., many years ago, who provided me with a not implausible etymology for the word

Kuranko. "It was from the kure tree," he said, "whose wood is very hard." Thus, to say *kure n'ko* is to imply that the speaker is tough-minded, able to withstand all kinds of hardships, and persevere, like the kure tree.

S. B. now continued his story from where he had left off the day before. It was 1956. "The first place we went to canvas support," S. B. said, "was Mongo Bendugu, in the heart of Kuranko-land. I met several Marah men, headed by the paramount chief Mongo Bala. The group included Fa Yimba Marah (who duly succeeded Mongo Bala), my brother Fara B. Marah, Braima Marah (now regent chief of Mongo), Momodu Kargbo (now court chairman in Mongo), Mansoud Jawarra (a businessman), and a cousin of mine called Faray. I can remember Mongo Bala saying, 'Oh, we did not know that our father Sergeant Major sent one of our children, one of our brothers, to school. We will support you.'

"I returned to Kabala, with high hopes that things would turn out well.

"There I met Arnold Nelson-Williams, who used to be a classmate of mine at the Government Model School. He wanted me to become a UPP (United National Party) candidate, and promised that I would be elected unopposed, because the man standing against me, Magba-Kamara, had a criminal record. But I was determined to campaign as an independent.

"I then appealed to my friend Sieh Mansaray for support. Sieh persuaded his father, who was a paramount chief, to send a message to the paramount chief of Yifin, who was my great uncle. In turn, a message was sent to Paramount Chief Kumba Fanko in Neya. They all came together in support of my candidacy.

"At that time, in Sierra Leone, only taxpayers had the right to vote. My opponent, A. B. Magba-Kamara, was a Big Man. He was an ex-serviceman who had traveled all over the world, and had the support of many paramount chiefs. But I had several chiefs supporting me, as well as all the teachers, and my own kith and kin. I told them that Magba was a finaba and that I was from a ruling house. We should not allow him to rule us. The Marah, as well as others from ruling families in other chiefdoms, came to my aid. I was a very young man then, only twenty-three years of age. But I was handsome. The girls liked me. And the young men liked me, and supported me.

"In 1957, Koinadugu was a large constituency, and unmotorable. So the election results came in slowly, over the course of a week. The count began on a Saturday morning, and it was announced that whoever won the election should travel to Freetown the following day for a three o'clock meeting at the Chief Minister's Lodge on Hill Station. Magba-Kamara stayed at home during the counting, but from time to time he would send someone in an old Land Rover to report to him. The first chiefdom counted was Diang. Magba got over 300 votes. Soon he had 1,000, and I had only 100. I thought he would surely win. He already had four cows tied in his compound — we saw them — and his people were also confident they would win. I was very young. I had nothing but my birthright. Magba continued sending his Land Rover. He now had 1,600 votes, but I had 1,200. He left his veranda, where he had been waiting, and came to the counting house. But at that moment, I started to catch him. Finally, there were only two places still to be counted. One was Firawa, my hometown, in Barawa; the other was Bandakarafaia in Woli, where my cousins came from. The Firawa vote was 587. The Bandakarafaia vote was 230. Magba got only two votes from Barawa. This put me ahead. Even if he got all the votes in the last box, I would win. In fact he only got 10, and I won by a margin of over 600 votes. As soon as I was declared the winner, there was dancing and jubilation all over Kabala.

"My first place of call was Paramount Chief Almami Yembeh's house. He had been threatened by Magba-Kamara's people and when he saw this crowd approaching his house he was afraid and went into his room. But we came dancing and drumming, and he came out, and I told him I had won. He gave me a bull to slaughter as my sacrifice.

"There was jubilation that night, but I was expected to be in Freetown the next day. The district commissioner, R. S. R. Beers, got me a lorry. The driver is still alive. He occasionally comes to see me for his pension — if I can put it that way.

"We left Kabala about ten at night and drove to Makeni, where we spent the night with the Reverend J. S. Mens, who was married to my cousin Saday. They didn't mind being woken up. They were overjoyed to hear my news. When I woke in the morning, my first thought was to go out and start canvassing again! It takes several days to get used to the fact that you no longer have to do this.

"We reached Freetown at about eleven, and I took a taxi in search of A. H. Kande, who had won the other Koinadugu seat. I looked for him all over town, unaware that he was living with my opponent

Magba-Kamara. Finally I went to see Pa Mustapha. He said, 'Oh boy, you know, we must vote for the old man, he's the only fit man to lead us.' But quite honestly, I didn't know what he was talking about. I was new to politics. I didn't know a thing. I asked Pa Mustapha if Kande was there. He said no. I then went to the Chief Minister's Lodge, to see if Kande was there. The police would not let me in. They said, 'This is no small boy's business.' I told them that I had won the election. They said, 'What is your name?' I said, 'I am Sewa Marah.' They said, 'No, we don't have any Sewa Marah listed here.' I repeated that I had won the election the day before in Kabala. They said, 'Look, the only name we have here is Magba-Kamara.' Then they asked if I had been to school. I said, 'Yes.' Well, they said, 'Come and look. Is your name here?' I saw that my name was not there, only Magba's name with a question mark beside it. I persisted. 'I am telling you I won the election in Kabala!' In those days we thought that politics was all about being aggressive. So I shouted. An English police officer heard the noise and came over. He said, 'Young man, what is it?' I said, 'Well sir, I won the election yesterday in Kabala and now I want to see Dr. Milton Margai [chief minister in the Legislative Council], but these officers will not allow me to go in.' The English policeman sent one of them to call Dr. Margai. I remember him as if it was yesterday, coming to the gate. He was wearing a blue shirt, white canvas shoes, and white trousers. I told him that I had won the election in Kabala and traveled all night to come to Freetown. I did not know it at the time but Dr. Margai was very much relieved to learn that Magba had been defeated, because Magba was one of his brother Albert's supporters [in the forthcoming election for the Legislative Council]. He took me into the parlor, and we sat there. But believe me, he did not once tell me to vote for him, or do this or that. I didn't know what I was about.

"When I left the lodge I went to see my cousin John Bangura at Wilberforce Barracks. John has been everything to me. He later became a colonel, then force commander, and was executed for his part in an attempted coup against the government in 1971. He welcomed me, saying, 'Cousin, we are very happy.' The news quickly went around that a small boy had defeated Magba. Everyone was staring at me. They could not believe what had happened. John said, 'I'm going to take you to meet Albert Margai, I want you to vote for him.' I had no idea there was a leadership struggle going on. But the question of independence was in the air, and some people felt that

Dr. Milton Margai was too old to oversee the transition from colonial rule, while others bore in mind that he was a man of great integrity who had worked tirelessly for the country's freedom. Anyway, we went to Albert's house, but his wife Esther was unable to find him, though she looked everywhere. In the end she said to me, 'Look, you who were born of a woman, I want you to vote for my husband.' But my cousin John Bangura said, 'It's all right, he's my brother, I've talked to him, he will vote for Albert.'

"Next time we found Albert at home. When Albert turned up we all sat down. Albert spoke to Maigore Kallon in Mende, saying, 'Tell this young man to vote for me.' He did not realize I could speak better Mende than he could, so I knew what he had said. Maigore told me he had attended the Bo school with my elder brother Kulifa. 'You know what?' he said. 'The old man does not want us to have independence. He's with the white people. But Albert wants us to get independence. He's dynamic. You should vote for him.' I said I was undecided, despite what my cousin had asked of me. I had stood in the election as an independent candidate. If they wanted me to take up their party's symbol, they should not ask me but the people in Koinadugu and Kabala who had voted for me. They should ask the people if I was a fit person to be supported by their party. I had it in mind that Albert had supported my rival, Magba-Kamara, you see. But because my cousin had asked me to support Albert, and I had given him my word, I voted for him. In fact, he beat his brother by only one vote. My vote.

"After voting, some of the Big Men in the party came together and said, 'It is good that we support Albert Margai, but it would not be a good thing if we removed the old man.' Siaka Stevens and Y. D. Sisay, who were Albert's main supporters, had left by this time, so people like John Karefa-Smart, J. C. O. Crowther, and R. B. S. Coker were talking now of the pros and cons of displacing Dr. Margai. Finally, it was agreed that Dr. Margai should not be asked to step down before Siaka Stevens and Y. D. Sisay had been consulted. They then searched high and low for Siaka Stevens and Y. D. Sisay who were, I am sure, trying to avoid the issue, because they did not want Albert to yield. But they were finally persuaded by Maigore and others, and particularly by one clever person who said, 'Now look, Dr. Milton led us into the election. It would have been all right had we removed him before the elections, but let us not make the mistake of removing him after the elections, because he is our leader and it was his name that was given to the governor. If we remove him now the governor will have to order another election?' Of course no one wanted this, and so people persuaded Albert not to contest the premiership, but allow his elder brother to continue as leader. Since time was running out, and we did not want to leave the matter overnight, it was finally agreed that Albert should be groomed for the leadership over the following six months, and that Siaka Stevens and Y. D. Sisay be informed of this decision later. But it was up to Albert and his brother. So Albert went to his older brother. Sir Milton was still wearing his white trousers, white canvas shoes, and blue shirt, and smoking his pipe. Albert knelt before him, and Sir Milton placed his hands on him, in the traditional way. Then Albert said that he accepted his brother ruling for another six months or three years. He shed tears. But there was jubilation among everyone present.

"When ministerial positions were being decided, Sir Milton appointed Albert minister of works, though he had been minister of Internal Affairs until then. Siaka Stevens received no ministerial appointment. Opposition to these decisions surfaced immediately. Albert refused his appointment, insisting that his friend Siaka Stevens be given ministerial office. Sir Milton then went to Albert's home at Spur Loop and offered his brother the position of minister of Internal Affairs, but Albert and some of the younger politicians still wanted to press the old man to give up the premiership. When Albert's supporters went ahead and published news of Albert's appointment without Sir Milton's permission, it was the last straw. Sir Milton withdrew his offer, and the battle started again.

"After my return to Kabala, Dr. Margai came to visit me. He drove his own car. But he had a minor accident at Mile 38 [a road junction thirty-eight miles north of Freetown], and hurt his chin. But he came to Kabala and asked for my support. He had known my father. When my father was working in Sefadu, Dr. Margai was a medical officer in Kayima. In fact, he had wanted to marry my elder sister, Ai. He had also worked with my father in Bonthe. I told Dr. Margai I would give him my support. So when the time came to appoint a junior minister, I was the man Dr. Margai wanted. But people did not know the difference between A. H. Kande and myself. So when Dr. Margai said he wanted that fellow from Kabala, they put Kande's name instead of me, and I missed the appointment.

"It was politically difficult in those days, because of the break between Albert and his brother that followed the 1957 elections. It was brother against brother, and Albert soon left the SLPP — the party his brother founded in 1951 — and formed the People's National Party [PNP]. It became known as Pikin nar Pikin [Brother against Brother]. But this party didn't last long. They made the elephant their symbol, and this was the same symbol Sékou Touré was using in Guinea, where people were shouting far and wide at the time, saying that they had won their independence, they were free, and we who were not independent were mere slaves. People in districts along the Guinea border came to believe that we in the SLPP did not want independence, did not want to be free, that we wanted to remain slaves under the white man. If some of those people were around today, perhaps they would prefer to be still in the hands of the white man. In any event, Albert and his group finally agreed to form a united front and go to England for constitutional talks on independence, which was achieved on 27 April 1961."

In December 1958, about a year before the British government announced its willingness to enter into talks on Sierra Leone's independence, S. B. attended the first All African People's Conference in Accra, Ghana. He was three months shy of twenty-four, and it was his first trip abroad.

"Tom Mboya from Kenya was elected chairman of the conference. Patrice Lumumba was there. Julius Nyerere. Dr. Banda. Kenneth Kaunda. Odinga Odinga. Ben Bella. Joshua Nkomo. All under the banner, 'Hands off Africa! Africa Must Be Free!' One meeting I shall never forget was with Kwame Nkrumah, who told me he preferred to stay in Owusu, which was the old governor's building, rather than a flat-topped modern building. He said he wanted his people to realize that power was now with the African. For that I admired him very much. Following this conference, the urge for independence became very strong in all of us, because you saw and heard these people talking with power, talking as real Africans, and when you came home you wanted to ask the white man to go away, you really wanted your independence. Everyone was gingered, everyone was inspired. It led me not to fear the district officers; I felt I could now challenge them in public. And I felt that as long as I was in the right there was nothing to fear. It was a great influence on me, and I can still remember some of those speakers, when they took the rostrum. Patrice Lumumba. Kwame Nkrumah. Ben Bella . . ."

And yet, when S. B. recalled the moment his country achieved its independence, I thought I detected in his comments not only the

Independence

exhilaration of being free but the anxiety of being now on one's own. "I remember the Recreation Ground where the stadium now stands," S. B. said. "I can see in my mind's eye, on that night of 26 April 1961, Sir Milton Margai and Sir Maurice Dorman, moving on to the stage. At five minutes before midnight, the two men are walking toward the flags. The Union Jack is flying. The whole place is in darkness except for a spotlight on the flag. At one minute before twelve the Union Jack is lowered, and from the stroke of midnight the Sierra Leonean colors of blue, white, and green are flying from the flagpole. There is drumming all over the city. Ships at sea blowing their horns, church bells ringing, Arabian drums. People dancing and shouting in the streets. I was so happy, so overwhelmed with happiness, that I shed tears. For what I could not say. But at the end of the ceremony we all thought, 'Now we are free men and women.' And we went home. That was it. Our independence. Whether it was the right decision we took, or whether it was the right time, only history will tell."

12   Going Abroad

One morning, a few days after recording S. B.'s reminiscences of the Accra conference, I was sitting in the parlor of his house among the numerous other visitors who had come to call—town chiefs and elders from the north in their country-cloth gowns, parliamentary colleagues, and several Freetown friends. S. B. sat in his chair, as if presiding over a court, occasionally cracking a joke, pontificating on the indolence and irresponsibility of today's youth, or discussing some minor political intrigue. Suddenly, he asked me how I felt as a white man sitting among all these black men. Did it bother me at all? I was somewhat taken aback by the question, and sensed that S. B. was simply voicing a sentiment someone else had expressed. "I feel at home here," I said. "After all, I've been coming here on and off for more than thirty years!" Then, in an effort to address the possible perplexity of some of the visitors who did not know me, I said the reason I was not participating in the conversation was that I had nothing to contribute to it. This did not mean I wasn't interested. It was because I hadn't come to Sierra Leone as a businessman, an authority of some kind, to tell people what to do; I was there as a visitor who wanted to understand the way people lived, and what they thought about the issues of the day.

"You see," S. B. said, obviously satisfied with my answer. "Just as I told you, he's not a white man like other white men!"

Yet later that day, walking down Signal Hill from Wilberforce Road, I realized that my response to S. B.'s question had been only half true—for I had never felt *entirely* at home in Sierra Leone. I was an outsider, a stranger, a guest, lacking fluency in any local language, and often as gauche as when I first arrived in the country in 1969. It was, of course, different when I was among friends, like S. B. and Rose, or in the company of Noah, but there were times when I experienced the acute vulnerability and aloneness of the interloper. Adopting the role of perennial listener and habitual note-taker gave me all kinds of insights into quotidian life, to be sure. But if I had played an active part in that life, my understanding would have undoubtedly been deeper. And this might have offset the besetting passivity that is the price we pay, as ethnographers, for our marginality—this eclipse of one's capacity to act, to call any of the shots. Susan Sontag writes that interpretation is the revenge of the intellect on art. It is also the revenge of the academy on life. For no one can postpone indefinitely the urge to be the maker and shaper of his or her own existence, having a starring rather than supporting role. The more passive one's life in the field, the greater the need to reverse the situation when one returns home, which is why the arcane and authoritative character of academic writing may be seen, to some extent, as a vengeful reaction to the inertia, uneventfulness, and waiting one had to endure as a guest at someone else's banquet. A way of redressing an existential imbalance, as it were—reclaiming authorial will by superimposing one's own meanings on theirs . . .

These were the fragmented thoughts that passed through my mind as I descended the hill toward Congo Cross, and that led me, the next day, to ask S. B. the same question he had asked me. Had he ever felt out of place, awkward or intimated, in the company of whites?

S. B.'s response was to recall his second trip abroad, to a Commonwealth conference in the United Kingdom and Northern Ireland, a few months after Sierra Leone became independent in 1961.

"Our delegation included the Honorable R. B. S. Coker, Mr. S. V. Wright, and J. C. O. Crowther. We left Freetown on the 28th of August, I think, and traveled by sea. It was nine days to Liverpool. I remember being amazed at how old the docks were, and how rundown many of the buildings seemed. This was not the England I had imagined. We boarded the train and got to Victoria Station. It was my first experience of so many white people gathered in the same place, and everything moving so fast. We were met by some officials and driven to the Savoy Hotel. Apart from the Ambassador in Accra, this was the first time I had stayed in a hotel. We were told that we were only the second group of Africans to have stayed there. It was a very nice hotel. I didn't feel that I was in a strange place. In fact, as a small boy, back home in the colonial days, we used to be scared of white people, but now, after independence, we had begun to feel that the white man had kept us backward, because we could now see their streets, wide and clean, vehicles, everything cleanly done, the hotels clean, and we went to their shops, many of them very big, with escalators and lifts, and some of them underground . . . and we felt they had done very little for us, because our streets back home were not good, they had potholes, the city had not been well planned, even the government buildings, with the exception of the Law Courts and the Secretarial Building, were not as good as the government buildings they had in London. We visited Whitehall. We went to Parliament. And after the conference we were taken on a tour of the country. We stayed a night in Coventry, where we saw the destruction from the war. At Stratford-on-Avon, we saw Shakespeare's birthplace, his house, his pen, his bed, his table. This impressed me very much, his belongings kept for all that time. And we attended a play. Then we were driven to Edinburgh where we stayed two nights. I saw Rob Roy's place. We went to Loch Lomond, where I thought of the words of that song we learned at school. And we spent a night at a place called Callander, where a dance was put on for us. One of our party was from Fiji, and during the dance a young fellow of about eighteen or so shouted at this man that he should leave the hall. I think his exact words were: 'Girls wear skirts, boys do not wear skirts.' The Fijian delegate was angry, very angry. Embarrassed to be talked to in this way. Yet what of the kilt they wear? It made me wonder why this boy said what he said, and shamed this guest.

"From Callander we went to Glasgow. I went out shopping one day with the then–Nigerian minister of education, Alhaji Yusa Keita. We tried to talk with some of the local people. One girl called me over to where she was standing, and asked, 'Who is that man? Is he a Mau Mau?' I said, 'No, he's a Muslim from northern Nigeria. The Mau Maus are in Kenya, not Nigeria.' This is how ignorant many people were about Africa. They kept asking me where I was from. When I said, 'Sierra Leone,' they said, 'Where's Sierra Leone?' After all these years, I still get asked the same thing.

"After Glasgow we were to go to Belfast, but there was a cyclone blowing over there, and our flight was delayed. Some of the delegates decided to go back to London. But when I talked to Mr. S. V.

Wright he reminded me that I was to be an after-dinner speaker in Belfast, and since we Sierra Leoneans were so few, and the Nigerians so many, we really should go to Northern Ireland to represent our country. So I agreed, even though two of our other delegates went to the Isle of Wight. On my way back to my hotel I picked up a newspaper. There was a big headline, "Dag Hammersjköld Dead in a Plane Crash," and at the bottom of the page was another report, of a plane that had crashed where we were going to land. So I became very worried. I couldn't sleep for the whole night. Next morning I went looking for some Sanalgen, thinking I'd drink it to calm my nerves, but I was really, really scared. I was shivering with fear as we boarded the plane. And though we landed safely, I was all the time thinking of how I could get back—whether I could go by sea to England and by train to London.

"The first few days in Northern Ireland I was not happy, thinking about this flight back that I would have to make. Quite honestly, I must say so. We went to many places. Port Rush, where I gave my after-dinner speech. Newcastle in County Down. One fellow, who was our guide there, was a priest in training. He'd come from Rome, and offered his services as a guide. We saw the name of an engineering firm. It was the same name as this fellow's. We asked him if he was related to the person who owned the firm. 'Yes,' he said, 'it is my father's company.' The most interesting thing for some of us, especially the Africans, was how could a fellow who comes from a wealthy family like this, and is the only child, go into the priesthood? To this day I have wondered about this. But he accepted it. He was very. . . . He didn't appear . . . I don't know how to express this . . . but that a man who is so wealthy, who is from a wealthy family, should leave it and become a priest. And he was a very humble man, very polite, ready to help. I'm sure he made a good priest. It was his calling.

"One place I loved was Londonderry, though the Irish preferred to call it Derry. St. Patrick came from there, and I went to St. Patrick's school in Bonthe. So I felt very much at home, very, very happy and excited to be there. Because people who went to St. Patrick's in Bonthe were very dear to me.

"When I look back on this trip, I remember thinking how we had been kept really, really behind. Most of the things we are trying to do in Sierra Leone today—building roads, dams for electricity, hospitals, schools—could have been done years ago when the white man was ruling us, so that today we would not be undergoing all these hardships. Roads and electricity were cheaper in those days. Labor was cheaper. In fact there was free labor; people were forced to work. But most of our wealth was scattered, maybe not by our colonial rulers themselves, though they let other foreigners take away our wealth. But I have never felt intimidated by Europeans. Rather, I will be aggressive, I'll be aggressive, I'll be aggressive. Definitely. And even now, when we go to Europe and some of these places, we find that people look low upon Africans. But we will do our best to eradicate such attitudes, where each race takes it upon itself to feel better than all the others. For me, God's creatures are all equal. Blood is blood. We are all human beings."

13   In Government

When Sir Milton Margai died in April 1964 and his younger brother Albert succeeded him as premier, S. B. became government whip, and a junior minister in the Ministry of the Interior under Maigore Kallon. Two years later, he married Rose Tucker. "I was in Form 2," Rose said, "when we first met. I was living in Bonthe with my aunt, my father, and my sister, Pat. S. B. said he intended to make me his wife, and he began to give gifts to my aunt so that she would approve the match. When Pat found out what was going on she was furious. She removed all my things from the house, told my father not to take them back inside, and took me to Freetown, where I completed my secondary schooling. I met S. B. again in 1966, a year after I left school. I was twenty-one at the time, and wanted to go overseas and study to be a pediatrician. In the meantime I was working in the prime minister's office with Pat. Pat was still dead set against the marriage. She pointed out that S. B. had been married twice already and that one of his wives had left him, and, besides, we were from a Christian family and therefore had very different backgrounds. It is strange to think that Pat [who died in 1998] should marry Tejan Kabbah, who is now president, and I should marry S. B., the president's most trusted friend."

Of his first few years in government, S. B. spoke with real pleasure, though the clouds of political strife and tragedy were already gathering. "Whenever Parliament was in recess," he said, "I would visit my constituency. In those days, most of Koinadugu was not motorable, so I would travel everywhere on foot, meeting my people, talking with them, telling them the value of communal work and of sending their children to school. Working together, we built many roads. We had then what they called the Colonial Development Fund, given by the British government. But this money had to be used before independence. Two bridges were gazetted for Koinadugu district—one to be built over the Mongo river, just out of Musaia, and the other over the Seli, a few miles from Kondembaia. The contractor asked the people from these towns to cut poles and put them at the riverside, to help with the construction. But while the people of Musaia did this, the people of Kondembaia did not. The contractor then informed the district officer, whose name was Osborne, that the Kondembaia people had failed to do what he had asked. Osborne was very angry and decided to put the bridge elsewhere. I was a member of the District Council at the time, and thought it a bit immoral that the bridge should be taken away from Kondembaia simply because the people had failed to cut the poles. I made this point at the meeting. But I could not really support the new proposal, because this would bring a road to Firawa, my hometown. If I argued that this was a good thing, people would say I was unfairly biased.

"As it happened, the bridge near Kondembaia on the Yifin Road was built first, and this opened up the Kuranko hinterland. I am still trying to have a road built from Firawa to Bandakarafaia, so that the Loma Mountains can be developed as a tourist area, and people can get to see the highest point in Sierra Leone. The vegetation in that area is quite unlike anything else in the country. Life there is very easy. The climate is excellent. I have been there myself on many occasions, and I love being with my people. I am trying my level best to develop those areas. Even though we now have roads from Kabala, via Yiraia, to Serekolia and Mongo Bendugu, and from Kabala right up to Kurubonla, and from Kabala to Alikalia and Yifin, these roads all need upgrading . . . We have schools now. When I started my political career, there were very few schools in the north. So it gives me great pleasure now, when I sit back and think of all the changes I made possible.

"In those days you had to walk everywhere. I remember once I had to walk from Sengbelero to Firawa, then to Kulanko, Alkalia, Kindaiya, Sunbara, right up to Yifin, then to Kruto, on to Bandakarafaia, and back to Firawa and Sengbelero. The whole journey took a

In Government

month. But I had many people to accompany me. One of them was my late wife, Rugiatu Touray.[1] I married her when I was a young teacher. We had a child, but it was born premature and did not live. God never gave us another issue. She was very helpful to me. We would walk fifteen to twenty miles a day in the bush. As soon as we reached a village she started cooking, fetching water. She worked hard. She did all my domestic work to my satisfaction. She entertained my guests. She was helpful to everyone she met. But she died very suddenly. She was asthmatic. She went to take her bath. She began screaming. But before anyone could reach her or find out what was wrong, she was dead. I was away at the time. I rushed to Kabala, only to find that she had already been buried. She did not live long, and there is nothing to show for her life. I pray that her soul may rest in perfect peace.

"When I joined Maigore Kallon's ministry," S. B. continued, "I traveled even further afield. We were both young, and almost every weekend we would go to the provinces to meet paramount and section chiefs. Maigore was very democratic. I would see him paying school fees for boys from the north, even though he was an easterner. I too fought hard to get scholarships for young people. As a matter of fact, as Maigore Kallon's deputy I was assigned to look out for jobs and scholarships for young people, and as a result I became very popular with the youth. When Maigore was transferred to the Ministry of External Affairs, he asked me to go with him as his deputy, but I preferred to remain in the Ministry of the Interior and let Pa Amadu Wurie, who had been one of my teachers, take the position. In the Ministry of Interior I was acting minister much of the time, and it was while I was there that I met Rose. Pa Amadu was very fond of her. He always called her 'my deputy.' Whenever he saw her, he would say, 'My deputy.' He was like a father to me, and I had great regard for him. He often told me stories of the people he had taught over the years, or who were with him at Bo school.

"As a young backbencher," S. B. went on, "I was very troublesome, I was very sharp. I was especially good at question time, and could embarrass ministers with my supplementary questions. Some did not like me for this, but they sought my friendship so that I would not embarrass them in Parliament. I remember one day I tormented the late I. B. Kamara, who was then minister of trade, by asking a supplementary question." As he recalled this incident, S. B. chuckled. "I. B. Kamara lost his temper and said, 'Mr. Speaker, you know what

Marah means in Temne? The word means 'disease'!'" Laughing so hard that he could not, for a moment, go on, S. B. then delivered his punch line. "I said, 'Mr. Speaker, I agree, and it is this disease I am giving him!'

"But seriously, Parliament was sacred to me. I can remember, as government whip, sending out ministers who were not properly dressed. In those days either you wore a two- or three-piece suit, or a native gown to Parliament. I have recently reinstituted this custom, and our parliamentarians are very presentable now. No one sits down in Parliament wearing an open shirt. And we are trying to return to the old system of having people sit in the gallery when debates are going on, and not just wandering around freely as they do today. We are trying to restore an image of real authority to Parliament. I've spent most of my life around Parliament, so it is very dear to me. I am the only person in Parliament today who saw that flag rising up the night we won our independence.

"Parliament was more secure, too, in the old days. Recently, you know, we have had some minor thefts. One time [S. B. chuckled again], the Speaker's secretary received an international call for someone who was not in the office at the time. She left to go and find the person, but by the time she came back the telephone had gone!"

On 8 February 1967, Sir Albert Margai made a radio broadcast in which he announced that a plot to overthrow the government had been discovered and the conspirators arrested. Among those detained in Pademba Road Prison were several of S. B.'s kinsmen and close friends, notably his cousin and mentor, Colonel John Bangura (deputy commander of the armed forces), who hailed from S. B.'s mother's homeland near Pendembu, as well as Captain Falawa Jawara, Captain Sheku Tarawali, and Lieutenant Abu Noah.[2]

"I had information that Sheku Tarawali was not involved," S. B. said. "I told the prime minister that Sheku was a Kuranko and my kinsman, and I asked him if I could have permission to talk to Sheku in prison. He gave me permission, and I went to the prison in the company of some police officers to take a statement from Sheku, in which he declared his innocence of any involvement in the plot. Again I saw the prime minister. I told him that I was worried for Sheku's life, and that he should be removed from prison and sent to

Guinea for his protection. I said, 'He is afraid he will be poisoned in prison.' The prime minister said that the food was checked by the prison officers. I said that no prison officer would ever eat prison food. But the prime minister refused my request."

Six weeks later, in March 1967, came the bitterly contested general election. Stalemate and controversy over the election results led to military intervention and the declaration of martial law. With the establishment of the National Reformation Council on 25 March, the constitution was suspended, Parliament dissolved, political parties banned, and newspapers prohibited unless they were government-owned. John Bangura and others accused of the coup plot to overthrow the Margai government were soon released from Pademba Road Prison. Bangura was appointed to a position in the Sierra Leone embassy in Washington, but toward the end of the year he joined Siaka Stevens in exile in Guinea, and from there, in April 1968, returned in triumph to Freetown and helped install the APC government. Though Bangura was promoted to brigadier and force commander, suspicion and acrimony between him and Siaka Stevens increased, and following a bungled coup attempt in March 1971, John Bangura and Falawa Jawara were arrested yet again, tried, and found guilty of treason.

S. B. would never forget the day of the executions on 29 June. "I couldn't drive," he said. "I had to take a taxi into the city. A Nigerian woman in the taxi asked me why I was crying. I told her that they had executed my cousin that morning. As for Major Falawa Jawara, he was considered a gallant soldier. He came from Mongo Bendugu district. I taught him in Kabala. I knew his father well. In the army he was my father's batman, and he later worked with my father on the Court Messenger Force. He was one of my staunchest supporters."

After its defeat in 1967, the SLPP went into the political wilderness. But as the 1977 elections drew near, politics reclaimed S. B.'s life.

"My people came out for me," S. B. said. "They told me that I had to contest the election, even though I was reluctant to return to politics. Delegations came from Kono, Kenema, Kabala, and pleaded with me. I said that Siaka Stevens would not allow me to stand as an SLPP candidate, and that I would not stand under the APC symbol, so I would run as an independent.

"Now Siaka Stevens secretly sent for one of my most able lieutenants, John F. Mansaray, otherwise known as John Saradugu, and offered him the APC symbol to run against me. John told Siaka

Stevens that he could not stand against Sewa Marah in that constituency. Siaka Stevens became very angry. 'You bastard pikin,' he said, 'nar me symbol I di gi you!' So John accepted. Late that night there was a knock on my door. To my surprise I saw John standing there, dressed in a Kuranko gown, with the *bambedon* [crocodile mouth] cap on his head. He dug deep in the pocket of his gown and produced the APC symbol. He said, 'Uncle, I have been given the symbol to run against you.' And he told me what had passed between him and Siaka Stevens. 'But I have come to assure you,' he said, 'that I will not run against you. You are our hero. I have pledged my support to you. So what I want you to do is this. Early in the morning of the day that nominations are submitted, I want you to have me tied up, taken to the bush, and kept there until after the day of the nominations is over. Only please don't let me get beaten up.' Then John turned to Rose and said, 'Do you have any food? I'm hungry.' Rose brought him some food and he ate it and left. He went to stay with my cousin that night. It was too dangerous for him to stay with me. This is African politics. In fact, my cousin, M. L. Marah, chastised him for even coming to see me.

"Before Siaka Stevens gave John Saradugu the APC symbol, Kawusu Konteh, Siaka Steven's minister of mines, had been scheduled to run against me. Now Kawusu's wife said, 'Why do you have to run away from S. B. Marah? You must fight him for that constituency.' So the APC changed its mind yet again.

"I was well prepared. Prior to nomination day I had informed all Kuranko everywhere in Sierra Leone what to do. We should converge on Makeni at ten in the morning and go on to Kabala together. People came from Kambia, Kono, Tongo, Kenema, Pujehun, Bo, everywhere. They converged on Makeni. By ten most of them were there—all in my support, singing songs. I left Freetown at one and reached Makeni at three. The honorable Edward Kargbo then joined us. I introduced him to the crowd, saying, 'This man is one of the best APC ministers. He is my brother.' Then they took him shoulder high and were dancing with him all over the place. After the nominations day, he returned to Freetown and told Siaka Stevens, 'If you do not send for S. B. Marah we are going to lose Koinadugu; I saw how ready people are to support him. Kawusu will never win. We must send for S. B. Marah.'

"We reached Kabala that evening. There were more than fifty vehicles. It was clear I was going to win. There was only one hitch. The

D.O. could not find my name on the Koinadugu electoral roll. I pointed out to him that I was registered in Freetown, so we had to send a car to Freetown to collect the list showing I was registered there. Then the crowd would not allow Kawusu to approach the place where nominations were being received. It was not until three in the afternoon that he was able to register his name as a candidate."

The tragedy that began to unfold the following day, which was a Sunday, had its beginnings in an arcane word and a ruler's death. In the three years before the 1977 elections, the people of Koinadugu had been urging S. B. to stand against Kawusu Konteh. This grass-roots support assumed many forms, including a song known as "Mal koenya" (our business) composed by Senewa Kamara, whose husband Mankoro belonged to a *jeliba* family from Firawa — praise-singers of the Marah rulers for hundreds of years — and a widespread mood of solidarity, summed up in the phrase *be ara kanye* — "we are all of one mind." As Noah once explained, APC was so aggressive at that time that no one could speak out against it, so mal koenya became a kind of code for S. B. Marah. S. B. was known as *mal kéké* — "the thing we like." (*Kéké* means "crawfish," but may refer generally to any fish or meat for which people have a strong appetite or desire.) Words of the song occasionally varied, but certain phrases recurred: "We are one voice (*ma be kan kelan*); let us move together, children of Kuranko; don't be afraid, death is better than shame; we must follow our leader, so Sewa, do not fear, don't look back, we're behind you, you will draw us on, and we will win." When S. B. was elected, the refrain was added, "*mal koenya na ra fanka le la* (our business came to power)." Yet it was, perhaps, the one word *ferensola* that most potently identified the popular support for S. B. Marah, and in the lead-up to the election men and women took to wearing rust-red country cloth, imprinted with ferensola motifs, and even my book, *The Kuranko*, which appeared in 1977, was adopted and distributed as the ferensola book. *Ferensola* connotes unity despite difference. "Like the sons of the same father but different mothers," as one man once explained to me. Literally "town of twins," the term had figured at two other critical moments in Barawa history — when three of the four Marah rulers who established themselves in the Loma region in the late sixteenth century entrusted the defense of their domains to their younger brother Yamisa, and when the Marah rulers of Neya, Mongo, and Morfindugu placed themselves under the protection of Bolo Tamba in the late nineteenth century. The underlying idea was that while power is given to one, that person remains beholden to all. In 1977, ferensola embraced not only all Kuranko, but all those in the north opposed to APC rule. It was this that led Kawusu to conclude that ferensola was a synonym for the SLPP, or a secret society with plans to bring down the government, a suspicion that Siaka Stevens would never completely dismiss from his mind, despite having been shown evidence to the contrary from my book.

The tragedy that began that Sunday also had its origins in the death of the Neya chief Kumba Fanko Marah in 1975. Rather than elect the chief's son and successor, Kawasu told the people to vote for his own preferred candidate, Bundo, who now adopted his father's name Madusu Lai. "This is the man that the APC wants in office," Kawusu said. And without further ado, he took the staff of paramount chieftaincy from the D.O.'s office in Kabala and gave it to Madusu Lai II. People were incensed by Kawusu's tactics, but were powerless to resist. As minister of mines, Kawusu had enriched himself and his patron, the president, as well as purchased guns and ammunition from China. In league with his brother Kemor, Kawusu would, it was rumored, lay his hands on the biggest diamonds from Kono, saying, 'Pa go like for see this,' and take the stones to the president. In Neya, the already unpopular Madusu Lai now became the enemy of his own people. Backed by Kawusu and the APC, he raided granaries and shipped the rice south. People starved, and Kurubonla became a ghost town. As for Kawusu, he was loathed as much as his appointee. "Kawusu is not even Kuranko," people said. "He is a Sankaran Kuranko from Guinea." Others pointed out that he was the son of a blacksmith, and not worthy of high office. Moreover, they said, he has done nothing during his years as minister but allow roads and health services to run down.

About this time, S. B. and Rose had their last child, whom they called Chel'manseh, the nickname of the late and revered Paramount Chief Kumba Fanko.

Within a day of the registration of candidates in Kabala, Kawusu's APC thugs began terrorizing the town. They drove about in trucks, firing their weapons, and threats were made against Kurubonla, which had ostracized Madusu Lai II and obliged him to take refuge in his own village of Porpon. People were frightened. The market closed. The police were intimidated. Realizing the situation was getting out of hand, S. B. asked the police to intervene, but the police protested that they were powerless to do anything. It was, however,

In Government

already too late. Kawusu, his wife, and Madusu Lai II left Kabala with nine trucks filled with armed thugs, their destination Kurubonla. It was here that Kawusu would launch his campaign. That night the convoy arrived in Mongo Bendugu, and early the next morning it went on to Kurubonla. Most of the men from Kurubonla were still in Kabala, where they had gone to support S. B.'s registration. The thugs were now high on cannabis, and when they encountered the women of Kurubonla, singing protest songs against Kawusu and celebrating S. B.'s candidacy, they lost control and fired into the crowd. No one knew how many were killed. Two bodies were subsequently taken to Kabala. Others were buried or thrown into the flames when Kawusu's thugs looted and sacked the town. They returned to Kabala that same night. Men were seen, bound and gagged, in the trucks that passed through Kabala. And reports quickly followed of the destruction of Kurubonla, reaching the ears not only of S. B. in Kabala but Kuranko soldiers in the various Freetown barracks. When a brigadier relayed the report to Siaka Stevens, the president immediately summoned S. B. from Kabala.

This much I knew already. So when S. B. touched on these same events, I was curious to know how he would remember and interpret them. "Kawusu had about nine vehicles in Kabala," S. B. said, "and his followers were driving around and firing guns. People were panicking, running away. I went to the police station and told them to stop Kawusu. People were defenseless. The police said they did not know what they could do. So I said, 'I would rather he killed me than he go and kill my people.' But nothing was done. The following afternoon I was sitting with the D.O. playing a game of draughts when a message came from the police. The D.O. went to the police station and I returned to my mother's house. I was sitting on the porch when they called me to the police station. 'Someone has been shot,' they told me. 'The body has been brought down from Kurubonla.' Then the police said, 'Ferensola.' I asked, 'Do you know the meaning of *ferensola*? You should get your facts right before you start accusing people.'

"Exactly what had happened, we did not know. But Kawusu and his APC boys had gone to Kurubonla and shot up the place, killing one or two people. Then they tied thirty-four villages hand and foot, put them in a lorry, and drove them to CID headquarters in Freetown overnight. In fact we saw the vehicle drive through Kabala, unaware of what was going on.

"Then the Kurankos converged on the police station. They came in their thousands. They were very angry. They demanded that I leave the police station. But I said, 'No, I will not leave. You want to send me to Parliament to make laws, so I must obey the law. Don't worry. I will remain here. I will be all right.' You see, I had to appease them.

"While we were there waiting, a wireless message came through from Freetown, ordering S. B. Marah, Paramount Chief Balansama Marah, and Kawusu Konteh to report to Freetown at once. A helicopter would be sent to fetch us. I said, 'I am not going by helicopter. I'd rather go by road.'

"I reached Freetown that night and went straight to Siaka Stevens. He said to me, 'Marah, I have called you to join me. I'll find something else for the other man (meaning Kawusu). I want you to be my friend now. But I must not abandon his friendship. I will look out for something for him. Many years ago I sent him to talk to the soldiers at Wilberforce Barracks when my life was in danger, and he talked to them, so I can't abandon him now. If I did so, you yourself, with our new friendship, will think I will abandon you after some time.' I said to him, 'No, sir, even the other man, I would say, is my brother, my elder brother. I call him *korto*. This is politics. And as far as you are concerned, sir, I will call you father because our own fathers are no more. I knew your father very well, and he and my father behaved like brothers when they were in Moyamba. And let me say one thing more to you, sir. My people came to you and asked if I could run as their candidate under the SLPP symbol, but you rejected them. But you know, in 1957, when I first came to Parliament, it was you I followed because you were my brother. You were the only person I knew among them all. I did not tell you this at the time, but I followed you as an elder brother. But when you formed your APC, I did not join you because I felt within myself that there was no need for me to fight the government. I had to associate myself with the government in order to be in a position to help my people. It was not that I did not like you. I simply wanted to find a position where I could help my people. As for my detention in 1973, I bear you no grudge. It was a question of law. The law had to take its course. I was found not guilty and you graciously released me, and I am now a free man.'

"Siaka Stevens said, 'OK, I want you to join me. I am going to appoint you minister [S. B. became the minister of energy and power]. But as I say, I will ask the other man to come. I will give him something. But there is one thing I want you to do for me. Go to Koina-dugu and tell those other candidates to withdraw.' I said, 'Sir, for moral reasons, I cannot ask them all to withdraw. I will not go to Koinadugu. I know the candidates, all of them, and I know their main supporters. You send a wireless message for them to come. Then I will appeal to them — though not the SLPP candidates, be-cause I am SLPP in Koinadugu. Let them go to the elections, but I can assure you that I will win. But I will not ask them to stand down.'

"So the candidates and their supporters all came to Freetown, and I told them all that the president regarded them as members of his party and that there was no need to have two parties standing for election. I told them that the president wanted them to withdraw, and that their expenses would be reimbursed. They agreed imme-diately, and Siaka Stevens paid their expenses.

"So I was sort of considered to be returned unopposed. Kawusu was later appointed ambassador to Ghana. And I went back to Ka-bala, where the people received me very proudly.

"Although Kawusu and I were political rivals, honestly I bore him no grudge. He was born in Kabala. He was an age-mate of mine. I called him *n'koro* [elder brother]. His father's family came from the Sankaran area in Guinea. His father was a blacksmith, and later be-came the Kabala town chief. Before Kawusu went into politics we were very close. He was very quiet. I don't know why he changed so much when he went into politics. When he died, I was in London. One Tuesday, at about eight P.M., my son Abu called me from Free-town with the news, and told me the funeral would be in Kabala that Friday. I did not sleep that night, but packed and flew to Paris. I got a flight to Freetown the next day. We traveled to Kabala where I was just in time to see him placed in his grave. I was in tears as we drove the last mile into Kabala. I asked myself, 'Why all this rush in the name of politics? Why do we rush so much with life?'"

S. B.'s recollections made me remember the dry season of 1979, when I was living in Firawa with my wife and daughter. Evidence of the Sierra Leone elections of 1977 was still very visible. On the doors, shutters, and walls of many houses, S. B.'s campaign notices were still exhorting people to "Vote for Your Own." There were APC posters, too. And a lot of people were wearing APC Youth Police t-shirts, although the flames on either side of the rising sun had been over-printed, I noticed, with S. B.'s initials. "This isn't the first time that the Marah have ruled ferensola," S. B.'s finaba, Yeli Maliki, told me.

"S. B. is a true son of ferensola. We all move in the name of ferensola. Ferensola extends beyond Kuranko, beyond Koinadugu, beyond Sierra Leone," he said. "This ferensola business unites us all." Nor could one refuse to go along with the crowd. "To do so," one old man told me, "would be to invite ill feeling. No one would greet you. No one would help you when you were in trouble. Ferensola is where we all belong; would one go against that?"[3]

It was at this time that Noah told me the story of what had happened in Kurubonla, and of how Siaka Stevens had brought S. B. and Kawusu together, urging them to make up and shake hands. S. B. refused, saying that the people of Kurubonla had received neither compensation nor apologies for the losses they had suffered. "But Chief Balansama was present," Noah said, "and he finally prevailed, speaking on behalf of the people of Kurubonla." S. B. was in tears when he took Kawusu's hand. He was only pretending reconciliation. His anger was only plastered over. And Noah cited the Kuranko adage, *Ninki nye gbale* (cow shit dry), to remind me that the sun-hardened crust on top of a cowpat belies the mess underneath.

In the wake of S. B.'s electoral success, the Barawa chief, Tala Sewa, brought all the young men of the chiefdom together to cut a vehicle track from Firawa to the Seli river. For two years the bridge did not materialize. The earthworks washed away, the log bridges, so laboriously made across tributary streams, collapsed under their own weight, and grass and scrub reclaimed the path, reducing it once more to a single, worn line of laterite blindly honoring the time-old contours of the land. But with S. B. in power, everyone now expected access to the benefits of the outside world, and a place in the nation state. When I visited Firawa in 1979 S. B.'s brother Abdul's wife Tilkolo expatiated eloquently on the matter. "As it is now," she said, "we have to carry everything from the Seli River on our heads. It is wearying to carry such loads, and we are exhausted from it. Indeed, if you saw us arriving with such loads you would feel sorry for us. But if the bridge was there, trucks would carry the loads for us, and we would no longer suffer. If it were possible to ask an unborn child what it most desired in this world, it would say 'bridge' so that trucks could come to Firawa."

Tilkolo's dream was shortly to be realized. As part of an international aid and development project for Koinadugu funded by the European Economic Community, the Seli would be bridged at Yirafilaia. The Sierra Leone government would put up 20 percent of the required capital, and a Peace Corps engineer would supervise construction. But even before these negotiations were completed, Chief Tala Sewa mobilized his people. Invoking the traditional right of a chief to exact tithes and take such initiatives, Tala Sewa collected money, cows, rice, and cement, and organized a workforce to construct concrete bridge pillars. The work was done in the space of only two months.

Tala Sewa explained to me that some people had stored rice in their granaries for two years, waiting for a chance to truck it to market. He pointed out that fruit went rotten on the trees or was eaten by monkeys because people had no means of transporting it down-country for sale. Stressing how liberating it would be if people did not have to carry headloads of roofing iron, bags of cement, and commodities into the village, he told me that the bridge would enable a school and dispensary to be built. The bridge would improve everyone's lot, he said.

14 Thinking Back

Every morning, as I drove with small S. B. between Lumley and Wilberforce, I would look across the valley toward Juba Hill and the remote, palatial residence known as Kabassa Lodge, built by Siaka Stevens for his retirement, inherited by his successor, taken over by the NPRC (National Provisional Ruling Council) in 1994, and now occupied by Johnny Paul Koroma, who led the junta that deposed Tejan Kabbah in May 1997. This extravagant dwelling, as domineering as it was distant, brought home to me the intimate connection between tyranny and abstraction, and put me in mind of John Berger's observation that "abstraction's capacity to ignore what is real is undoubtedly where most evil begins."[1] I remembered how Siaka Stevens's motorcade would speed unimpeded through the cleared streets of the East End, the police in dark glasses, the flashing lights on their motorcycles, women dressed in white robes and red taffeta head-ties, the APC Pioneer Youth in dark khakis and red berets, a brass band playing a Sousa march, but no contact between the president and the people. Only the tinted windows of his car — through which the squalor of the East End must have appeared almost exotic — and the air-conditioning that kept at bay the stifling humidity of the streets, the stench of a dead animal and the open drains, the acrid smoke from smoldering trash, the whiff of peeled oranges, the odor of shish kebabs and charcoal braziers. This separation from the lived reality of the country was not just a prerogative of power, but its very condition — for to rule implied an absolute divorce from the masses one ruled, a divorce that was at once social, physical, and moral. Rule was, in fact, a form of divine kingship — the ruler less a mortal than an otiose god, withdrawn from the very world whose sweat and blood sustained him.

This "pathos of distance" unsettled me.[2] There were times when I wondered whether S. B. ever regretted the estranging effects of high office, and the mask of authority and imperturbability that he was obliged to wear. Yet, to observe him holding court in his home, or joking with his peers in his office at Tower Hill, was to see a man for whom power was as gratifying as it was natural. Perhaps this was why, when I asked S. B. how it was possible to reconcile being a politician with being a man of the people, he laughed. "Unless you are in a position of power," he said, "you can do nothing for the people." And he cited the road between Makeni and Kabala that would never have been built had he not been in government. "But you must also maintain your position," he added, meaning that a Big Man would command no respect unless he possessed the accoutrements of power — charisma, clothes, title, wealth, and women.

One day in November 1985, I happened to meet S. B. in London where he was seeing his doctor and concluding some business. After a visit to Harrods, where I helped S. B. buy a bicycle for his youngest son Chelmanseh, we took a taxi to Brixton, where S. B. knew a Nigerian customs agent who would arrange to ship his purchases — two Mercedes sedans (one "a gift for Rose"), various home appliances, and several padlocked suitcases of clothes, toys, and household bric-a-brac — back to Sierra Leone. I remember how critical Joe the Nigerian was of S. B.'s view that a person could achieve anything with hard work. "You need contacts, too," said Joe, "and a lot of luck." "Yes," said S. B., "but you must work hard, you must persevere, and then you will be given your just reward. That is why I help people who make an effort to help themselves."

Would Prince have concurred? Prince worked for S. B., and when I had been in Freetown a few weeks earlier, Prince had often talked to me about the difficulties of his life. The shed in which he slept. S. B.'s irascibility and harsh reprimands. "We are all afraid of S. B.," Prince said. "This is why I do not like politics. Politicians lose touch with the common people." Prince went on to explain how he wanted to go to the United States and study to be a marine engineer or lawyer, if only God would help him. "Batuke wolo!" he exclaimed in Sherbro, "God is great. He rewards our efforts. That is why I work hard. That is why I don't give up." But without some divine intercession or a benefactor, Prince saw little future for himself. He envied his age-mate, John Sisay, who also worked for S. B. and had reaped his reward. A born follower, John had campaigned for S. B. in 1977, though his wife had tried to dissuade him, fearing for his safety, and left him when he refused to comply with her wishes. Recently, John's wife's family had said that his wife would like to come back to him. John told me about this as we were walking along Lumley Beach, nearing the stretch of buff-colored sand where my wife Pauline and I used to bring our daughter at the end of my first year's fieldwork in Sierra Leone. "I consulted with my brother, S. B.," John said, "and S. B. said that would be all right. But we Africans have many girl-friends," he added. "The trick is to keep the business from your wife."

"What if you have a love child?" I asked.

"That is up to God," John said. "So far God has been on my side, and I have had no love children to take care of."

We were now approaching a group of fishermen on the beach. A semicircle of floats marked the position of an offshore net, one end of which had been tied to a coconut tree. A line of chanting men and women were hauling the other end of the net onto the beach. We watched for some time as the net was brought inshore, and glimpsed the catch like silver knives lacerating the smooth green surface of each collapsing wave. As each wave withdrew in a hiss, the next emerged, unfurling with the sound of a sheet snapping in the wind, until it ran foaming and effervescing up the beach. "God is powerful," John said, "to make a sea like this." And it was then that I recalled Prince's poignant attempt to commend himself to me one day when he saw me reading in the parlor, saying that all good novels contain meta-phor and personification, and that plays could be classified either as comedies or strategies.

My previous visit to Freetown had been six years before, in October 1979, and I had stayed with S. B. and Rose on that occasion too. At first sight, the city had seemed unchanged. Vultures wheeled high overhead against the rain clouds, and downtown the traffic tooted, lurched, and splashed through the potholed streets. In the garden, variegated and mottled shrubs blended with flimsy mimosas and casuarinas that stirred sluggishly in the wind. A rooster crowed hus-

Thinking Back

kily, and a gecko skittered across a rain-mildewed wall. In the evening, the trill of cicadas in the garden mingled strangely with the squealing and mewing of bats as they massed in the darkening trees. When I talked to old friends, however, I heard only of worsening times. Albert Tuboku-Metzer, a doctor in the children's hospital, said he now lacked even the most basic medicines. His wife Cathy enumerated the inflated price of rice and food. No one was in any doubt as to how this parlous situation had come about. The president had negotiated huge loans with the IMF and World Bank to host the OAU summit, due to take place in Freetown in 1980. Every head of state would have a chauffeured Mercedes, and be lodged in one of the sixty Moorish villas being built on the slopes above Hill Station. New hotels and a conference center were being built at Cape Sierra, together with a bridge across the inlet. Lungi airport would have a "Presidential Lounge," and three new ferries would bring delegates from the airport to the city in comfort. But "OAU today, IOU tomorrow" was the slogan on everyone's lips. S. B. was unfazed. Now minister of energy and power, he proudly described his plan to have street lighting installed from the ferry-landing, through the city, to Cape Sierra. One day, he drove me to the Bintumani Hotel in his new Mercedes — a gift from his Lebanese friend and associate, Tony Yazbeck. In my journal from that time, my cynicism is undisguised. "Together with three parliamentary secretaries, we sat on the hotel terrace drinking cokes and bitter lemon. The conversation turned to health issues. The Establishment Secretary related how he had suffered from dizzy spells and recurrent fevers that no local doctor could diagnose. He flew to London and consulted specialists in Harley street. 'They told me there was northing wrong weeth me, northing,' he said. 'I said, "well, do you think I've come here on a wild gorse chase." "Northing," they said. At times, you know, at times it is advisable to go to the weetch doctor and make a sacrifice.'"

A few days later S. B. took me to see the site of his new house at Thousands Bay. The long grass had been cleared, exposing blackened granite boulders. We sat in the shade of some big mango trees, looking out over the inlet. The tide was turning. That night we watched a Burt Reynolds movie on S. B.'s new TV — a montage of stunts and car crashes, images of invincibility. "It has better color than the old one," S. B. explained. "I will have the old set sent to my new house in Kabala." Perhaps he saw the expression of incredulity on my face. "It's for Rose and the kids," he added. "I want them to be happy after everything they have been through over the last few years." And so I watched the ailing stunt man in hospital, saying, "Someone said your body's a temple, but the temple's all busted to shit now," while outside in the corridor, the broken stunt man's daughter confessed to Burt that she loved him.

The daily newspapers also conveyed a sense of impending catastrophe. These stories, for instance, from *The Tablet* of 13 October 1979:

"The government has banned a popular political satire Poyotogu Wahala, which attacks false promises etc. of rising politicians, and self-interest."

"Khalil Kamara, a journalist with the Daily Mail, cabled a despatch to the BBC Network Africa in which he referred to Vice-President S.I. Koroma as a 'trouble-shooter.' Thinking this meant trouble-maker, the Vice-President had Kamara thrown out of his job."

Fofona "Bigbelly," one of S. B.'s loyal supporters, whom I would subsequently write about as "the man who turned into an elephant," was also staying in S. B.'s house at the time. One day, he pointed at the portrait of S. I. Koroma on the wall. "Thees man straightforward pass all," he said, meaning that the first vice president had no assets or savings salted away in foreign banks. He then pointed to the portrait of C. A. Kamara-Taylor. "Thees corot man," he said. He then turned to the portrait of Siaka Stevens. "Thees corot Pa," he said, rubbing his forefinger and thumb together, as if to indicate money passing hands.

Often at loose ends, I would raid S. B.'s bookshelves for something to read. That I found consolation in Epictetus says something about the mood of disenchantment that gripped me at that time (Epictetus began his life in slavery and ended it in northern Greece in poverty, which he preferred, having only earth, sky, and a cloak to his name. He wrote nothing but was so revered that after his death an admirer paid 3,000 drachmas for an earthenware lamp he had used).

S. B., however, was determined to show me a good time.

One evening, Rose, S. B., and I drove to Tony Yazbeck's for dinner. Yazbeck was one of S. B.'s closest and wealthiest friends, and owed much of his recent fortune to his close personal relationship with the president. The conversation before dinner touched on political intrigue, international conference trips, the comparative merit of a £100 per diem for two months and a £300 per diem for three weeks, and the importance of traveling first class "to show the flag." The Yazbecks were gracious hosts, the food superb. And I congratulated Tony on his magnificent home — the classical portico, the semi-circular terrace, the ornate balustrade, the breathtaking view. "How did you acquire such a site?" I asked. "My cousin's father was living in South America," Tony said. "The cousin came here in 1938, when he was fourteen. During the war they were passing down the road on Signal Hill and saw that there was to be an auction of a block of land. They made their bid, and purchased it for £26." As Tony drifted away, I fell into conversation with a French cement manufacturer. "You British never developed a liking for West Africa," he said. "You knew that all the best colonies were in East Africa and Asia." I tried to extricate myself from the categorical "you" and express my own affinity for West Africa, but the Frenchman had more to unburden. "There is no use pandering to their love of gadgets," he said. "We did not install a computer in our Togo plant because labor costs are low, and if there was a fault it would be too costly to send for an expert from France. To compensate our workers we installed a bright red steering wheel in the console, pretty much functionless, but a toy, you see, to amuse them. Zeh are just like children. Vraiment, you ave to amuse them like that."

I was only too happy when we were called for dinner, and the French cement manufacturer was seated at the other end of the table. I found myself next to Tejan Kabbah, who was with the UN in Tanzania. He described a visit to Uganda a couple of days after Kampala was liberated. One night shots rang out close by. The Swiss consul's house was being raided. Glass shattered, and gunfire crackled intermittently all night. The consul was well-armed, and finally the mob was driven away. But nearby a luckless Englishman, married to a Filipino woman, was killed in his house when the mob broke in. His wife begged them to spare her and the children. Isn't my husband's death enough for you; can't you let us live? They teased her cruelly and hung about undecided. At last they said they would not kill her and the children, but they required a small souvenir. The leader took his knife and cut a piece of skin from her chin.

When I now think back to that time, I like to remember not the pervasive sense of despair and foreboding that made such a disconcerting contrast to S. B.'s optimism and good fortune, but the times I spent with the children. The way Abu and Aissetta would bash the mimosa bushes by the gate, chanting "Go sleep, go sleep, go sleep" as they whacked—the leaves blenching and curling, the whole bush darkening as they closed. "Tie you lapa, you man dae kam, tie you lapa, you man dae kam," they cried in the same singsong voice. And then the laughter from the bedroom where Aisha and Fatmata—S. B.'s daughters from his first marriage—played together for hours, or brushed and braided each other's hair, or did their homework in the early morning before leaving for school. Or the way Abu, whom S. B. called "the Playful One," took care of his baby brother Chelmanseh. And the afternoons when S. B. came home from his office with Smarties, pistachios, plastic toys, and ice cream, and stood there grinning as his small son toddled up and grabbed his trousers. "You want to fight me, you want to fight me!" S. B. would say, before picking the child up. As much his favored child, as S. B. had once been, perhaps, the favored child of his mother.

15 Seeds of Conflict

Most mornings I would wake at first light, have a cold shower, dress, and go down to breakfast at seven. I prolonged everything I did, pacing myself as if in a monastery, for I knew I could not rely on small S. B. to pick me up when I was ready, and in Sierra Leone nothing could be hurried, nothing planned. I watched a lot of CNN those mornings, waiting for small S. B. to arrive, or stood at the window idly observing the people who came and went along the path that had been worn by bare feet, across the laterite and into the trees. One morning I noticed a young woman on this path, carrying a pail of water on her head. She stopped to take her bath behind a white UN tarpaulin that had been tied around a frame of lashed branches. She threw her lapa over the tarp. The watery sunlight rendered the outline of her body barely visible. I heard a rooster crow, and a UN helicopter waffling its way out to sea from the Mammy Yoko Hotel. Then I quickly looked away.

No ethnographer or journalist can ever escape the suspicion that he or she is a kind of voyeur. An eavesdropper. For are we not always half-hoping to catch our quarry unawares, as if a person's truth is revealed in his or her least guarded moments? And are we not ourselves slaves to an intellectual tradition whose distrust of surfaces is equaled only by its preoccupation with abstraction? Perhaps this is why I have always shared Walter Benjamin's aversion to the logic that seeks to cover the particular with the universal, and been drawn to his use of epiphany.[1]

When I arrived at PK Lodge that morning S. B. was installed in his chair, clad in boxer shorts, shirtless and unshaven. There were already several visitors in the parlor, sitting together in amicable silence, though the Kuranko villagers, wearing kola-dyed, rust-colored country-cloth tunics, looked out of place — their rigid faces and wide eyes betraying their awkwardness. The television was on, replaying yesterday's game from the Africa Cup of Nations. But the volume was turned up so loud that I found it difficult to follow the desultory conversation as it touched on political quandaries and minor crises, with S. B. holding court like an emperor, by turns joking, pontificating, upbraiding a houseboy, and asking me if I had eaten breakfast or was comfortable in my hotel.

I often heard disturbing stories from the people who came from up-country to petition S. B. or pay their respects. This particular morning, the Kuranko men told me about the case of Paramount Chief Mongo Bala's grandson. When the RUF invaded his chiefdom, Mongo Bala sought the help of Guinean troops to drive the rebels away. In the course of their successful operation the Guineans captured several rebels, among them some kids from Mongo chiefdom. Mongo Bala pleaded with the Guinean soldiers to spare the rebels' lives, saying, "They are our sons, our children, our grandchildren, do not kill them." The Guineans agreed to release them. But when the rebels regrouped some time later, the Guineans suffered several casualties, and in revenge they took Mongo Bala to Faranah. "Your children and grandchildren killed our brothers," they said. And then, reckoning the cost of their own losses, they killed him.

When S. B. had showered and dressed, he suggested we move out to the veranda, and record another chapter of his story. But no sooner had we begun recording than the phone rang, and S. B. was called away to talk to the president about some constitutional matter related to the forthcoming elections. Though we tried again, we were again interrupted, this time by Paramount Chief Sheku Magba Koroma III from Kondembaia, who had arrived from Kabala the previous night.

I had spoken to Sheku at the ferensola meeting in Kabala. I recognized his fly whisk as the same one his father always carried, and I talked to him for some time about the impact of the war on Kondembaia. In turn, Sheku remembered how I used to come to Kondembaia to see Keti Ferenke. As a ten-year-old, he would run out with the other boys to meet my Land Rover, calling, "Mr. Mike is coming, Mr.

Mike is coming." Sheku's mother Fina died when he was eight, and he was raised by one of his mother's cowives, Tina, who happened to be S. B.'s younger sister, and had inherited their father's mother's name. Sheku did well at school, and went on to complete a degree in mechanical engineering in Washington, D.C. After the death of his father in 1996, he returned home to contest the Diang chieftaincy. In the past, primogeniture would have determined the succession, but nowadays democratic elections are held. In the fiercely fought campaign, S. B. preferred Abu, his sister Tina's son. But he did not want to appear partial or pushy, and deferred to the family's decision to support Sheku, who was duly elected on 16 June 1996 at the age of thirty-six.

Just as dreams of diamond wealth had proved to be the undoing of so many Sierra Leoneans, so Sheku's position was jeopardized by gold. In the 1980s an international consortium had begun mining gold in Diang chiefdom. As the RUF overran the country, this gold became a prime target, and so the American mining engineers suspended their operation and left Sierra Leone. For a while, Sheku was able to appease the RUF by giving them some of the mining equipment he had ordered brought to Kondembaia for safekeeping. Now, with the war over, the mining company was taking Sheku to court. Sheku wanted S. B. to contact the head of the consortium, and persuade him to call off the legal action, or find a way of settling the matter out of court.

"I'm busy right now," S. B. responded irritably. "I don't have time to talk."

As Sheku implored his uncle to hear him out, his demeanor became increasingly plaintive and abject.

S. B. abruptly lost his temper. "This is not my business," he cried. "Go away, you're a nuisance."

"Don't push me away, don't push me away."

"You don't know anything," S. B. said.

"I have fifteen years' experience outside the country," Sheku retorted.

"It doesn't count for anything in this country."

"Don't molest me, don't embarrass me," Sheku pleaded.

"You stop! Stop! Behave like a chief! You never talk sense. Talk like a chief!"

"I have been urging people to support you 100 percent in the elections," Sheku blubbered. "We are grateful to you. Everyone in ferensola looks up to you. But you are too tough on me. You're down on me because my mother wasn't your sister."

Sheku was now too distraught to speak, and small S. B., who had been standing morosely in the doorway, observing his brother's humiliation, now embraced Sheku, tears streaming down his face too. S. B. was as unmoved by their display of emotion as a stone. After the two young men had drifted away to lick their wounds, he defended his tirade. "Sheku smokes too much cannabis," he said. "Their father spoiled them." S. B. then picked up the phone and dialed the United States. The person he needed to speak to was not available. "Then tell him that S. B. Marah called," S. B. said. "Tell him it is urgent. Have him call me back as soon as he can."

The irony of power! How blatantly it seeks to control time. One minute making a lesser mortal wait, or enjoining an underling to exercise patience, the next minute exhorting some minion to hurry up, and not keep the master waiting. Pierre Bourdieu was right: "The all-powerful is he who does not wait but makes others wait. Absolute power is the power to make oneself unpredictable and deny other people any reasonable anticipation, to place them in total uncertainty by offering no scope for their capacity to predict."[2]

There are, I think, times when we accept the omnipotence of those who hold our destinies in their hands, in part because we are powerless to do otherwise, in part because we believe that this is in the nature of things, and that things will change. But there must surely be conditions under which we can no longer endure tyranny, and begin to harbor thoughts of rebellion or revenge. There must be a threshold beyond which we suspend normal moral constraints, and seek extraordinary means of restoring some semblance of justice to the world. And I thought of Noah's resentment at the way his elder brother had treated him. Selling him into slavery, as Noah put it, in 1953, by pledging him to a Fula trader as a way of discharging a debt. Disrupting his secondary schooling by obliging Noah to help him in his 1962 and 1964 election campaigns. Not surprisingly, S. B. saw these events in a very different light, insisting that Noah had left school for reasons of his own, and that he, S. B., had tried to persuade him to stay on. Whatever the truth of the matter, it had always pained me to observe the way Noah deferred to S. B., addressing him as sir, circumspect and self-effacing, even in the face of S. B.'s scathing comments. Calling Noah a wastrel. Accusing him of having squandered his opportunities. Telling him not to expect others to take care of him. Was it possible to see, in this vexed relationship between S. B. and his younger brother, Nietzsche's contrasted moralities—the

Seeds of Conflict

ruthless self-affirmation of the noble, driven by the will to power, and the self-abnegating *ressentiment* of the slave, who, unable to act, reacts, making himself small and submissive in order to preserve what little power he has? I also wondered how small S. B. felt when his uncle criticized him for laziness, or for walking with too much swagger. "Don't walk about in that kingly style! It will get you into trouble. You must move more modestly, as befits a small boy. Take my advice before it's too late. It's for your own good, not mine. When you're young you have to move fast. Later in life there'll be plenty of time to sit down." My heart would go out to small S. B., standing in the shadows of the room, eyes averted, head bowed, as S. B.'s reprimands broke over him like a wave. But when I asked him what he felt when S. B. upbraided him, as had happened that morning with Sheku Magba, small S. B. made light of the event.

"S. B. always bullshits like this," he said. "He has to show everyone who is boss. That's why he's always bawling us out. One day we'll sit around and laugh about all this, about the things he says to us. In fact, our father used to shout at us in the same way when we were kids, but now I miss him a lot, and we laugh at the way he used to behave."

As if to drive this point home, within minutes of S. B. leaving the house for his office at Tower Hill, small S. B. was instantly transformed. Laughing and joking with the other houseboys, he ensconced himself in his uncle's chair by the telephone and made a long call to his girlfriend. "When the cat's away!" I joked. "In fact," said small S. B., "we were waiting for you to leave too!"

Perhaps I had taken the morning's fracas much too seriously. When small S. B. used the word *bullshit*, perhaps he meant that I should see these exchanges as forms of theater, in which people played out their opposing roles without losing themselves in them. It was in this vein that S. B. had exhorted Sheku to behave like a chief—to act the part, to comport himself in a way that was consistent with the role, and overcome his weakness, set aside his own feelings. It was in this same spirit that people had urged me to rise to the occasion and throw myself into my honorary role of paramount chief—to play the part, to choose a woman for my comfort. It wasn't a question of how I felt; it was all a matter of entering into the spirit of things, of donning the masks, of playing the game. Thus, while Big Men performed their status in public, young men satirized them behind their backs, opposing power with cunning. Quotidian life in Africa was, I reflected, a good deal more expressive and histrionic than the way I had been encouraged to live as a child. I grew up in a world that regarded authenticity as something deep within one's soul — governed by one's conscience and measured against one's true nature. A question of being true to oneself. Of avoiding artifice. Kuranko do not fetishize the ego as we do, but emphasize a person's social nous. As such, authenticity is consummated in the way one realizes one's given destiny or plays one's social role. The name of the game is not self-knowledge, but knowing one's place *and making the most of it.* For this reason theatricality implies something very different from acting out. Rather than spontaneously giving vent to one's feelings, one learns to perform the gestures and emotions appropriate to one's role. It was this element of role-playing that explained why small S. B. could so easily distance himself from the drama that morning, as indeed S. B. had done, after asserting the status distinctions between them. There was, as it were, nothing personal about it. Nor did their contretemps imply a criticism of these distinctions. It was simply a matter of dramatizing the power relations that should ideally obtain between master and minion, and of both accepting their places in the scheme of things.

Later that afternoon, as I walked on the beach, recollecting the events of the morning, it occurred to me that this theatrical element in social relations was perhaps nowhere more in evidence than in Kuranko storytelling. And I recalled the numerous folktales I had heard in Kuranko villages, over many years, of the hyena and the hare. In these tales, Fa Suluku — the hyena — is always the elder, the bigger, the senior, and, by implication, conservative, inflexible, covetous, gluttonous, and corrupt. While Hyena is the dupe, Fa San — the hare — is the trickster. Like Epimetheus and Prometheus they exemplify the contrasted attributes of gravitas and levity, hindsight and foresight. Young, nimble, quick-witted, and full of guile, Hare redresses the injustices and restores order to the chaos that Hyena creates. Almost invariably the tales begin with a situation in which Hyena has used his superior social position for selfish ends. Thus, in a time of hunger, he hogs what food there is, letting his children starve. Or he imposes a law on the community that is to no one's advantage but his own. Or he kills and eats a lion cub that has been left in his care. In such stories, Hare humbles and outwits Hyena,

Seeds of Conflict

restoring moral order to the world. But he does so by having recourse to duplicity and chicanery — behaviors that are ordinarily condemned. Thus, the notion of retributive justice implicit in these stories suggests that all manner of antisocial behavior is licensed, so long as it returns moral order to the world. In extraordinary times extraordinary means are justified.

But stories aside, what behavior would Kuranko consider so outrageous that extraordinary means were justified in reaffirming the moral norm? Certainly not Sheku's momentary humiliation at PK Lodge. Or Noah's lacerated pride. Not the abject misery I had seen in a young Kuranko woman's face some years ago, as she sat impassive and without the right to speak at a court hearing that would order her to leave her lover and return to her husband. Not even the grief in the voice of a young man who told me how his father badgered him remorselessly for his ineptitude and immaturity. "When I am in my grave," the father declaimed, "who will shoulder responsibility for the family?" And the young man — an eldest son and therefore heir — complained bitterly to me of his father's carping and constant criticism. "Nothing I do pleases him," he said. "Even my mother sides with him, though I beg her to intercede with my father and plead my case." Poor Tamba! He took his father's displays of hostility far too personally, unable to see that the old man was obliged to display this kind of disdain and distance lest his younger sons resent the elder's privileged destiny. Nor did the proverbial resentments that young wives felt toward their senior cowives constitute grounds for revolt. Nor the rancor of women, obliged to respect husbands for whom they felt no affection.

None of these petty miseries of everyday life entailed a flouting of social codes. They simply inspired devious, tactical means of getting around the obstacles placed in one's path. Subterfuge in love. The search for a patron or mentor who would give what one's immediate family could not. Recourse to witchcraft and sorcery, possibly, to prosecute a feud. The irksomeness of life was simply the cost one paid for being born into a particular period of history, a particular social class, or a particular role. But the situation of a person taken captive in war and made a slave was very different. Likewise the plight of a people under an oppressive regime. Perhaps the political situation of Sierra Leone in the late 1980s had, for many, crossed a threshold and become intolerable. No one would question the rightness of the slave revolt in 1838, for example, when Kuranko slaves, commanded by Bilalé, the son of a Susu chief and a Kuranko slave woman, rose up against their overlords at Kakuna, in the Upper Scarcies. Few would argue against those who led the 1898 Hut Tax Rebellion against the British. And perhaps, in fifty years, when the harrowing experiences of personal loss begin to be forgotten, history will not judge harshly those who fomented the rebellion of the 1990s.

16 The War

The most conspicuous thing about suffering is, as W. H. Auden once observed, its banality.[1] The day is green, the sun is shining, someone is eating, or opening a window, the torturer's horse is scratching its innocent behind on a tree, and in a mere second someone we love is dead. But the cosmos does not comply with our grief, the sun going into eclipse, clouds lowering, rain falling in sympathy. And we are dumb to comprehend what has occurred, and how suddenly and irreversibly our life has been changed. When we try to describe it we are reduced to a spare recitation of events that moves the listener only because it so obviously fails to convey a fraction of our pain. In relation to others, and to language, our suffering is like an island lost in the mist, or an ice floe whose mass is all but invisible. This is why, when we talk about war — those of us who have not been touched directly by its horrors — we tend to fall back on the statistics, names, and dates that float like so much jetsam in its wake, as if the experience of human suffering were at once too deep, too elusive, and too ineffable for us to fathom.

In Sierra Leone, I encountered not only people's difficulty in communicating what they had suffered, but also a cultural reluctance to voice their inner feelings. I remarked this often, listening to refugees' accounts of the war, or when S. B. arrived at a critical juncture in his narrative. "You can imagine how I felt," he would say, as if leaving it up to me to fill in the gap, to flesh out the emotions he felt unable to express himself. Perhaps this was why, when I talked to Noah about the war, he was more at ease expatiating, as a spectator might, on the history of events, rather than recounting his own losses.

"In a nutshell," Noah said, "the root cause of the war was bad government," and he recalled how, as early as 1971, Siaka Stevens had recourse to violence as a way of consolidating his hold on power. Indeed, so effective was the APC Youth League in intimidating voters in the run-up to the 1973 elections that the SLPP withdrew its candidates, allowing the government to be returned unopposed. "Because voters did not have to provide proof of identity," Noah said, "APC thugs and stooges could vote in the name of registered voters, and do so in different polling booths several times over. If a registered voter complained, APC red shirts bullied him into withdrawing his complaint. At the same time, the APC installed chiefs who were favorably disposed to the party, even though they were neither sons of the incumbent nor from a ruling house." In 1978, faced with a failing economy and increasing opposition, Siaka Stevens established a one-party state. Over the next ten years, government funding for social services, hospitals, and schools steadily declined, and an insidious shadow state expanded in which the president exploited the country's natural resources, particularly gold, rutile, and diamonds, to create a loyal network of commercial allies, yes-men, and foreign opportunists.[2] Some said that his credo was the Krio adage, *wusai den tai kaw, nar dae e dae eat* (a cow grazes where it is tethered), for under the APC, people with access to public money were allowed to use it unabashedly for private ends. "Under the APC," Noah said, "we had no civil, constitutional, or natural rights. Favoritism, nepotism, and cronyism were rife. If you were not a member of the inner circle, you did not get paid, and you were lucky to have a job." Unable to remove the APC from power, or even protest the state of the nation, people began to see no alternative to armed struggle.

Noah recalled the student demonstrations against Siaka Stevens and the APC on 29 January 1977 as a turning point. Within a day or two, the president's Mr. Fixit, S. I. Koroma, had rallied the APC youth league at Victoria Park, and armed gangs of red-shirted APC youths, high on cannabis and alcohol, invaded the Fourah Bay College campus. While police stood by, laboratories, dormitories, and lecture rooms were ransacked, staff and students were beaten, and at least a hundred were arrested and detained by the CID. By March — with students, schoolchildren, and workers demanding change — Siaka Stevens called a general election, and appointed several new and youthful ministers, including S. B., who became minister for energy and power. But nothing really changed, and seven years later, Fourah Bay College was still a hotbed of dissent. Following a student demonstration in January 1984, truckloads of APC hooligans, armed with cudgels, whips, and stones, again invaded the campus. Rooms were looted, students beaten, books destroyed. For some of the protesters, this was the last straw, Noah said, and they traveled to Libya for training in guerilla warfare. But the revolutionary movement that became the RUF attracted not only dissident intellectuals, but malcontents and opportunists.[3] One critical error, Noah said, was allowing Foday Saybana Sankoh — an army corporal, cashiered and sentenced to seven years in Pademba Road Prison for his alleged role in the 1971 conspiracy to overthrow Siaka Stevens — to lead the armed wing of the revolution. Sankoh nursed an abiding hatred for Joseph Saidu Momoh, who had succeeded S. B.'s cousin and mentor, John Bangura, as army force commander, and become president in 1985 — holding him personally responsible for Bangura's execution. In his embitterment, and his resolve to see the APC destroyed, Sankoh reminded me strongly of Dostoevsky's abject hero in *Notes from Underground*. A man who feels himself so downtrodden, thwarted, and humiliated that he becomes consumed by a cold, poisonous craving for revenge. Indeed, he is so in thrall to his ressentiment that nothing can cure him of it.[4] More imperative even than power was this self-defeating need to keep his hatred alive. This is why, Noah said, when Foday Sankoh had an opportunity to realize his revolutionary ideals in government he argued that the RUF had not fought a war to secure posts; its sole objective had been a kind of cleansing or purging — to remove a corrupt regime from power.

On Wednesday, 29 April 1992, the APC era came to an abrupt end when a small contingent of soldiers traveled overnight from the war front in the east, ostensibly to present to Siaka Stevens's successor, Joseph Saidu Momoh, and his commanders-in-chief, a list of their grievances. While the RUF were armed with new AK-47 assault rifles, rocket-propelled grenade launchers, heavy machine guns, and an inexhaustible supply of ammunition from Charles Taylor's stocks in Liberia, the army lacked food, arms, ammunition, fuel, medical supplies, and vehicle spare parts. Nor were soldiers being paid, for the simple reason that funds for the rank and file were being clandestinely diverted into the bank accounts of the officer corps.

A day later, President Momoh fled the country, and a military junta known as the National Provisional Ruling Council (NPRC) came to power.

Almost immediately, S. B. found himself again under arrest and in Pademba Road Prison. Though he was never told why he had been detained, he imagined it was because of the large number of Kuranko in the army. The NPRC were afraid they might, with the proper leadership, engineer a countercoup. "But prison conditions were considerably better than they had been during my 1974 detention," S. B. said. "I was locked in my cell between seven P.M. and eight A.M., but during the day I was free to exercise, wash, mingle with the other detainees, and play draughts. After a year in prison, I was placed under house arrest. I was not allowed newspapers or visitors, and spent much of my time reading books from my home library. One year and six months of my life was wasted. I had not committed any crime. And like the time Siaka Stevens locked me away for a year, I received no compensation, nothing."

While S. B. languished in prison, the RUF broke out of the Kailahun and Kenema districts in the southeast, and in October captured the diamond fields of Kono. Though the army counterattacked and temporarily regained control of Koidu, thousands of civilians fled the battle zones, spreading stories, not of rebel atrocities but of pillaging soldiers whose main interest was recapturing the diamond field for their own benefit. As disenchantment with the army grew, so did the belief that the rebels possessed supernatural powers. It was about this time that the people of Koinadugu formed the first Civil Defense Force, the tamaboros.[5] Though Noah explained that *ta ma bo aro,* loosely translated, means "go and free us" (i.e., from this war, this mess, this plight), S. B. asserted that the Kuranko term means "walkabout-bag," because hunters never say they are going to the bush, only that they are going walkabout. Under the leadership of Komba Kambo, the tamaboros enlisted the support of hunters and others with special powers like Mariama Keita from Senghe, who possessed powers of witchcraft, and two Yalunka men known as Field Marshal and Dembaso Samura. Noah mentioned one woman who could change herself into a bird, and thereby reconnoiter RUF positions. Other shape-shifters attacked the rebels as leopards or bees. And magical medicines, as well as incantations, were also used, Noah said, to pierce or immobilize the enemy, to protect one's own body against bullets, to make guns shoot straight, to help one see in the dark, and to render oneself invisible. The tamaboro used the same secret skills that one acquired in the hunters' society — stalking, ambushing, and killing the rebels as if they were dangerous animals. And like hunters, they imposed a strict code of conduct on themselves, abstaining from sexual intercourse before and during combat, trusting and respecting their brothers, and refraining from looting. Most Tamaboro casualties came from infringing this code, Noah said, and so becoming vulnerable to RUF bullets.

After the success of the tamaboros in repelling the RUF from Kono and forcing them back to their base in Koindu, there was a ceasefire and the tamaboros returned home. When fighting broke out again, the tamaboros refused to take part, saying that the NPRC vice chairman, Captain Julius Maada Bio — had come to Kabala and insulted them, accusing them of stealing weapons. The NPRC leaders were uneasy about the tamaboros, since their rationale for staying in power was their own vaunted ability to destroy the RUF. Accordingly, they ordered the tamaboros to disband, describing it as a "rogue army," and sending Komba Kambo back to Koinadugu. It is very likely that when the RUF sacked Kabala in November 1994 — the same attack in which small S. B.'s cousin was killed — it did so in complicity with the Sierra Leone military. Traveling over mountainous terrain and avoiding roads, an RUF force of about seventy youths walked 110 miles in seven days, from Kalmaro, northeast of Magburaka, and entered Kabala with some of the government troops that locals had seen pass through the town in uniform only three days before. One of the objectives of this raid was to punish the town that had given birth to the tamaboros, which explains why certain houses were targeted for destruction and why Dembaso Samura was stabbed and beaten to death.

During the years of the NPRC regime, Noah worked within the military for the CID, and gained many insights into the way corruption bred inequity and dissent. Between April and August 1991, for example, a total of Le 2.6 billion was expended on the military, excluding Le 200 million per month for salaries. But upper echelon officers cooked the books, Noah said, giving the impression that there were 15,000 rather than 8,000 soldiers, while secretly selling a portion of the 40,000 bags of rice allocated each month to the military. This was easy enough to do because the army was not audited. When the NPRC relinquished power in 1996, the newly elected president, Ahmad Tejan Kabbah, alienated the military by insisting on a proper audit, as well as an exact tally of military personnel, and by placing his trust in local militias to win the war—the Kuranko tamaboros, the Temne gbethi, and the Mende kamajoisia. It was then that the army began to turn against the government and those who had voted for it. Officers lied to the lower ranks, telling them that government cutbacks now meant that a single bag of rice would have to be shared among two to four men, and, to rub salt into the wound, alleging that quotas to the army had been reduced so that the kamajoisia could be fed.

In a military coup on 25 May 1997, President Tejan Kabbah was deposed, and the new junta formed an alliance with the RUF under the banner "the people's army." The coup triggered, if not licensed, an orgy of looting, robbery, and destruction by pauperized rank-and-file soldiers and impoverished rebels whose targets were the vehicles and possessions of businessmen, government ministers, foreign diplomats, humanitarian aid workers, and journalists.[6]

After sharing a platter of rice and fish sauce that Rose had prepared for us, Noah took a taxi home, and I went out onto the veranda to write up my notes. What had struck me most forcibly in Noah's account of political life in Sierra Leone were all the wrongs and resentments that demanded retribution, the social debts that cried out to be repaid. Students demanding an end to the one-party state. Subalterns conspiring against their commanding officers. The RUF/SLA seeking reprisals against the Civil Defense militias. Not to mention Foday Sankoh's grudge against the government that had imprisoned him for seven years. And then there were the countless personal grievances and gripes, born of the inequalities of everyday life.

Up to a certain point, people cling to the hope that things will change. That the resources, opportunities, and futures they feel that they are owed will magically or miraculously be made over to them. In lotteries and games of chance, in fantasies of possessing divine or occult power, people resist what Pierre Bourdieu calls "a fatalistic submission to the forces of the world."[7] But when nothing happens, young men turn to death-defying games in a desperate attempt to generate a sense that they exist, that they can act, and that they are more than mere playthings of fate. And it is at this moment that the fantasy is born of reversing the situation that has condemned you to nothingness.

Almost always, acts of violence are prepared over a long period of time, often in the subconscious, as an aggrieved individual licks his wounds, composes his self-justifying story, and contemplates revenge for the injury he feels he has suffered. Though violence makes its appearance suddenly — as if it is an eruption of irrational or primitive impulses — its rationale and necessity have usually been deeply contemplated. This is why it is impossible to assign any one cause to an episode of violence, though defining moments there may be, last straws as we say, which are invoked in retrospect to justify the act.

At some time or another, we all find ourselves struggling to reconcile the gap between expectation and reality — to explain the sense of disappointment and unfairness that oppresses us whenever fervent desire comes up against limited opportunity. Sometimes we say the fault lies in the nature of things; it is fate, and we must accept it. Sometimes we blame ourselves. Mostly, however, we blame others. According to a Kuranko adage, the *lenke* tree — a species of acacia, whose pods explode in the heat, scattering seeds far and wide — does not benefit the ground directly beneath it. I have heard the adage used when a person is complaining of the way an older brother or Big Man has given favors to friends and strangers, rather than look after the welfare of his own immediate kin. In a country like Sierra Leone, where popular expectations continue to rise, even as local resources and opportunities decline, a man of means and influence like S. B. is the focus of both adulation and resentment. Although Abdul Bangura had told me during our trip to Kabala that S. B. was a powerful man, and that power was defined as "the ability to accommodate people," it would be absurd to claim that any one individual, no matter how powerful and wealthy, could accommodate all those who made demands on him.

Perhaps it was different in the past. The modern idea of progress — of developing into something different, better, greater — had not yet taken root.[8] An older generation sought only to conserve the social order, not to transform it. One's horizons of expectation were delimited by what one knew from past experience, not what one imagined the future might hold. In Tina Kome's time, all this changed, so that nowadays young men, looking beyond the village, face confusion — a nation in name only, summarily carved out of the continent by colonial powers, a place whose center had never held and whose infrastructure is as fragmented as it is surreal — a modern highway that runs eighty miles through the middle of nowhere, a fleet of unused ambulances rusting away in a city yard, a school without teachers, a clinic without pharmaceuticals, a gas station with no gas. Young men drift into opportunism and fantasy as orphans sometimes do, hoping for some fantastic change of fortune, of a second chance in another country, or a powerful benefactor or political leader who will guide them out of the wilderness.

There is no one word for what these young men crave. Perhaps *power* comes closest, if we allow that the word covers a vast array of imperatives, any one of which an individual may consider vital to his very existence — manhood, wealth, work, education, status, strength, renown — though it eludes his grasp.

But what of the village? Was this not also a source of power?

In the villages, life is a matter of reciprocity — the expectation that what you give in the course of your life will somehow be given back, and that whatever you receive will be shared. You respect your elders, parents, and rulers; in return they protect you and see to your welfare. To the lineage from which you take a wife, you give bridewealth in return. And you offer guests food and lodging on the understanding that they will do you no harm.

Lapses in these everyday protocols of give and take are the concern of Kuranko stories, where, like stories everywhere, all problems are happily resolved in the end. An exploitative chief is overthrown, a jealous cowife punished, a duplicitous guest unmasked, a liar hoist by his own petard, a recalcitrant bride reconciled with her lot. Everyone gets his due, or his just desserts. But for many young men, there is no natural justice. For them, the time-honored roles of gender and of age, together with hereditary chieftaincy, cult associations, and labor collectives, are no longer binding or viable. The dreams of the village are no longer their dreams.

As for the new sources of power that preoccupy them — diamonds, commerce, education, Islam, and the military — these seem to belong to a world apart, where justice is subject to no known laws.

Even if you landed a job — as Noah had done — you were often paid sporadically or not at all, and then, like everyone else, had to fend for yourself, or be driven into desperate schemes. Noah spent a lot of his time playing draughts. Sometimes I thought of that board of painted squares, with bottle top counters, as an image of his world. The tried and tested moves, the gambles one might take. A person could have, as we say, more than his share of good luck, just as another could suffer unfair setbacks — as though singled out by some cosmic power for Jobian punishment. "Haven't we endured enough," people would say. "Don't we deserve a break?"

In the villages I used to meet young men who had returned from the diamond districts of Kono. Having heard so many stories of sudden riches, they were baffled as to why luck should desert them while smiling on others. Mohammed Fofona, for instance, had joined the army as a young man. He saw it as a kind of initiation. "The army gave you discipline, made you a man, made you feel a real force," he said. "In those days, a soldier was like a white man in the villages; he commanded great respect." After a few years in the military, Mohammed drifted south into the diamond districts. But things didn't pan out, and as he became more and more dissatisfied with his lot, he lambasted the bribery, bias, exploitation, and cronyism he saw in the government, and began to dream of radical political change.

Others imagined that Islam might provide the answer to their prayers. In the dry season of 1979 one of my nearest neighbors was a young man called Abdulai Sisay. After many fruitless months digging and panning for diamonds in the alluvial fields of Kono, he returned home bewildered and disappointed. "My hands are empty," he told me. Some years before, he had consulted a Koranic diviner who had given him good advice. He had then gone to Kono and made enough money to fund his elder brother's pilgrimage to Mecca. Now the same diviner told him that his run of bad luck was about to end, and advised that he should sacrifice a sheep to Allah and share the meat among his neighbors. But even after dutifully taking the diviner's advice, Abdulai was nagged by doubts, and desperate for further insights into the cause of his fluctuating fortunes.

And then there was the mystique of literacy—the subject of my initial Kuranko fieldwork in 1969 and 1970. What struck me, talking to students in the Kabala Secondary School, or reading their responses to my questionnaires and TAT (Thematic Apperception test) protocols, was the poignantly impossible gulf between their dreams and their reality. Though most were the children of farmers, they showed their disdain for farming in the zeal with which they laundered their uniforms, washed their bodies, manicured their fingernails, and, at one time, wore white gloves on their hands. Thirty years have passed, but as I leaf through the tattered stacks of paper that I have lugged around the world for so long, in the vague hope that I might one day find a use for them, I read of ambitions to become a doctor, a teacher, an engineer, "to help my people," "to help my parents," "to help my country," and wonder what became of these dreamers when they left school and found their hopes dashed. Of sixteen-year-old Marie Kandeh, for example, who wrote: "As we all know that education today is the key of life, anyone who does not try to be educated will just be like a slave." Or twelve-year-old Daimba Koroma: "I want to be a doctor to free people from death." Another thing arrested me as I read through my old notes, and this was the clandestine care with which many students used magical medicines, either to tie the hands of a superior student or to protect themselves from such attack. It brought to mind a story that Rose once confided to me. Her brother was the top student of his year. The day after sitting his Cambridge entrance exams in 1956, he attended a celebration party at which he fell desperately ill. He died the following day. One day later, his best friend also died. Autopsies revealed that both boys had been killed with a traditional poison, and though suspicion immediately fell on a fellow student who had made no bones about his dislike of Rose's brother, nothing was ever proved. Rose's parents died four years after the death of their son. "They never got over it," Rose said. "They died of broken hearts."

These idle thoughts and recollections were not unrelated to the recent war, for, as Unisa, Kaima, Rose, and several others had told me, many of the rebels had sought out erstwhile schoolmates in order to avenge remembered slights.

For years I observed these anxieties of powerlessness and marginalization — villagers working through an entire dry season to build a road through the bush, or a bridge across a river, in the expectation that their collective fortunes would improve, only to find that nothing changed; young men, like Abdulai, back from the diamond fields, with little to show for their efforts; others back from the cities where they had hoped for a windfall, but found none; students unable to find the money to finish their schooling, or thrown out of college for protesting against the government; men frustrated in their attempts to ally themselves with a powerful mentor and patron. At the same time, I was witness to the fantastic avenues to self-esteem and empowerment that had begun to fill this existential vacuum, particularly among young men. An alliance forged with a powerful bush spirit. The acquisition of powerful medicines, or the ability to transform oneself at will into a powerful animal. Or the hope that Islam and the spiritual authority of the *alhajis* — those who had made the pilgrimage to Mecca — would usher in a new age. And then, as corrupt governments and coups destroyed the civil state in Sierra Leone, and the economy collapsed, these thwarted dreams had assumed increasingly violent and vengeful shape, mixing indigenous fantasies of magical power with images from kung fu movies, fixations on invincible trickster heroes, and the possession of lethal weaponry.[9]

That evening, as I wandered along the beach at low tide, my bare feet on the hard, ribbed sand, I recalled an experimental artwork that I had seen in New Zealand some years ago. The artist had taken a series of photographs that documented the same stretch of beach sand at low tide at the same time over a period of thirty days. What this series of snapshots revealed was that no two tides were ever the same. We may get the impression that a beach is a beach is a beach, but the ribbed patterns, interlacings, and shallow depressions that the ebbing tide leaves behind are always slightly different. You simply need to be curious, and to have a means of satisfying your curiosity, to bring this phenomenon to light. What troubled me about Noah's account of the war, and my subsequent reflections, was how quickly one lapsed into impressionism and generalization. The truth is, however, that no two people ever experience the same period of history, or the same event, in exactly the same way. In striving for some general explanation of the war in Sierra Leone — some antecedent cause, some predetermining factor — we can all too easily forget that only a few of the young men who became frustrated, embittered, and angry at the decline in their country's fortunes during the 1970s and 80s embraced armed struggle. And we can all too readily ignore the tens of thousands of young men who fled the country rather than risk being press-ganged by the RUF. As my mentor George Devereux noted of the 1956 revolution in Hungary: "The simple fact is that, as a Roman commonsense 'psychologist' pointed out long ago, *'Si bis faciunt idem, non est idem'* (if two people do the same thing, it is not the same thing). Where one man revolts because he has been exploited, another because, twelve years earlier, the Russians raped his wife, another because he hates all authority, still another may revolt because he wishes to impress his girlfriend with his patriotism and valor and so on."[10]

17 Day into Night

Sometimes, as I sat on the veranda with S. B., recording another installment of his story, my gaze would wander to the distant spur of Mount Aureol, and the rain-stained concrete buildings of Fourah Bay College among the besieging acacias and casuarinas. Since I had promised to help Kaima with his university enrollment, and needed to do some research of my own in the Fourah Bay College library, one afternoon I asked small S. B. to drive me to the campus. As we began the steep climb to Mount Aureol, I was surprised at how familiar everything was — the uniformed schoolchildren waiting for poda podas at the corner of Circular Road, the young women washing their clothes in the stream that tumbled down the hillside among rust-colored granite boulders, the city below us, smudged by dust and smoke — and this impression was reinforced when I reached the campus and observed well-dressed students strolling to and from their classrooms, waiting at the bus stop, or bent over their books in the university library. Given all the destruction I had seen in Sierra Leone, I marveled that the campus had been left untouched, though this was not, of course, true of the young men and women who lived and studied there. After finishing my business, I returned to where small S. B. had parked the Mercedes, and found him deep in conversation with a cousin, now a third-year journalism student, whom he had not seen for several years. "Abu was shot by rebels," small S. B. explained. "I was lucky," Abu added. "I received medical treatment almost immediately, which saved my life." After Abu had unbuttoned his shirt and shown me the disfiguring scars on his torso and upper arm, I excused myself, saying I would be back in an hour or so, and set off up the road toward the Guest House where I used to stay on my way up-country or recuperating after months in the field. As I trudged up the steep asphalt road in the heat, I found myself thinking about people I had all but forgotten, as if their spirits still haunted the vicinity. Like Jim Blair, whom for many years I confused with Leo Blair (who also taught at Fourah Bay College in the 1960s), and whose son became prime minister of Great Britain. And Moses Dumbuya, who was doing his Ph.D. at the University of Toronto at the same time as I was at Cambridge, though he never, as far as I know, published his research on Pepel Island, where iron ore from the Marampa mine was shipped overseas. Moses and I spent a lot of time together, talking about our fieldwork, and the kind of anthropology we wanted to write, and when my daughter Heidi was born on 15 May 1970, we went on a memorable nightlong bender, drinking *omole* (distilled palm wine). Though Moses was incensed by the exploitation of Sierra Leone's mineral wealth by multinational corporations and foreign entrepreneurs, his tirades against neocolonialism soon began to include expatriates and anthropologists. One night at the Guest House bar in 1979, after my wife had pleaded tiredness and I said I would accompany her back to our apartment, Moses pursued us, shouting: "Heidi is a proper Sierra Leonean. Michael, you are one by adoption, but Pauline, you are only 50 percent." The next day, he apologized. "I have to carouse and booze," he explained. "If I spend the weekends at my mother's place at Bullom, my *compin* [companions] get resentful. They say my Ph.D. has gone to my head and given me airs." As the years passed, I gradually lost touch with Moses, though I knew that he had left the sociology department at Fourah Bay college and entered politics — as minister of education in the APC government. When the APC years came to an end following the NPRC coup in April 1992, Moses was one of the many politicians, including S. B., detained in Pademba Road Prison. After his release, he committed himself to the promulgation of Islam, and wrote two tracts — "Why Muslims Fast During Ramadan" and "Marriage in Islam." He died in his mid-fifties, a tragic loss. Another regular at the Guest House was Milan Kalous. Milan, who hailed from Czechoslovakia, toiled day in and day out in the university archives, documenting in meticulous longhand 1,000 cases of cannibalism and human sacrifice, allegedly carried out by various secret societies during the colonial era, particularly in the southeast of the country. As Milan saw it, his mission was to bring to light these "starkly brutal" facts of the African past, and thereby counter mistaken liberal views of traditional Africa as "a sort of political utopia where chiefs and people closely cooperated and shared common interests, including, of course, the anticolonialist spirit."[1] I see him now, in his cream-colored, short-sleeved shirt, his drill trousers, Roman sandals and socks, ambling down the road from the Guest House to the archives, then climbing back uphill at the end of the day to a Guest House dinner of hamburgers, chips, and peas, and afterwards a drink at the bar, where he often, inevitably, fell afoul of some local academics who would take him to task for his inability to distinguish between fantasized and real forms of rebellion. Undaunted, he completed his work in that cramped and musty archive, then left the country to take up a teaching position in the history department of Auckland University, where I saw him once or twice in 1973, after I returned to New Zealand, and not long before he published his compendium of incriminating documents, *Cannibals and Tongo Players of Sierra Leone,* in Wellington at his own expense. I remember being mystified as to how a person could bury himself so completely in the past, venturing beyond the walls of the campus only when absolutely necessary, and continuing to believe that history reveals abiding, if momentarily hidden, compulsions, so that the reappearance of human baboons, human crocodiles, and human leopards was inevitable, because they were, so to speak, in the racial unconscious, in the blood.

I sometimes despair that, after one hundred years of painstaking empirical research, anthropology has had so little success in persuading us to abandon popular stereotypes about savagery and civilization. One would have hoped that by now we would have broken the habit of magnifying those traits which seem to make us ostensibly unlike others — the color of our skin, the language we speak, the food we eat, the beliefs we espouse — and come to terms with what all human beings have in common, for better or for worse, and seeing, beneath the surface of cultural differences, comparable imperatives, logics, and dispositions. In 1993, when I was living in Bloomington, Indiana, I received a letter from Richard Dooling, who worked as an attorney in Omaha, Nebraska. Rick explained that he had lived in

Sierra Leone in the early 1980s, and was about to publish a book, based partly on his memories and experiences of that time. In researching *White Man's Grave*, he had, however, availed himself of details from one of my books about Sierra Leone, and hoped I would not take offense at the liberties he had taken with this borrowed material. He also made some generous comments on my work, and said he hoped I would like his book, even though it was fiction. I wrote back, telling him that I believed in artistic license, and joking that I would not be seeking a cut of his royalties by taking him to court on some trivial, if litigious, issue. When Rick's book was published he kindly sent me a copy, marking the pages where my own work figured. In one passage, Rick's main character is in a Mende village, suffering from amoebic dysentery. "Each knot in the lower abdomen," the author writes, "each tremor of nausea, each aimless blast of fecalia took fluids, nutrients, strength, and hope from him. He tore a page out of a book called *Paths Toward a Clearing*, by Michael Jackson, and read it by candlelight: 'Traditional African thought tends to construe the unconscious as a forcefield exterior to a person's immediate awareness. It is not so much a region of the mind as a region of space, the inscrutable realm of night and of the wilderness, filled with bush spirits, witches, sorcerers, and enemies.'"[2]

For years, I misremembered this episode, thinking that the ailing American had torn the page from my book to use as toilet paper while squatting over a pit latrine. This mistake undoubtedly reflected my misgivings about Rick's book, which, with its echoes of Conrad's *Heart of Darkness* — a white idealist becoming prey to primeval fears and beliefs — pandered, I thought, to base stereotypes about Africa as a stamping ground for witchcraft, sorcery, cannibalism, and untamed libido, a place bereft not only of modern amenities but of modern sensibilities as well. Despite poking fun at American litigation, medicine, and the insurance business, by comparing these to primitive magic Rick's novel failed to challenge the power inequalities that require our view that *we* are natively superior to *them*.

Nowhere is this distinction between reason and unreason more evident than in the way we talk about warfare. While *our* wars are waged for good reasons and just causes — defending civilized values and human rights, or making the world safe for democracy — African wars are all too often seen as outbursts of instinctive, tribal savagery.

In 1967, not long after the outbreak of civil war in Nigeria, the federal authorities arrested poet and playwright Wole Soyinka and imprisoned him without trial. In solitary confinement, summoning all his resources to stay alive, the thought occurred to Soyinka that "some (albeit warped) logic is involved in acts of inhumanity."[3]

But how is one to understand this logic?

All violence is a form of retribution. A form of payback, driven by the need to reclaim something that one imagines to have been wrongfully taken, that one is now owed.[4] One's very existence is felt to depend on making good this loss—a legacy stolen, a promise broken, a loved one murdered, one's honor impugned, a dream betrayed. Often, these existential wounds are so deep and degrading that material indemnification is considered inadequate. The injured party demands satisfaction, and this, as Nietzsche observed, commonly involves punishment inflicted on the debtor's body—by branding, amputation, rape, and mutilation.[5] The logic of this kind of exchange, Nietzsche writes, rests on the fact that "instead of a direct compensation for the damage done (i.e., instead of money, land, possessions of whatever sort), a sort of *pleasure* is conceded to the creditor as a form of repayment and recompense—the pleasure of being able to vent his power without a second thought on someone who is powerless, the enjoyment *"de faire le mal pour le plaisir de le faire,"*—the pleasure of violation. Sadly, one finds little difficulty in finding evidence for Nietzsche's unusual insight, whether in the medicalized brutalities to which the Nazi doctors submitted the inmates of the death camps, in the stylized processes of dehumanization, disfigurement, and dismemberment during the genocide in Rwanda, or the RUF practice in Sierra Leone of cutting off people's hands because they had, allegedly, voted in the wrong way.

When war breaks out, the thinking that provided its initial justification is quickly eclipsed, and the conflict takes on a life and logic of its own.[6] Though this logic is increasingly alienated from the political ideology to which the high command continues to pay lip service, its origins may be traced to the everyday life that preceded the war.

The morning after my visit to Fourah Bay College, I asked small S. B. why the rebels sometimes wore comic-book masks, women's underwear or wigs, carried children's toys, and adopted nicknames like Black Jesus and Captain Blood. "When I was taken captive in Kabala," small S. B. answered, "there was one rebel who called himself Born Naked, and went about without a stitch of clothing. Another was called Arab. He dressed in a *djellaba* and *keffiyeh*, like a sheikh. And then there was Albila'u, which means 'dangerous thing'

Day into Night

in Mandingo, and Kill-Man-No-Law, because there was no law in existence that could prevent the RUF from doing whatever they liked to you. They dressed up," small S. B. added, "because no laws or rules applied to them; it was to show that they could do anything."[7]

Small S. B.'s remarks were reminiscent of what Isa had told me at Freetown Airport. "During the war, everyone was alone. Everyone had to fend for himself. *There was no order.*" And hadn't Pierre Bourdieu written that "absolute power has no rules, or rather its rule is to have no rules — or, worse, to change the rules after each move, or whenever it pleases, according to its interests: heads I win, tails you lose."[8]

In all human societies, order and disorder are mutually entailed. Image creates counterimage, in the same way that figure becomes ground and ground becomes figure in those ambiguous and illusory images from first-year psychology textbooks.

Among the Dogon of Mali, the figure of Yourougou is associated with extravagance, disorder, and oracular truth, while its opposite, Nommo, represents reason and social order.[9] For the neighboring Bambara, a similar contrast is posited between Nyalé — who was created first and signifies "swarming life," exuberance, and uncontrolled power — and Faro, or Ndomadyiri, who was created next and signifies equilibrium and restraint. For the Kuranko, the contrast between bush and town signifies the same extremes. Because the bush is a source of vital and regenerative energy, the village must open itself up perennially to it. Hunters venture into the bush at night, braving real and imagined dangers in their search for meat. Farmers clear-cut the forest in order to grow the upland rice that is the staff of life. And initiation rites — which take place in the bush, and whose ostensible goal is the disciplining and channeling of the unruly energies of children so that, after a symbolic death, they are brought back to life as moral adults — simultaneously affirm community bonds and encourage intense individuation, since each initiate must now live in the world into which he or she was born as a world for which he or she is personally responsible.[10] But to see the world as something one has the power to create is to see it for the first time from the outside, from the standpoint of the bush, and this opens up the possibility of contemplating this same world as something one may destroy.

Whenever the boundary between town and bush (or their symbolic analogues — day and night, domestic and wild) is transgressed, disorder and confusion momentarily reign. Walking through the forest at night, one does not speak, for fear that a djinn might steal one's name and use it for bedevilment. During initiations, people fall prey to similar anxieties, and consult diviners to see how they may safeguard themselves from witches, who, it is said, can leave their bodies and go forth in the shape of night animals. At such times, some people send their children to the homes of medicine masters, so that they will be protected from the nefarious powers that are abroad, while others redouble the protection of their bodies and their houses with magical medicines. And day in and day out, role reversals and masquerades give outward expression to this inner disquiet and uncertainty—a consequence, informants told me, of the normal order of things being momentarily in abeyance.

I used to devote a lot of thought to this relationship between ourselves and our environments, trying to understand why our consciousness, composure, and self-control are so easily disturbed when the routines and rhythms of ordinary space-time are suspended. I became particularly interested in how we cope with such disconcerting experiences by literally taking on ourselves—incorporating, internalizing—the disorder that lies about us, before playing it back to the surrounding world, as it were, in the form of feigned madness, possession, abusive speech, role reversal, and ritual inversion. In doing this, we not only mimic the chaos that surrounds us; we master it, for it is no longer something that has befallen us from without but something we have decided from within. So, during Kuranko initiations, women don the clothing of hunters, act aggressively toward men, or pretend to be soldiers, marching up and down with fake rifles, while one woman, known as the mad Kamban, or Sewulan, dressed in a man's clothes, dances clumsily with distracted gestures and deadpan expression, occasionally chasing away men and children with the switch she holds in her hand *(see overleaf)*.

Disorder is probably the wrong word for what is occurring here. More accurately, we should speak of inversion or reversal. In initiation the passage of human life from birth and death is played backward. First, the neophytes are separated from their parents (a symbolic death), and sequestered in a bush house, where they will be reborn as adults. This entire process—in which the older generation tames the raw and unruly energies of the young, and so brings into being a new, vital, but biddable generation of adults—is played out as a journey into the bush, where the power of the wild is tapped and

Day into Night

domesticated before being brought back to the village. Rebellion and revolution spring from the same desire for rebirth that underlies all rites of passage, including death and burial.[11] At such junctures, time stands still, fraught with possibility and filled with peril. Indeed the RUF leadership sometimes invoked initiation rites in justifying its revolutionary method of preparing young boys in bush camps for the violent, but necessary, cleansing of corrupt towns under such code names as "Operation Pay Yourself" and "Operation No Living Thing." For many of the kids who went to the bush and joined the RUF, this desire for initiatory rebirth as men of power (purified of the taint of childhood) may have been stronger than their commitment to the RUF cause.

Certainly, their sense of impunity, of which small S. B. had spoken, was reminiscent of the license enjoyed by neophytes. And the abduction of children by the RUF, and their adoption by rebel leaders — who were regarded as fathers, and called Pappy or Pa — recalls the initiatory seizure of children, whose ties with their parents are symbolically severed so that they can be reborn, in the bush, as men. This idea that war — like initiation, or play, or an adventure — is a moment out of time, spatially separated from the moral world, may also help explain why many combatants anticipate a remorse-free return to civilian life. But the analogy between rebellion and initiation can be pushed too far.[12] For in initiation, as in play, the ritualized disordering of the mundane world, with its dramatic negation of hierarchy and distinction, is but a prelude to its symbolic reintegration — a reaffirming of the bonds that make a community viable. Initiation is a drama of restoration, not revolution — which is why rebirth is its central metaphor. In war, by contrast, disorder breeds disorder, and death is the dominant image. War is playing with fire, or "playing for keeps" — a phrase we used when playing marbles as kids, to declare that gains and losses would henceforth be irreversible. In playing for keeps, one's honor, one's pride, one's possessions, one's manhood, one's life, are on the line. Players stake everything. Winner takes all. In war, one must kill or be killed. Coping with terror, bolstering one's courage, surviving to fight another day — these consume one's waking hours and pervade one's dreams. Any attempt to drop out of the game, to escape, is to invite immediate punishment, which in the RUF meant mutilation or death.

18 The Reversals of Fortune

Thornton Wilder's half-forgotten masterpiece, *The Bridge of San Luis Rey,* begins with a tragedy that seems to defy explanation. A rope bridge gives way as a group of travelers are crossing a deep canyon, and they are thrown to their deaths. A Franciscan priest who witnesses the accident is both stunned and mystified. *The bridge seemed to be among the things that last forever; it was unthinkable that it should break.* How could a benevolent God allow this fate to befall innocent people? There must surely be some reason for their deaths. *Why did this happen to those five?* Wilder's book recounts Brother Juniper's attempts to research the backgrounds of the victims, and arrive at a theologically meaningful explanation of why they should have died at that time, and at that place. For we who repudiate the idea of divine omniscience and design, it is still not easy to accept that life may be devoid of ultimate meaning, and that accidents happen for no good reason. Though we may receive windfalls without much questioning, ill fortune tends to provoke considerable soul-searching. It seems outrageous, for example, that a young and beautiful woman should die of cancer, or that a brilliant writer, at the height of his powers, should perish in a car crash, while a corrupt tyrant enjoys health and happiness. Surely life is more than just a lottery. Surely the good do not deserve to suffer, and evil go unpunished. Surely there is some reason why some of us should live in hell, while others inhabit paradise. In Sierra Leone, one was constantly reminded of these age-old questions of theodicy.

In 1977, faced with economic crisis, student protests, and widespread discontent, Siaka Stevens dissolved Parliament and called a snap election. The violent APC campaign was orchestrated, as it had been on previous occasions, by the first vice president, S. I. Koroma. In March, however, driving to Magburaka for an election meeting, S. I. Koroma was seriously injured in a motor accident from which, despite being flown to Germany for immediate medical treatment, he never recovered. Eight years later, his dream of succeeding Siaka Stevens was dashed when the APC Delegates Conference elected Joseph Momoh leader and secretary general of the party. In his history of the APC, Abdul Koroma describes the moment:

> As S. I. Koroma sat there now on the dais, with the cheers and admiration of the crowd focused on Momoh, the thought must have passed painfully in the subconscious — the great organiser and master political tactician had at last been outwitted. He shifted constantly and uneasily in his seat. His eyes were moist with an occasional far-away look as he fought back the tears. Whether it was superior political manoeuvering, or political reality or just plain treachery or all three rolled into one that had brought S. I. Koroma low, it is hard to tell with certainty. But this can now be said without a shade of doubt, that the fates had been activated and now treated him cruelly.[1]

As for the second vice president, C. A. Kamara-Taylor, divine retribution would soon cut him down too. He suffered a paralyzing stroke in 1984, and died the following year. And today, even as I write, rumors circulate that Foday Sankoh's trial in Freetown may be compromised by his increasingly unstable state of mind.

One afternoon, as I was walking down Spur Road toward Lumley, a heavy lorry, belching black smoke, lumbered up the hill toward me. Painted in large letters above the windscreen were the words *Hard Work*. No sooner had the lorry passed, than a red poda poda appeared. Its logo was *Blessings*. This coincidence started me thinking about the very different ways in which S. B. and Noah explained the forces that shape a person's destiny. While both brothers shared the view that the course of any person's life is influenced by the decisions and efforts he or she makes as well as by luck and contingency, S. B. and Noah placed very different emphases on the importance of hard work and blessings.

"You are what you make of yourself," was S. B.'s constant refrain, when upbraiding the young men who fetched his bathwater in the mornings, washed and ironed his clothes, helped him dress, carried his bags, and attended him. "If you don't work hard you'll get nothing in this world. You must be honest and straightforward. Young people today want something for nothing. They are not serious. Even my own children," S. B. confided. "I often think about them all night long. I don't sleep for thinking of them." And S. B. told me how much he wanted his sons to "do well," to be men of substance, status, and influence. That they were waiters filled him with shame. "Would I want people to know my sons are servants?" he asked. "These useless jobs. Living underground because they do not have residence visas." When I pointed out to him that Abu and Chelmanseh were doing courses in hotel management in London, and were not simply waiters, S. B. said he wanted to be proud of them, he didn't want his sons to disappoint him. "These things weigh on my mind," he said. "After I am dead, what will happen? I wish Rose would speak to them, urge them, tell them these things."

Driving past the amputee camp in Murraytown on our way to Cape Sierra one evening, S. B. made a strange comment. "They sell everything they are given," he said, as if to suggest that I should not pity the amputees, since they were very capable of exploiting their situation to their own advantage.

Noah found these views difficult to accept. "It's painful," he said, "when people tell you that you are not serious. Because often there is no work; often people have nothing, and they have no connections. I would have gone into politics myself in 1967, but our mother pestered me, crying to me all the time that she would be blamed, and people would mock us if I ran as an APC candidate against my brother in the SLPP. 'People will laugh at us,' she said. 'They will say, "Oh, look at these two brothers fighting each other."' Mindful of this, I dropped out of the race. But at times, I feel very bitter when S. B. tells me I am not serious. I bear him no grudge, but it pains me when he makes these remarks about my not being serious, for if I were not serious I would not have gone all-out to support him in his campaigns in 1957 and 1962, and when he contested the paramount chieftaincy in Nieni in 1964."

Where S. B. invoked the Kuranko notion of *wale* — which meant both work and duty ("What you have to do," as S. B. put it, "doing your duty by others") — Noah spoke of the overriding importance of *duwe,* or blessings. Blessings were not earned or gained; they were a direct reflection of one's mother's behavior toward her husband. A hardworking, faithful, and dutiful wife brought blessings upon her children, who became *duwe dannu* (blessèd children). But women who were unfaithful could be cursed with childlessness, or their children severely disadvantaged. "You might be wealthy, well-educated, or well-born," Noah explained, "but if you lack blessings, nothing will work out well for you in life. In the old days, it wasn't easy to command respect, to have people heed your words at a public gathering. If you were not blessed, you would not be able to impose your will on people, to speak with authority, or command respect, and you would be called *danka dan* (accursed child). But if you *were* blessed, this would make up for what you lacked in wealth, education, or social standing. Thus," said Noah, "I tell my children that though I am not educated and am poor, I have blessings, and this is why people listen to me, heed my advice, and respect my opinions."

When I asked Noah if education, wealth, and hard work could compensate for not having blessings, he said no, and cited the Kuranko adage, *latege saraka saa* — no sacrifice can cut fate; nothing a person does can alter his destiny.

Noah's fatalism undoubtedly explained his formidable patience. Paradoxically, it also explained his tendency to place his hope in others, to look for rescuers, benefactors, and saviors. And it underlay his habit of complaining bitterly about the people who had disappointed him in life, or shut him out. But where Noah set great store by retributive justice — whereby people ultimately pay for their errors, and the meek inherit the earth — S. B.'s outlook was very different.

Although, by his account, an impatient and emotional man, S. B. had a remarkably sanguine attitude toward life's vicissitudes, and there was often an ironic edge to his comments on political fortunes in Sierra Leone, as when, for instance, he spoke about being in opposition.

"When I decided to accept a ministerial position in the APC government in 1977," he said, "it was because in Africa to be in opposition is all right, but if you really want to help your people you have to come to the government side of Parliament. You have to have the advantage of being a government official. People don't doubt you then. So that is what I did. I needed the backing of government.

"In fact, there is one thing I do not like in African politics, and that is to sit on the opposition benches. Definitely, I would not want to do this. I would sooner leave politics than to be in opposition, because I have a belief that people should come together and share their ideas. If I have my own idea, and it is different from other people's ideas, then we must come together and put our ideas on the table, so we can decide which is best. That is my belief. Not that I don't want to oppose, just that I like constructive, not destructive, opposition.

"All through my political life I have thought about those in Parliament and those who are no longer in Parliament. And there is one idea we must try to eradicate in Africa. When people leave Parliament, after serving their nation, we must not dump them, because this means that when someone loses an election he is finished, or is thought of as a bad man. But it is often circumstances that determine if a person wins or loses an election, and we should try to make better use of talented people, regardless of whether they are in opposition or in government. If someone has been a leader, you don't have to dump him down the drain because he's no longer in power. But this is what happens. People in high positions—even doctors, lawyers, permanent secretaries, and senior civil servants—when they leave office we tend to forget them. When there is some public occasion, we don't invite them to attend. I mean, how does his wife or family feel? They don't feel good. That's why we should change this idea that a person is only worthy of respect when he's in power, and that out of power he is a nobody.

"I suffered this myself some time ago. This is why, when I am invited to official functions, I don't go. Because I know that if I was not in power, I would not be invited. Unless we change this idea that when a person is not in power we can forget him, I am not going to attend any of these social functions.

"And we must always keep our leaders. In some countries you see photographs of all the past leaders, whether good or bad, but in other countries, as soon as a new leader comes along, they drop all the photographs and things associated with the former leader. That, I feel, is not good. We have to stop it. A leader is a leader. He may not be 100 percent. For instance, there are certain people now who like the way Siaka Stevens ruled. You can't stop people thinking in their own ways. But we must not forget the past. Even though most Sierra Leoneans know nothing of British rule, when you ask the ones who knew of that time they say it was better. Things were cheaper. You could get newspapers from London the same day! And nowadays there are many people who only know of the military regimes. Spencer, I mean . . . what do you call that chap, the fellow that seized power in 1992? I can't even remember his name [the April 1992 coup was led by Captain Valentine Strasser]." And S. B. laughed out loud at this lapse of memory, before adding: "The military doesn't appeal to me, military rule doesn't appeal to me at all . . ."

A few days later, when we were discussing ferensola, S. B. spoke in a similarly bemused way of an incident in 1991 when Parliament was debating whether or not to return to multiparty democracy.

"Toward the end of this debate," S. B. began, "I signaled to First Vice President Salia Jusu-Sheriff that he should join me outside the chamber.[2] We went to the members' lounge where I spoke to him in Mende. 'Salia,' I said, 'now that we are going to get rid of this one-party system of government, I think we should re-create the SLPP.' He asked me, 'You want it so?' I said, 'Yes.' Then we returned to the chamber. Though I was not a close friend, I had enormous regard for him. Until the coup he had been first vice president in the APC government. But he now resigned from the APC and declared himself once more for the SLPP. The revival of the SLPP was mainly his doing.

"Our first party meeting was held in the town hall, which was quickly filled to overflowing. Many people remained downstairs or in the street. There was music and dancing, and the SLPP emblem was displayed. While we were waiting for the meeting to begin, Dr. Alpha Lavalie, who was then secretary of the party, told me that the Reverend Paul Dunbar, who was to have chaired the meeting, could not be found, so would I agree to take his place. I immediately agreed.

"I was sitting in the front row, getting ready to be called upon, when for some reason I turned around and looked toward the door. I saw several Kurankos there. Assuming they had come for the meeting, I beckoned them to come forward, and I asked some of the people sitting near me to give them their seats. But the men said to me, 'We have been sent by the chief to come and call you.' I said, 'What chief?' They said, 'Chief Dabo.' Chief Dabo was our tribal headman in Freetown; I had been instrumental in getting him elected after we lost confidence in the previous man, who was a drunk, and once vomited in the Wilberforce mosque, disgracing us all. So when they said Chief Dabo I said, 'Well, I cannot go now, I have to chair this meeting.' But I asked them again, 'What does he want me for?' They said, 'For a ferensola meeting.' I said, 'I am the person who originated ferensola meetings. I have always been the person to call ferensola meetings, yet you are calling me to such a meeting? That's a change!' I told them again that I was busy with the SLPP meeting and could not leave it. They said, 'Did Daniel Koroma not tell you that we were going to hold a ferensola meeting today?' I said, 'No, he did not tell me.' They said, 'Well, he said he went to your office but you were not there.' I said, 'That may be true, but he is a near neighbor of mine; he could easily have gone from my office to my house and left word with my wife, who is always at home. But he did not. Anyway,' I said, 'if you have decided to hold a ferensola meeting today you will have to do it by yourselves.' They said, 'Well, give us a time when you can convene a meeting.' I told them I could not do so at that moment. I was concentrating on the meeting that I had been asked to chair.

"So they went back and reported to the others that I was not ferensola any more, and that I had joined the Mendes, and so on. They were confused. They thought ferensola was a Kuranko political party, and SLPP was a Mende party, and that I had therefore gone over to the other side. They called a meeting of chiefs in Kabala, and I was chastised for having left ferensola and gone over to the Mendes. I explained to the few I met that ferensola was neither APC nor SLPP. One could be both an APC member and part of ferensola, or an SLPP member and part of ferensola. But if they were saying that I was not of ferensola, if they actually knew the meaning of what they were saying, they were in effect telling me that I was not a Kuranko. If I am not a Kuranko, then let them tell me who my father is! Everyone knows I am a Kuranko, that I come from a ruling house, and that I support chieftaincy in Kuranko-land. So when they said they were going to expel me from ferensola, it was a great joke.

"Only a month ago a group of young Kuranko men came to my house to pledge their support for my leadership. They told me they had got it all wrong. I was right. It was a good thing that I decided to remain in the SLPP. Had I not done so it would have been a great loss for Kuranko and for Koinadugu. They said how wrong they were, and how right I was to be in government with President Alhaji Ahmad Tejan Kabbah, who had promised to end the war and give us back our freedom.

"So you see," S. B. concluded with a laugh, "I cannot tell you for sure whether I was expelled from ferensola or not!"

That evening, walking on Lumley Beach, my thoughts turned from the capriciousness of fate to the fervor with which Kuranko had embraced the idea of ferensola. I thought of it as an expression of people's need to feel a part of something greater than themselves. It was perhaps an instance of that perennial search for belonging and rebirth that lies, as Hannah Arendt has noted, behind all revolution. I had seen this same fervor when Kuranko embraced Islam — this sense of being part of a wider world, of tapping into a new source of vision and vitality. It was reminiscent of how an older generation described the spirits of the bush. Not only did the djinn provide a source of power, but the cults that centered on these mysterious creatures — part-human, part-animal, part-divinity — gave adepts a sense of solidarity with others, a shared secret, a common cause. It enlarged one's sense of who one was and what one was worth, and made up, in some measure, for the losses, humiliations, miseries, and exclusions of everyday life. Perhaps the RUF held out for many young Sierra Leoneans the same promise — of initiation into a movement, a cause, that would carry them beyond their present, oppressive situation, into a world where they had power, wealth, and recognition.

Then there was this question of "development." In both Freetown and in the north, people had impressed upon me the importance of "development." When I asked what they had in mind, I was told that improved roads would bring development, for along these roads would come the benefits of the outside world. The attitude was naive, if not magical. But it is typical of human beings everywhere that when we are mystified by a phenomenon, and lack the means to grasp it, we have recourse to magical thinking to provide a simulacrum of understanding and control. Still, it was not this relative ignorance of the outside world that troubled me, so much as the outside world's ignorance of the village world with which it was increasingly preoccupied — particularly where NGOs and other aid and development agencies were concerned. In the hotel bar, I would encounter these expatriates, with their proliferating paperwork and reports, and occasionally fall into conversation with them and hear the new catchwords of their field — *partnership, participation,* and *empowerment.* "But participation on whose terms?" I wanted to know. "How can you participate in the life of a village of which you know nothing?" I would be quickly reprimanded for my indifference to the life and death issues faced by villagers — the appallingly high rates of infant mortality, the spread of HIV-AIDS, the lack of potable water, clinics, schools. But for me, this was not the issue. Nor was it the lack of evidence that these endless reports entailed any real amelioration of the situation faced by the people I had met in the refugee camps or villages. Rather, it was the way these experts defined Sierra Leoneans solely in terms of what they lacked. I would try to argue that if *participation* and *partnership* and *empowerment* meant anything, they meant entering into dialogue on equal terms, of getting a sense of what is important to the other. And I would endeavor to remind my now-cynical interlocutors of Amartya Sen's argument that a person's well-being should not be made synonymous with his economic welfare, since it may be affected through various influences, and it is the assessment of the nature of the life the person himself leads that forms the exercise of evaluation of the living standard.[3] Sometimes I would point out, for example, that honoring the dead might come before improving the lot of the living, and once I mentioned Fina Kamara's plight, her child taken to America in order to improve her life chances, but at the cost of the relationship between mother and daughter — as if this social bond were secondary.

Because my mind was elsewhere I did not, at first, notice the girl who sidled up to me as I walked past Binta's beachside bar. She had a can of beer in her hand. Despite the makeup and the sexy dress, she looked no more than sixteen. "Can I walk with you?" "No," I said, "I don't want company today." "What is your name?" she asked. I repeated what I had said, and walked on. Along the tide line, a litter of torn plastic, charred wood, dead leaves, tin cans, and broken shoes. For a moment I asked myself what gave me a sense of worth and well-being. A sense that life was more than a lottery. But then I glimpsed, ahead, a line of men and women leaning against a rope, hauling a net inshore. As I passed them, the women were already beginning to gather the flapping karé from the wet sand, throwing them into enamel basins.

19 The Value of Shade

The morning I congratulated him on his appointment to the National Electoral Commission, Fasili told me he owed everything to S. B. "But it was not for nothing," S. B. interjected. "Fasili's good fortune is well deserved. He has stuck with me through thick and thin, and it is only right that steadfastness and loyalty should be rewarded." There were several Kuranko elders at S. B.'s house that morning, and all concurred. One man added, however, that Fasili's success reflected the qualities of his mother, for, as Kuranko see it, the duwe that one receives from one's paternal ancestors is contingent upon one's mother's behavior toward one's father. A woman who alienates her husband by being lazy, disobedient, or unfaithful jeopardizes her children's future. Hence the Kuranko adages, *ke l dan sia; muse don den; ke l den wo bolo* (A man has many children; a woman raises them; his children are in her hands), and *i na l kedi sebene, i wole karantine kedi* (The book your mother wrote is what you are reading now) — which is to say that one's actions and disposition are direct reflections of one's mother's actions and disposition. One's destiny is in one's mother's hands.

Concepts like duwe and *baraka* (blessedness) are well-nigh universal, and though they often defy exact definition and may be dismissed as illusory, they can rule our lives. Thus, baraka bears a family resemblance to the Kuranko notion of luck (*hariye*), the Rom notion of *baxt* (luck/destiny), the Melanesian concept of *kago* (cargo), the migrant's vision of pastures of plenty or of gold mountains, the adventurer's dream of El Dorado or Shangri-la, the exile's longing for the promised land, and oppressed peoples' yearning for freedom or independence. It goes without saying that all such existential values promise more than they can deliver. Yet their very scarcity increases our desire, and strengthens their hold on our imaginations. People will often harbor resentments against those who seem to be possess more than their fair share of luck, willingly risk everything to gain more of it, and readily fall prey to thinking that their own ill fortune can be attributed to their own moral failing or to the machinations of others. Among the Kuranko, these emotions are nowhere more intense than among children who share the same father but have different mothers. Known as *fadenye* (father-childship), sibling rivalry has its genesis in the qualitatively different relationships between cowives and their husband. If the child of one wife prospers while the child of another suffers, incriminations and envy often follow. But the notion of fadenye had wider connotations, for in a country like Sierra Leone, oppressed by acute scarcity and entrenched inequalities, fantasies of improving one's fortunes through supernatural means are as common as anxieties about losing them through witchcraft. And everywhere, this acquisition of luck or benefit depends not on the possession of talent, knowledge, or merit alone, but on earning blessings through a dutiful relationship with a status superior, such as a husband, a teacher, a politician, a businessman — paying him respect, working for him without complaint, serving him faithfully, and doing his bidding.[1]

In stories, this benefactor is sometimes fantasized as a djinn, or otherwise imagined. And baraka, as its Arabic derivation suggests, tends to be associated with the world beyond. When I lived in northern Sierra Leone, I often heard rumors of a fabulous town somewhere in the hazy savanna regions to the northeast, known as Musudugu — town or place of women. No men lived there, and the women of the town were famed for their skills in divination, medicine, and sorcery. Traders and travelers told of great wealth bestowed on men who had found favor with the women of the town, though none could confirm whether this place was identical with the town of Mousadougou which lies in the Konyor country at the edge of the forests that border Ivory Coast and Liberia.

If these myths of Musudugu taught me anything, it was that the imagined wellsprings of a person's fate and fortune easily elude his or her grasp. This is the penumbral domain that William James speaks of as "an ambiguous sphere of being, belonging with emotion on the one hand, and having objective 'value' on the other, yet seeming not quite inner nor quite outer."[2] These "fields of experience," he observes, "have no more definite boundaries than have our fields of view. Both are fringed forever by a *more* that continuously develops, and that continuously supercedes them as life proceeds." Yet for all its mercurial, distant, and indefinable character, this field of vital being obsesses us.

As long ago as 1824, when the first white man entered Kuranko country, people's desire for things from the outside world was so great that Major Alexander Gordon Laing reported on it in detail. "The jelimusu sang of the white man," he wrote, "who had come to their town; of the houseful of money which he had; such cloth, such beads, such fine things had never been seen in Kooranko before; if their husbands were men, and wished to see their wives well dressed, they ought to take some of the money from the white men."[3]

Echoing the praise-singer's words, the Barawa chief Marin Tamba, alias Sewa—who incidentally would be the first of his lineage to embrace Islam, presumably because it also promised access to the bounty of the outside world—sang of Freetown, which he called Saralon, and of houses a mile in length filled with much more money than Laing possessed, money they might receive if they left Laing unmolested, for whoever wants to see a snake's tail must not strike it on the head. In Sengbe, people sang the same refrain. Chief Balansama declared the road from his country open, so that Kuranko and Sankaran men with gold, ivory, camwood, and kola might travel to the saltwater with the white man.[4] And in token of his earnest, Balansama ordered his brother, as well as his son Denka, to go with Laing to the coast.

Though there is no suggestion, in Laing's account, of a link between wealth and knowledge, Kuranko were undoubtedly aware of it.

One rainy afternoon, many years ago, in the course of an aimless conversation with a group of Kuranko elders, I was asked if I thought of them as my kinsmen. Assuming they meant this literally, I said no. The old men reproached me, asking was I not aware that Africans and Europeans had the same ancestral parents, and that our forefathers were brothers. "Adama and Hawa had three sons," they said. "The eldest became the ancestor of the whites, the second the ancestor of the Arabs, the third the ancestor of the blacks. The first two sons inherited literacy and the knowledge of books, while the last-born son, the ancestor of the blacks, inherited nothing." When I asked why this should be so, one of the elders said, "If you uproot a groundnut and inspect the root, isn't it always the case that some of the nuts are bad and some good?"

The myth, I would later discover, was widespread and very old.[5] Winwood Reade heard a version of it in northern Sierra Leone in the early 1870s. "When God made the world he created a Black man and a white man. He offered to the black man his choice of two things: gold and a covered calabash. The black man took the gold, and the white man got the calabash in which a book was contained; and this book has made the white men powerful and wise, and the lords of the earth."

These notions that the missing element in one's life lay elsewhere, beyond one's immediate grasp, had governed people's thinking for a long time.

For Tina Kome, it had been a matter of literacy and colonial power. "My father wept the day I left to go to school," Noah once recalled, "but he had vowed that his sons should read and write." For Noah's son Kaima, education remained the key, and when he brought photocopies of his school records to my hotel, so that I could write letters in support of his application to Njala University, I saw in his hopefulness not only an echo of his father's youthful dreams, but a distant memory of my own. In his *Report on Experience,* the New Zealand writer John Mulgan observed that we inhabit our country like strangers, lacking the confidence and wherewithal to shape our own future. "That is why," says Mulgan, "we are restive and unhappy. Though we come from the most beautiful country in the world, it is small and remote, and after a while, this isolation oppresses us, so that we go abroad. But we *roam the world looking not for adventure but for satisfaction.*"[6]

But what we imagine will satisfy our cravings, and make us happy, is always changing. For Noah it was most urgently a matter of having a benefactor on whom he could pin his hopes. For Rose it was a question of starting up her dressmaking business again, and reclaiming her independence. For small S. B. it was having the resources to keep a girlfriend. Love wasn't enough these days, he told me — mindful, perhaps, of the growing number of girls making the most of the countless UN and NGO personnel now pouring into the country by working as prostitutes. To keep a girlfriend you had to give gifts, small S. B. said, and have the means to do so. For the faithful Fasili, who came to the house every morning, clutching his briefcase and attending his master's bidding, it was a matter of position. For Abdul Bangura, it was a matter of waiting to be assigned a piece of land on which to begin diamond digging again, and getting S. B.'s help in securing a license. As for S. B., it was, I suppose, a matter of being in power, and of not being dumped or written off when one was not in power.

But what of the people I met every day who had no prospects at all? Like the young mother of four whose husband had left her, who sold fruit on the roadside at Brookfields, oblivious to the outrageous graffiti on the wall behind her. Early every morning she would buy bananas and oranges from people who had come from up-country, then wait for hours on end for a sale. She fed her family on her earnings, though many days she did not break even. Or the people I talked to in the refugee camps, who had lost everything in the war, and waited with diminishing hope for a change in their fortunes.

The displaced people's camp in Cline Town had once been a foundry. Only a stone's throw from the warehouses and workshops of the waterfront, it was now a complex of semi-derelict buildings and laterite yards. Abandoned lathes and metal presses lined the

interior of a vast corrugated iron shed. Outside, in the shade of similar buildings, scores of women sat on wooden stools, selling tomato paste, onions, magi cubes, okra, and cassava leaf—ingredients for sauces that few could afford. Meat and fish were nonexistent.

I picked my way past a group of kids playing soccer with a half-deflated ball, and headed toward a row of makeshift huts—white plastic UN tarps over frames of lashed poles—hoping to go on with the conversations I had begun with small S. B.'s assistance the day before.

My aim was to write down what people wanted to tell me. As it turned out, some people wanted to recount their stories of the war, while others simply wanted me to record their names in my notebook and leave them my name and address, as if this would create a tenuous connection with the world outside the camp, a glimmer of hope.

"I was in Kono," Adama Sisay began, "when the rebels entered there. I was a businesswoman. I lost everything. We left Kono and walked on foot to Makeni [about eighty miles], and then to Kabala [another seventy miles], where I started over. When the rebels attacked Kabala in 1994 we ran away to Freetown. During the intervention in 1997 [when President Tejan Kabbah's government was overthrown by a section of the armed forces, led by Major Johnny Paul Koroma], soldiers looted everything we had. I went back to Kabala. That same year we were attacked again. We fled to the bush. We had no food to eat for a week. We came back from the bush and were told to stay in town. I had two sons. One is here. The other is sick. We have no money, no ointment, no medicine. I lost everything. When we came back to Freetown I was staying in Kabba town. I tried to start another life there. On January 6, 1999, when the junta entered the city, they burned down our house. They wanted to kill me. But God stayed their hand. We ran into the bush. When we came back to the city, they brought me to this camp. That is my whole story."

"Did you know any of the rebels, or did any of them know you?" I asked.

"Some school friends of mine in Kabala, I had to hide from them. They would have killed me."

"Did they have anything against you?"

"Well, if you have seen them, you know who they are, and if you get away you might tell others I saw such and such a person there."

"So they kill to keep their identity secret?"

"Yes."

"What is the hardest thing about your life here now?"

"The hardest thing is that I don't have money. I can't do any business. I used to do business. Now I am only living by God."

"Let me tell you what happened to me," Abu Kamara said. "I was at Lunsar, attending school there in 1994, when the rebels entered and we had to flee. It was the end of my schooling. We had to leave Lunsar. The place was not safe. I went to Kambia. In Kambia I spoke to some missionaries, and asked them to help me continue my education. But then we had to flee Kambia too. We went to the bush, to surrounding villages. From there we made our way to Makeni. We were searching for somewhere we could settle and start a different life. We were there for a while, but on the road to Kono one day we were ambushed by the RUF. We were with some ECOMOG soldiers. Many ECOMOG and RUF were killed. We went back to Makeni. We stayed there for three years. When Makeni was attacked we went back to Lunsar. The RUF attacked Lunsar. We came down to Freetown here. But we were in the east, and the rebels came and stopped us going to the west. They said they did not trust us. Whenever people came from the west they were killed."

Even before Abu had finished, his friend Amadu was taking up the refrain.

"We are suffering," he said. "We the youths do not have work. We don't attend school. We have nothing to do. They give us food, but it is not enough for us. After two or three days it is finished and we have nothing. Our families are scattered. We have nowhere to live together. Everyone is living on his own. We have no hope, no progress, no job, that is our problem."

So many people were now crowding around that it was impossible to allow each individual the time and space he or she wanted. So we talked together.

"The more we explain our stories," Abubakar said, "like that woman there [Adama], the more we are puzzled."

"What puzzles you?"

"That we have no work, no money, nothing to do. That we have to leave our wives. That we are useless. Before this time most of us were working, some of us doing business, some of us farming, but now they have brought us to this camp we are doing nothing. They cut off some people's hands, burned our houses, killed many people, but still, everyone in the country has said, 'Let us come together and build another Sierra Leone.' There is nothing we can say."

I was intrigued by this conflation of the RUF and those who ran the camp. This sense that one's life was hostage to some force beyond one's comprehension or control. The ubiquitous *They*. The degrading state of passivity, bewilderment, and waiting into which the people in the camp had been thrown.

"We sleep on the floor," said one young man.

"Where you're sitting right now, we sleep there," said another.

"Who runs the camp?" I asked.

"We know only one man, but he does not stay here."

"Sometimes," a woman interjected, "they give us a card on which our names are written. It is to get food. We make a line. Sometimes we spend the whole day waiting in that line. Sometimes it is two or three days before we get anything. Twelve cups of bulgur. Half a pint of oil. Sometimes they tell us, 'You are not registered.' The very same people that gave us the card."

"Who gives you the food?"

"One agent they call Share. The truck stops in the street. There is a forty-foot container. They open the door. They take out the sacks one by one. Sometimes you get something, sometimes you don't. After twenty bags . . ."

"What do they tell you, the people who run the camp?"

"They say we have to be patient before we go back to our homes. But we are suffering. We have been told we have to forgive and forget, that we have to look up to the government now, and see what the government can do for us. The government says the war is over, but for us it is still going on."

"We would be only too happy to go home," another young man added, "but what would we do? I am a mechanic. All my equipment was destroyed."

"I am a driver," said another. "The Big Man I worked for lost everything. I am trying to get another driver's license, but it costs money. So I am sitting down here, no work, no clothes to wear, no food to eat."

As if in response to these piled-up images of confinement and deprivation, Eddy Shuma pressed forward. "We have many stories," he said. "They wanted to burn me and some others in a kiosk on January 6. They locked eight of us in the kiosk. I thought I was going to die. We could not tell you all the stories we have. They are too much. If we started telling our stories it would take a day. You wouldn't go anywhere. You would be doing nothing but listening to all our stories."

I thought of Keti Ferenke Koroma, whose stories I had recorded in Kondembaia thirty years ago. Keti Ferenke had also liked to boast that I had neither the time nor staying power to hear all the stories he knew. Stories that were often about bloody conflicts, which inexplicably I did not think of as memories of actual events or as presaging the possibility of real violence.

Several of the young men wanted me to see inside their hut. They wanted to show me their cramped living conditions, the dirt floor, the bed made of lashed poles and a thin Styrofoam mattress, the makeshift towel rail on which were draped a couple of shirts, a blanket, and a towel. "Look at this place," they said, "look at the dirt here. At night we cannot sleep for the mosquitoes. The bedbugs. The rats that gnaw the soles of our feet."

Outside the hut, someone had written on a scrap of wood: "You only know the value of shade when the tree has been cut down."

As I copied the words into my notebook, Abu was saying, "I want to go back to school."

"I need tools," Mohammed said.

"We need help to get our licenses," Tony added. "Le 150,000. Where could we find that money now? Who would give me 50,000? How long will it take? We need help."

I shelled out all I had.

What overwhelmed me was not the demands, nor the sense of impotence I felt, but the realization that these people needed so little to resume their lives, and that, rather than dwell on what had happened in the past, they desired only to move on, to start over. It was this that made their immobility so painful. Driving back to my hotel through the thronged, polluted streets of the East End, I kept thinking of how these people were no less imprisoned than S. B. had been, when a smuggled message, a piece of meat, or a memory of his children's voices was enough to sustain him for several days. In such dire situations we do not hope for much. We scarcely dream. Explaining, judging, blaming are luxuries we cannot afford. It takes all one's will simply to endure. "In these circumstances," Odo Marquard writes, "theodicy is not an issue, because a mouthful of bread, a breathing space, a slight alleviation, a moment of sleep are all more important than the accusation and defence of God."[7]

If there is one thing that reduces a person to nothingness it is waiting without hope. Fasili's long wait had admitted the possibility of a payoff, sooner or later. Even S. B., in prison, believed his detention could not go on interminably. As for the street traders, who sat for hours on end waiting for a customer, experience had taught them that one or two sales were enough to put food on their table. But for the camp people, their waiting was as endless as it was empty. This was what they suffered. This was their pain.

That night, in my hotel, I read in a local paper that the EU had allocated 17 million euros to aid displaced persons in Sierra Leone, Liberia, and Guinea. I wondered if, and when, a portion of this money would reach the people I had spoken to at the Cline Town camp.

20 Exile

When S. B. recounted how he had fled to Guinea in 1997 on the same day that Tejan Kabbah was deposed in a military coup, it was the first time he had mentioned Lois in my hearing. I had known of his "second wife" for many years, though I had never met her, and had always assumed that S. B., mindful of my affection and regard for Rose, saw no point in broaching the subject of his marriages with me. Enough pain and embarrassment had already been caused. Still, I think I know what he would have said in his defense — the same rationalization he offered whenever his conduct was called into question: "I am not a white man. I am a Kuranko."

"The minister of Internal Affairs, David B. Quee, and I had agreed to go to Makeni for the swearing-in of the court chairman of the Northern Province," S. B. began. "We were due to leave Freetown on a Thursday, but Mr. Quee said that he had heard reports of rebels on the road, so he would travel by air. I said that I would go by road because I wanted to go on to Kabala after the swearing-in and visit my mother. I took my Toyota 4-Runner. My twin sisters, Tina and Dondon, accompanied me, as well as Lois. As we were passing Makolo Junction, I recognized my niece's vehicle going in the other direction. My niece recognized my vehicle too, and stopped and reversed so that we could talk. She said, 'Uncle, there are rebels on the road. They are stopping all vehicles. We were on our way to Makeni, but we've decided to go back to Freetown.' Musukura had three soldiers with her — Staff Sergeant Mansaray, who was driving, and two others. I said, 'Since you aren't going north, let the soldiers travel with me.' So they got in the 4-Runner.

"When we reached Masiaka we drove straight up to the checkpoint. There were about seventy cars and lorries stopped there. I asked the gatekeeper, who was in plainclothes, to let us through. He said I would have to get clearance. The staff sergeant made the same request, but the man at the barrier said he was busy. I said to him, 'Wait, what rank are you?' He said he was a sergeant. I said, 'Then you can't talk to your superior in the way you are doing — that's insubordination.' I became very stern. He said, 'I'm sorry sir, we will let you through.'

"We passed many villagers walking along the road with bundles on their heads. Even though we'd been told to watch out for rebels at Magbele Bridge, we saw none. We saw some soldiers, but in those days many rebels were dressed in soldiers' uniforms, so they could have been rebels. You never knew. I gave the soldiers with us Le 10,000 and asked them where they were going. They were going to Makeni. That made me happy, it meant we would have security as far as Makeni. Not far from Batkanu Junction I met my cousin, Lieutenant K. D. Marah. He told me that the rebels had burnt down sixty-four villages in that area, and he named them. We went on to Makeni. People were surprised we had not been troubled by rebels on the road.

"Next morning we swore in the court chairman. This was on Friday, 23 May. On Saturday morning I took a portmanteau of gowns and trousers to my cousin, Paramount Chief Kande Sayo, whose house had been burned by the rebels, leaving him with nothing. In the afternoon we went on to Kabala, where we arrived at 5:30. That evening, people came to the forecourt of my house to dance, but I felt dull, as though I had malaria, and I couldn't watch the dancers for very long. I went to bed early. But we agreed to hold an SLPP meeting in the morning, just by the side of my house.

"We were at the meeting when the district officer came and sort of whispered in my ear that there was trouble in Freetown. He said he did not have the full details of what was happening, but it seemed that there had been a coup. He would try to confirm this, and let me know. I did not want the others at the meeting to know what the D.O. had told me, so after he had gone I said that we should be

181   *Exile*

united, that we should stay together and uphold the principles of the SLPP — this sort of thing — until Mr. Melvin Caulker, the D.O., came back to tell me that there had indeed been a coup and that the president had flown to Guinea. I then informed the crowd. You can imagine how they all felt. Then I asked that they pack my things so we could return to Freetown. My things were packed, but the D.O. and the CPO tried to prevail on me not to return to Freetown, but to go to Guinea immediately, because I might be listed among those who were wanted by the coup leaders, who would know I was in Kabala. They urged me to leave at once. Salo, my second driver, who drove the Land Cruiser, was asked to come with me. Poor chap. Before we left Freetown, he had told me that his wife had just put to bed. I said to him, 'I'll give you some money.' So I gave him some money to send to his wife before we left. I did not want to make him go to Guinea with us. I thought of driving myself. But there was really no other way. So I left the second vehicle with my brother, Alhaji Fatmata Balansama Marah, though the soldiers later came and harassed him for it, and took the vehicle away. There was a large crowd at my house. And because my house was on a hill, we were visible from other parts of the town. Then my twin sisters decided that one of them should go with me. So Tina decided to come. She asked her son, Sewa, to join us. Then Fasili Mohammed Marah decided to come too. He said, 'I'll go with you, sir.' But the crowd was urging me to leave, and Fasili got left behind. Almost everyone was in tears when I left, saying goodbye [Lois remained with Dondon]. There were hundreds of people in the forecourt of my house. I came down the steps, and waved my hands to say goodbye to them, and they waved back. Over the heads of the crowd, I could see my mother was praying for me. Raising her hands, placing them on the ground, raising them again. I know she always does this when she wants to pray for me.

"We went to Paramount Chief Balansama Marah's house. He was alone on his veranda. I went to him and said, 'Brother, I have come to say goodbye. I'm going to Guinea.' He said 'Why?' I said, 'There's a coup, and I understand that the president has gone to Guinea, so I am going to join him there.' He shook his head and started crying. Tears ran down my cheeks. I went and held his hands, and he blessed me. He too was crying. I did not know it at the time, but this was to be the last time I would ever see him. We went on to Alhaji Masi Baré's place, where I stopped to bid him farewell. He was a Yogomaia elder. Then I went to the Sherif's house, and to Karimatu's and Nafisatu's, to bid them farewell. They were all surprised when I told them what had happened. They too were in tears.

"We drove north to Sinkunia where I had sent a message that we should be given food. We ate. I left my gun and cartridges with them. By now the soldiers knew that we were around. They had a motorbike, and had sent someone ahead to Gberia Fotombu. We saw him ahead of us, going at top speed. Just after the school at Falaba we stopped and went back, and took the road to Ganya. We didn't want to stop. At Ganya we picked up a guide who could take us to the border, but he took us the wrong way, and we had to return to Ganya. We got new directions, and drove on to Kaliere where we arrived at nightfall. The chief at Ganya had told us that we would be able to buy fuel there from the town chief. We bought five gallons, enough, we thought, to get us to Faranah. That night in Kaliere, we did not know if the villagers had heard of the coup in Freetown, or suspected that we were fleeing the country.

"We drove on into the night. We did not know where we were. That night is memorable. We were driving into the unknown. There were thunderstorms. We got to various junctions. God directed us to the right or left. We came to one. Another road cut across. God directed me to go right. One mile further on we came to a big village. I think it was called Sanya. The road was hard going and we were strangers. We didn't want to stop and ask if we were going the right way. So we carried on. Then we heard a faraway sound as if a *balafon* [xylophone] was being played. A little further on we began to see an electric light. I started thinking of my boyhood stories, because they said there was a devil, something like a light, that would seize hold of you and take you to the bush and transform you . . . so I thought it was this. As we continued, the sound of music became louder. Then we heard people singing. We stopped near a bridge. Tina said, 'I'm getting down now.' She went with her son toward the place where the music was playing. She disappeared into the darkness. Suddenly the music stopped. I was alarmed. I was afraid. There was complete silence. I got down from the vehicle and said to the driver, 'Wait for me, I'm going to find out what has happened to my sister.' As I started walking away from the vehicle, I saw my sister and her son hurrying back toward us. They said, 'Oh, we have seen tire marks, we must be on the right road.' You can't imagine how I felt, because we were lost, and I was responsible for everything that had happened.

We were tired and hungry. It was eleven at night. So we got back in the vehicle and continued on our way.

"When we reached Faranah we drove straight to the police station. I gave them my name, and said there had been a coup in our country, and that I was trying to join my president in Conakry. We waited about an hour before word came that we could stay in the old OAU village. We went there, but the man said we needed documents from the police. We went back to the police station. After some time, a senior authority was found who gave us the OK. On our way back to our lodgings we changed some leones into Guinea francs and bought some meat. The driver and I slept in the bed, while my sister and her son slept in the parlor on the settees that were there. Believe me, the mosquitoes and bedbugs were terrible! Early next morning, my sister heated some water, and I had a bath. I felt so good, scrubbing my skin. Then we drove to Dembaso Samura's sister's place, where they prepared some breakfast for us [Dembaso Samura was one of the leaders of the tamaboros, and Tina's boyfriend; he was killed in Kabala by the RUF in November 1994]. After we had eaten we returned to the police station. They took us from office to office. I did not know what they were doing. But we went from office to office until in the end I asked if I could speak to my president. It was not easy to get the call through, but finally I did so. I told him I was in Faranah, 410 kilometers away, and that I was on my way to join him. We left Faranah at about 2:30. We had many stops on the way, so many stops. They would ask us for documents, this document or that document. Fortunately I had some official-looking typed documents with me in the car, and I would wave these. But Tina and her son and the driver didn't have any papers at all. It was a big task to convince the people who stopped us that there had been a coup in my country, and to get them to allow us to pass. We did not get to Conakry until ten P.M. I reported to the police again, and they sent me to the Lovoten Hotel. I was given a room. My sister had another room. My nephew and the driver had another room.

"In the morning I asked my sister to go back to Freetown to get me some clothes. Salo, the driver, went with her. I gave him a very good letter of recommendation, and asked the management of the IPC travel agency to donate something to him on my behalf. That was the last I saw of him. He was killed in the RUF invasion of Freetown in January 1999. After my sister, her son, and the driver had left, I called Rose. She was not in. I was given another number. It was our cousin,

John Tucker's place. He had been one of my classmates in Bonthe. I called and spoke to Rose. She was scared. She said, 'I'm afraid of the gunshots.' She said she had taken the children, Aisetta and Cadi'lai [Lois's children], with her to our aunt's place, which was nearby, so they would be safe. I then told her that I had sent Tina to bring some clothing for me. And I asked her to transfer all our belongings to Daha Yazbeck's place in case the soldiers stole it. Although she did this promptly, a young Kuranko soldier called Momori Mansaray, who had once driven for me, had joined the junta, and he led some soldiers to the house where Rose had hidden our things. They carted away everything I had worked for in the forty years of my working life. Everything. Shoes, clothing, cars, everything was carted away from that place. That was one of the prices I had to pay for that coup.

After calling Rose, I went straight to the president. He was alone. That was real leadership. This loneliness of command. Only he knew at that time what was going through his mind, but there I was, and he received me cheerfully. He said, '*m'berin* [in-law], welcome.' Then he said, 'We will go back in a week.' But that week turned into a month, and that month turned into another month and another month, until ten months passed. We could easily have knocked down those fellows who made the coup. All we needed was about 350 men. But because he was a lawyer and respected the rule of law, he did not. He did not want to upset the British. But that's the kind of person he is. You can't change that. Even today, when he is governing us, you can see that he is democratically minded. Before he takes a decision he always reviews what will be the outcome of that decision. Nobody pushes him. But when he said we would be going back to Freetown in a week's time I was very happy."

21 In Conakry

After a brief pause, S. B. continued his story. "Fasili, who we'd had to leave behind in Kabala when we made our escape, actually reached Conakry before I did! He had got hold of a motorbike and driven the entire distance, and he remained with me for the entire ten months I was in exile. I pay tribute to him for this steadfastness and honesty. Not once, in all the months we were together, did he ask me for money, despite the fact that he had nothing. He would be there every morning, just as he is in Freetown now, prepared to run errands, to help in any way he could. When he was made electoral commissioner for the Northern Province, many people were very happy for him. It showed that sooner or later, loyalty, honesty, and steadfastness are rewarded.

"It was not easy for any of us in Conakry. We would meet almost every day at our embassy, trying to work out how we could get back to Freetown. I also made arrangements for Rose and the kids to come to Guinea in a trawler. They were supposed to leave Freetown at about five in the afternoon, and arrive at midnight. The Lovoten Hotel was near the gateway to the harbor, so I could keep watch from my window. I sat there from eleven at night. Nothing came. Twelve, one, two, three, four in the morning, I was still waiting. All kinds of thoughts ran through my head. Then, at seven, I called Mr. Ali Baka, who was deputy ambassador. I said, 'I have seen one boat pass; I don't know if my wife is on board. Can we go and check?' "

Rose later told me what had happened. Large numbers of refugees were arriving in Guinea at this time, and the boat trip turned out to be a nightmare. Though the vessel had a capacity for 250, it carried 400 this particular night, and a trip that normally took six hours took twenty-two. Moreover, there was neither food nor water on board, and only one toilet — so filthy, Rose said, that she refused to let the children use it. Cadi'lai, who had typhoid fever, vomited throughout the trip. The boat reached Conakry at midnight, but the port authorities, aware it carried refugees, would not allow it to berth.

"I was very anxious," S. B. continued. "I went down to the harbor at 7:30 with Fasili and Ansu Kaka, and we saw this boat going round and round in circles. We were told it was from Freetown, but it could not dock.

"By 10:30 that morning I was praying the fuel would not run out. But then the boat docked, and I finally saw Rose. I said, 'Thank God.' I held her hands. I helped her up out of the boat. The first thing she said was: 'I am thirsty, I want a drink of water.' We helped Aisetta and Cadi'lai up onto the quay. Fortunately I had a cooler in the car, filled with water. I gave it to Rose, and I sent someone to buy milk for her. Unfortunately we had to wait then for the officials, and it was some time before I could take Rose and the children to the hotel. We had only one bed. I slept on the floor.

"Rose had also brought two of the girls who had been with her sister Pat at the lodge [Pat was married to Tejan Kabbah]. We took them to where the president was staying. A little later, Rose's sister arrived from Lebanon to join her husband.

"I didn't have enough money. I would go out every day and buy some roast meat and some bread for Rose and the kids. At the hotel, I slept on the floor. Rose and the two children slept in the bed. Life was not easy for any of us."

The anthropologist Chris Coulter, who was in Guinea at the time, working with Sierra Leonean refugees, remembers that the Sierra Leoneans were everywhere.[1] The streets teemed with Sierra Leonean shoeshine boys, and street vendors selling cooked food, while the embassy compound was crowded with people sleeping, peddling whatever belongings they had, waiting to be repatriated, looking for relatives and friends, selling bags of ice water, Kool-Aid, and food. "Many young men," she writes, "were making a living by selling international phone calls from stolen cellular phones for US$1 per minute," and the streets outside the embassy and the alleys surrounding it also housed a large black market for currency exchange.[2] S.B recalled the same scene. "Most of my colleagues were scattered around the city," he said. "People were even sleeping on the floor at our embassy, where I went every morning. I felt particularly sorry for one woman, a Miss Wright, who I had known very well in Freetown, where she owned several houses. In Conakry she and her mother were living in a leaking garage. She took me there one day. 'S. B.,' she said, 'this is where I spend the night.' Though I was comfortable in the hotel, I told myself that I would have to leave, or people would say that I was comfortable while they were suffering [In Rose's recollection the management of the hotel asked them to leave, presumably because they had difficulty paying their bill]. So I moved out of the hotel," S. B. said, "and went to stay with a chap whose parents I had known in Faranah. About three days later, I ran into an old friend of mine, Alhaji Daklala, who asked if I had somewhere to stay. He was also from Freetown, but he had family in Conakry, and he immediately made arrangements for Rose and me to stay in an air-conditioned, self-contained room, with two beds. Rose slept with Aisetta on one bed. I slept with Cadi'lai on the other. It was a heaven-sent blessing. Not only did the Daklala family give us lodgings and food; they provided us with transportation whenever we needed it.

"Rose would prepare food for us every day. Very good food, I must say. She really did well. We always had food at the correct time. This was one of the things we enjoyed while we were in Conakry. I pay tribute to her, especially for taking care of me, Fasili, and Lois's children.

"After we'd been in Conakry for several weeks, Lois and her son Sheku arrived with my sister Tina. I spotted them one afternoon as I was driving down the main street. They said they had decided to come and join me in Conakry because the situation in Kabala was getting dangerous. I found a place for Lois to stay with Fasili. Tina stayed with her son-in-law, Mr. Sumansa, who had been one of the most wanted men on the junta's list. He was a police officer, and had been prosecuting Johnny Paul Koroma for plotting a coup when the junta seized power. They came looking for him at police headquarters, but he was in plainclothes and they didn't recognize him. They asked, 'Where is Mr. Sumansa?' They said, 'Upstairs.' How he escaped is a mystery to me.

"While we were in Conakry, where so many Sierra Leoneans shed tears, the President's Lodge was not far from our embassy. Whenever we knew he was going away, we'd all stand on the traffic roundabout to bid him farewell. We'd sing all sorts of songs, especially Negro spirituals, that slaves used to sing. And some of us would shed tears. This happened on many occasions. And when we knew he was coming back, we accorded him the same honor. We recognized him as our president, our dear president. Everyone did. Honestly, I had great regard for the Sierra Leoneans, both young and old. I would see these little children, young boys and girls, who had fled the country because they did not like the junta . . . all upholding the principles of decent citizenship. They behaved very well while they were in Guinea. We had no problems. Rather, it was they who were subject to molestation, even inside the embassy compound. I remember one day, the local police tried to arrest some of us inside the compound, in spite of the fact that we had diplomatic immunity. I told the police, 'If you arrest these people, then arrest me too, and take me to prison with them.' Believe me, it was not easy. But we knew that one day we would return to our lovely Sierra Leone, where we guarantee freedom to everyone, where we do not molest strangers, and where everyone is welcome as long as he does not go against the laws of our land. We don't ill-treat people. We are not like that. We take care of strangers. That is how we are raised. That is how we want to remain."

In October 1997, S. B. left Conakry with Tejan Kabbah to attend the Commonwealth Conference in Edinburgh. "Rose came to the airport to see me off," S. B. said. "Aisetta and Cadi'lai were with her. Because we did not know what fate had in store for us in Sierra Leone, we had decided that it would be best for them to be with our children in England. Just before our plane for London took off, President Kabbah said, 'M'berin, I don't know whether you have been told, but I have heard that your house in Freetown has been burned to the ground.' All I said was, 'Oh, I wish you had told me when Rose was here; she has now gone home.' I do not know how she took it, seeing the house in ruins, everything destroyed. But on the plane I thought of all I had. I thought of my belongings. I said to myself, 'Well, the almighty wanted it so, so be it. He gave and he has taken away. This happens to human beings. These are only material things. I can always get more.' So I forgot about it.

"I was in the U.K. for two weeks where I got the children settled, and attended the Commonwealth Conference. I then returned to Conakry." When a meeting was arranged in Abuja, Nigeria, toward the end of 1997, between President Tejan Kabbah and General Sani

Abacha, S. B. was one of the most vocal advocates for using external military intervention to defeat the junta in Freetown and destroy the RUF with whom it was allied.

"President Kabbah and General Abacha were sitting some ten feet away from the rest of us," S. B. recalled. "I got up and kneeled down before Abacha, and said to him, 'Mr. President, we have come because we have just escaped a coup. We have come to sympathize with you. At the same time we want to thank you for the honest and brotherly way you have been taking care of our president, and of all of us. Without you we would not be alive. But there is one thing I must tell you, sir. Those boys in Freetown, those rogues, will not give up power as a result of negotiations. The only language they understand is your language—the barrel of a gun. Sir, your brother here would be ashamed to say this. But we are his lieutenants. We like him. We respect him. We are prepared to follow him. That is the way we are. But since you are the elder brother, we are pleading with you to use all your might, to do whatever you can, to get rid of those boys. No negotiations will ever remove them.'

"Y. M. Koroma followed suit. Abdul Kamara, who was a very tall fellow, lay on the ground and held Abacha's feet, in the same way that I had done. L. S. Koroma did the same thing. Abacha didn't say a word, but I am sure he understood, and knew already what he was going to do. After the meeting, I remember saying to Mr. Bujama, who was the Nigerian foreign minister: *wen push don kam pan shove* . . . meaning, when push comes to shove, one can do anything to get oneself out of a mess.

"Back in Conakry, the president and I met to discuss further plans. There was only the two of us. He said, 'S. B., you are my brother, I am going to take you into my confidence; I don't want you to say anything about this to anyone.' I said, 'Mr. President, we've been together for forty or fifty years. In all this time, nothing of what has passed between us has come to the hearing of a third party. You can rest assured that whatever you say to me will be kept secret.' So he told me the updated plan for how we were going to get rid of those chaps [the ECOMOG operation in Freetown on 12 February 1998].

"When the junta was overthrown, we returned to Freetown. It was March 9, 1998. Rose went ahead with her sister Pat and the president, and stayed with them at the lodge. I drove to Freetown, and arrived late at night. After dropping Sheku and Lois off at the Stadium Hotel, I went to the Cape Sierra Hotel. When I got to the junction of Aberdeen Road and Wilkinson Road, I said to myself, 'After seventeen or eighteen good years of returning to the city from overseas or up-country, this is the first time I have turned right instead of going left.' My house was no more. I shed tears, and drove on, across the Aberdeen ferry bridge to the cape. There was no booking for me, but the manager gave me a room, and I stayed there for several months while PK Lodge was being made ready for me—the house in which I am staying now."

22 Trust and Truth

Hardly a day passed during my stay in Freetown that I was not confronted by the vexed issue of trust. It might be something as banal as the slogan on a poda poda — "White Teeth Black Hearts" — or graffiti on a wall — "No Hypocrite in Our Deep Secret." It might be an offhand remark of S. B.'s about the houseboys, how they could not be trusted, and would steal from his room given half a chance. Or the issue might be broached by one of the houseboys himself, angered by this suspicion, humiliated that S. B. should make such comments in the hearing of distinguished visitors, and moved to set the record straight for me. Biru, for instance, who told me how the endemic lack of trust in Sierra Leone made development so difficult. "It is why Sierra Leoneans avoid business dealings with each other," he said, "and prefer outsiders like the Lebanese." Undoubtedly Biru would have felt confirmed in this view when a security system was finally installed at Lungi Airport and the operating contract went to a South African firm.

Secrecy and suspicion are so much a part of everyday Sierra Leonean life that practically every ethnographer who has worked there has tried to explain it. Many years ago, Noah told me that he had given his son Kaima — then only a toddler — a lesson on the importance of not trusting anyone; he had urged the little boy to jump from the veranda into his arms. When Kaima did so, Noah stepped back and let his son fall, then berated him for not heeding the advice he had just been given. "Trust no one. Not even your father." Fascinating too was the Kuranko men's association, known as Doé, that specialized in techniques for reading a stranger's mind, and for divining what Mariane Ferme calls "the underneath of things."[1] The black hearts behind the white teeth. As for men's distrust of women, it was proverbial, and the subject of countless stories. Never let a woman know your secrets. All quarrels can be resolved except those caused by women. And just as young Kuranko men were exhorted to think before they speak or act, and to be wary of women and strangers, so they learned that others are also Janus-faced, their appearances not to be trusted, their words not to be taken at face value. Perhaps social life is universally a matter of necessary masks and expedient lies. As the Kuranko put it, "A person has blood inside him but it is saliva he spits out" — meaning that what a person says tends to belie what is in his heart and mind. I used to see this preoccupation with transparency and trust as a consequence of scarcity — of the "hungry time" during the last couple of months of the growing season, when people tell "white lies" about how much rice they have in their granaries lest the little that is left for their own needs will be claimed by hungry neighbors and distant kin. Or as a fear of in-marrying women and visiting strangers, whose loyalties and intentions can never be readily divined, even by the *Doé dannu* (the Doé children), who specialize in such matters. Or as a diffuse memory of Samori's *sofas*, who laid waste to Kuranko country a hundred years ago. Other ethnographers, struck by this same preoccupation with trust and betrayal, this world of clandestine desire, greed, and envy that so readily finds expression in witchcraft suspicions and fantasies, have sought to explain it in terms of slavery and endemic intertribal warfare.[2]

In my own ethnographic work, I had often noted the value that Kuranko attach to transparency (whiteness), straightness, and truthfulness between neighbors and kin. Informants would tell me that the hearts of those who live together should be open. One should strive for a consonance between inner disposition and outward behavior. That images of swamps, impenetrable forests, blocked paths, and murky waters pervaded Kuranko stories, dreams, and conversations was an indication of how often deviousness and duplicity compromised this ideal. "Neighborliness is not sweet," people would say, pointing out that adulterous affairs make men suspicious of one another, pollute sacrifices, and prevent conviviality. And so evil is ever-present in the form of witchcraft, dissimulation is commonplace, promises are broken, conspiracies hatched, and agreements dishonored.

In S. B.'s opinion, there had been more trust in the past, and people stood by their word. But today, a person's circle of family and friends is so much wider, and this increases the likelihood that one's actions will be misconstrued, one's words misinterpreted, and one's good fortune begrudged. At the same time, the absence of state institutions for the welfare and protection of citizens means that one is wholly dependent on family and friends for security and support. Accordingly, personal connections and loyalties take precedence over abstract principles — whether these are enshrined in the law, written into the constitution, or espoused by the church. To many Westerners, the resulting personal and familial claims lead inevitably to corruption. But honoring obligations to kinsmen, friends, and tribesmen is not corruption, S. B. pointed out. "Corruption is," as he put it, "stealing public money, or using someone else's money without his permission, for your own profit."

"But it must be very difficult," I said, "for any politician to satisfy all the personal demands made on him."

"This is true," S. B. said. "This is why I don't believe in numbers. If we have too many police, or too many soldiers in the military, it is impossible to provide good conditions for them all, and they grow restless. You never know what they will be thinking or planning. This is why I believe that the military should be very small and very efficient. Make them few, pay them well, and make them take care of the civilian population in case of emergencies. But don't let them go to war. Let the UN peacekeepers handle that."

It surprised me how often, in S. B.'s telephone conversations with the president, this issue of trust would crop up. "You are my brother," S. B. told Tejan Kabbah one day. "But let me tell you, there are certain people you rely on who are not reliable. We are all concerned about this. There are always more things than catch the eye. Don't trust anyone. Anyone at all." And S. B. cited a recent instance in which he had given a kinsman a large sum of money, only to hear, a few weeks later, that the man was bad-mouthing him and supporting the APC. Ironically, according to Rose, Tejan Kabbah was constantly making the same point to S. B. — urging him to be more careful what he said and to whom he said it, since an idle boast or careless comment could have dire repercussions. One never knew when today's ally would become tomorrow's turncoat.

One morning, S. B. was discussing the security situation in Sierra Leone with one of his nephews when, again, the question of trust was raised. "Would you put a person you didn't trust in a position of trust, a position where that person has the power to harm you?" S. B.'s nephew asked. "This is what Tejan doesn't always understand," S. B. replied. And he observed that Tejan's background as a lawyer and diplomat made him unduly respectful of Anglo-American directives. For instance, rather than have the AFRC junta leader Johnny Paul Koroma court-martialed for plotting a military coup against his government in 1996, Tejan Kabbah argued that Johnny Paul was a citizen and deserved a civil trial. Koroma was found guilty, only to be sprung from Pademba Road Prison while awaiting his appeal. "The destructive rampage by the soldiers and rebels would never have occurred," S. B.'s nephew argued, "if Tejan had not been so soft, so conciliatory," and he was equally critical of the induction of ex-combatants into the Sierra Leone army in the name of "reconciliation," for none of these renegade soldiers and erstwhile rebels was loyal to the SLPP — which was proven at the 2002 elections, when the ex–junta leader, Johnny Paul Koroma, standing in the western district of Freetown (the location of the Wilberforce and Juba army barracks), won the seat with a significant majority. "Democracy is one thing," S. B.'s nephew concluded, "but putting your enemy in a position where he can harm you doesn't make sense."

"I tell Tejan this," S. B. replied wearily. "He doesn't know these things."

When S. B. described his relationship with Tejan Kabbah, he began by reminding me that he and the president were brothers-in-law. "My wife and his wife are sisters," he said, "though we are like brothers. We have known each other for fifty years, and have always been very close.

"In 1967, Tejan's wife, Patricia, had to go to London for medical treatment. At the time, Tejan was permanent secretary in the Ministry of Education at New England, and had just got his leave. He said to me, 'Let's go to Conakry for the weekend.' I said to him, 'No, please, you have to go to England; your wife is not keeping well.' Then he said, 'M'berin, I have some money, let's go to England and study law.' I said, 'You go, I will stay.' I don't know whether he got wind of something, but he took his Mercedes-Benz car along with him, and believe me, the very day he left several of our colleagues were arrested, charged with treason, and condemned to death — Berthan Macauley, John Kallon, Maigore Kallon, Ella Koblo Gulama, Thomas Decker, George Panda, and others. I said to myself,

'Bless his stars, because if he had been here he would definitely have been arrested as well.' Maigore was soon released and went into a long exile in Liberia. Once, before going to Ghana, I sent word that my flight would be stopping briefly in Monrovia, and he came to the airport to see me. We had not seen each other for several years. It was very emotional for us both, and when we said goodbye we had no idea when we would meet again. There were several APC people on the same flight. I prayed to God that on their return they would not report my meeting with Maigore. People might think we were plotting. Although my conscience was clear, I was scared. As for the ones who were detained, they were defended by lawyers from England and won their appeal after three years in jail.

"I next saw Tejan when I was in England, after my release from Pademba Road Prison in 1974. He was about to take his little boy Junior to school and asked me to come along. I don't remember the name of the place, but we went by train. It took about an hour. All the way there I was crying. I said, 'Tejan, this boy is too young to be taken from you; why do you have to do this?' I was really angry with him, really sad. But there it was; he and his wife had decided. She was Catholic and wanted the boy brought up by the Catholic sisters. He's a big boy now. He's around. Junior. Anytime he sees me he hugs me, kisses me, and so on. That I like of him. He says, 'S. B. how are you doing?' And he will smile.

"Tejan remained abroad for some time. I did not hear from him, though I knew he was working for the UN Development Programme. Then, after many years away, he began to make trips home. Anytime he came, I would be the first person he'd look up. I was at the Alitalia agency, marking time there, waiting for the day I could return to politics. It was during one of these reunions that he offered me his house. Rose and I were living in Murraytown. I had moved there when I was kicked out of my ministerial quarters in 1967. Our daughter Aisetta was born there. So we moved to Tejan's house at 29 Main Motor road and lived there until I became a minister in 1977. Tejan's mother was also very fond of me. Haja Adama, née Coomber, was a princess from Mobai in the Eastern Province. She would prepare food for me, bring it to me, especially during Ramadan. She was like a mother to me. And the little I could do for her family when Tejan was away, I did, and this was always reported back to him.

"When Tejan finally came home for good in 1992, I was in detention. When I saw him after my release, he said, 'M'berin, I have come. I thought of you often when I was in the U.S. The kind of friends I have here I couldn't get there. I have come home so we can be together. We can go into business.' I don't think he had any plans at that time to go into politics; his only thought was in coming home to be with his kith and kin. But then, in 1995, the SLPP needed a leader. A meeting was arranged at Tejan's house, at which John Karefa-Smart was asked if he was interested in leading the party. I was not at this meeting, though I am sure that Karefa-Smart rejected the offer. When I and others heard what had gone on behind our backs, we were very angry. Karefa-Smart had left the SLPP twenty years ago to form another party. Why should we meet with him, and plead with him to lead us, when we had loyal party members fit for high office? Men who had served the party faithfully for many years. Some wanted to expel the three who had arranged this meeting, but others warned against the danger of splitting the party, and we took their advice. It was at this time that I thought of running, and I actually began canvassing for support. I had been in politics a long time. I knew every part of the country, spoke all its dialects, had good party stalwarts backing me in every area—especially the northern, southern, and western areas—and everyone knew of my dedication to the party. I had never changed colors. I had stood firm. During our days in opposition I had even been in jail because of the party. And so on. Nothing scared me. So I had a lot of support. But then Tejan expressed an interest in running.

"It was Alhaji Mahdi Sisay, the father of one of my best friends, M. B. Sisay, who was later killed by the rebels, who told him that if he wanted to go into politics he should go and see S. B. Marah. 'If he says yes, then go ahead; if he says no, then you must withdraw, you must not continue, you must drop the idea.' So one morning Tejan and M. B. Sisay came to see me at my residence, and they told me what Alhaji Mahdi Sisay had said. I thought at first it was a joke. I said, 'Come on, just get out of my sight!' Because we never thought of Tejan as a politician. I said, 'Tejan, you are not the type.' But when I saw how serious he was about it, I said, 'OK, if you're not joking, I'm not joking. I will see what I can do.' It was then I decided to give him my support.

"But I saw him going with the wrong type of people. He did not know them, but I did, and I knew they were after him to chop ['eat,' steal] his money. I could see this happening. So I took charge and stood by him. First, because he had been my brother and friend for many years. He had been very generous to me, and whenever he came back to Sierra Leone from the U.S., or when he was UN representative in Tanzania and Uganda, I would be the first person he'd look up. So we were very dear to each other, and besides, we were married to two sisters, he to the elder, I to the younger one. According to African tradition, when the parents are dead, the eldest takes on the role of the parent. So Tejan's wife was like a mother to my own wife—which meant there was no competition between them. My second reason for supporting Tejan was that he had been abroad, and made many friends while working for the UN. So I thought, if we supported him he would have more people around the world than I had who were in a position to help us. So I threw in my lot with him, and have supported him ever since. Even in exile.

"When we were preparing for the 1996 elections, I told the party that if SLPP was going to win, after being out of power for thirty years, we should get a northerner to lead us. We had always been accused of being a Mende party, even though SLPP was a party for all. This time, we should elect a northerner as our leader. And so I argued for the election of Tejan Kabbah, whose father was a Mandingo from Kambia, and whose mother was a princess from Mobai, a man who also had local experience of the north, where he had been a young administrative officer before independence, and who had subsequently worked as a district commissioner in the northern, southern, and eastern areas. Freetown-educated, he was an all-rounder, and the best man to lead our party at that critical time."

Whatever differences of temperament and political philosophy existed between S. B. and Tejan, it was abundantly clear how deep was the bond between them. Each tolerated the other's viewpoint, however dissimilar. Each friend assumed that the other would do nothing to embarrass or harm him. And these expectations were extended to friends, family, and associates, which was why S. B. was so taken aback when the president phoned one morning to say that S. B.'s niece, whom S. B. had named as one of his three choices to be sponsored by the president's office for the hajj, had already been to Mecca. The president had immediately ordered her plane ticket cancelled. Dismayed to learn that his niece had lied to him, S. B. apologized to the president, saying how hurt and embarrassed he was to receive this news. A couple of minutes after his conversation with Tejan, S. B. called his niece and told her that her ticket had been cancelled, and why. Although she protested her innocence, alleging she had never been to Mecca, S. B. said she had brought shame on him and the family. In conversation with other friends and family later that morning, S. B. made no bones about how angry he felt. The hajj was something you had to work for, he said. It was a reward for perseverance and hard work. For it to come easily, as a gift, detracted from its spiritual value, and "made it seem less of a blessing." S. B. concluded that he would never again petition the president for such sponsored pilgrimages.

In the days that followed I often found myself wondering how I could possibly reconcile the competing truths that had emerged in the course of my work with S. B., and I thought of the observation Lawrence Durrell attributes to Pursewarden in his novel *Justine*: "We live lives based upon selected fictions. Our view of reality is conditioned by our position in space and time — not by our personalities as we like to think. Thus every interpretation of reality is based upon a unique position. Two paces east or west and the whole picture is changed." That S. B. sometimes cautioned me against setting too much store by the memories and critical comments of Rose and Noah was a reflection of his understandable desire to privilege *his* truth, for, after all, I was ghost-writing his biography, not theirs. Yet all were equally dear to me, and I could not see myself doing justice to all without, in some measure, violating the trust S. B. had placed in me. Oscar Wilde put this quandary succinctly: "Every great man nowadays has his disciplines, and it is always Judas who writes the biography."

I suppose anyone who recounts the story of his life will want to make himself appear, in retrospect, to have been the author, if not the hero, of events that were, in truth, often out of his hands. Few of us can escape the tendency to create an impression that the things that have befallen us in life, that we experienced as inexplicable and accidental, were in some way our own doing, or part of some design. And so we ascribe to ourselves more mastery and insight than we ever, in fact, possessed, and declare that we have no regrets, while surreptitiously weeding out events that would not redound to our credit, errors of judgement that caused pain to our loved ones, and misprisions that might, if they were remembered, impair the image that we hope to leave for posterity.

That there are always others only too ready to correct our misrepresentations and set the record straight does not help us arrive at the kind of truth an omniscient God might conjure; it only offers the possibility of replacing one biased perspective with another. This is why the stories we tell ourselves and the stories we tell others, or that others tell about us, are all, to a degree, violations of a lived reality that can never be reduced to a single narrative, a valid theory, or even, I sometimes think, put into words. And this is why it may be best, finally, to allow each author to be his own judge and executioner, and find his own way, if he is willing, to the closest we can come to truth — which is silence.

23 The Hotel

When the Cape Sierra hotel was built, I would sometimes come down to Freetown from up-country and fantasize about staying there — swimming in the pool, eating in the restaurant, walking on the beach, sleeping at night between clean sheets *(see overleaf)*.

It was ironic, therefore, that after all those years, when the hotel was but a mirage, I should find myself living there in splendid isolation, often killing time — longing for the eventfulness of PK Lodge, and a chance of catching S. B. when he wasn't preoccupied by affairs of state. But would it really have made much difference had I stayed with Rose and S. B.? Listening to S. B.'s story, day after day, questions occured to me that I was reluctant to put to him. Certainly I did not want his story to be affected by my preoccupations, and I was sensitive to those occasions when my questions about his wives, various military coups, his relations with Lebanese friends, or current government business invaded his privacy. But my hesitancy also reflected the deepening and unspoken trust between us, as well as my longstanding conviction that individuals (and societies) differ less in their essences than in where they draw the line between what is made public and what is not. On our trip to Kabala, I had found myself mimicking Noah's deference toward his elder brother, or slipping into the role of griot, almost obsequious in the master's presence, though furtively empowered by my possession of the knowledge on which his public persona depended. But in the weeks we had worked together on his story, a seal had been set on our friendship, and I

had come to accept S. B.'s reticence as he accepted mine. Despite his force of personality, S. B. was possibly more vulnerable than I was—politically, physically, and emotionally. At the same time, as a Big Man, he did not want to cheapen or compromise the appurtenances of power by appearing too common. In public, his anxieties, his sensibilities, his doubts, were all masked. One of my unasked questions concerned the costs of my long stay in the Cape Sierra Hotel. S. B. told me I should not worry about this; he would take care of everything; I was his stranger, his brother, his friend. But I did find out, one way or another, that during the RUF invasion of Freetown in January 1999, sobels destroyed the Bintumani and Mammy Yoko hotels, even stripping them of their tiles and electric cable, but left the Cape Sierra unmolested, presumably so that some of the junta leaders would have a place to stay. When Tejan Kabbah's government returned from exile there were calls to take over the hotel and have the manager deported from Sierra Leone. S. B. argued successfully against this action, with the result that the management was now beholden to him.

Driving along the beach road from Cape Sierra one morning, small S. B. was playing one of his reggae tapes. "What's the name of the group?" I asked. "Culture," small S. B. said. "*Three Sides to My Story.*" Captivated by this title, I wondered for a moment or two if I could use it in the book I planned to write, interleaving S. B.'s narrative with others, and showing how all were constrained by custom as well as foreshadowed by history. Suddenly, small S. B. turned up the volume louder. "Listen to this track," he said, a broad smile on his face. "The NPRC used to like this one. They made the radio station play it all the time. They'd get stoned and dance to this one. They used to weep." "What is it called?" I shouted. "'No war,'" small S. B. said. "This was their favorite. Whenever I hear this track I think of that time."

Whenever there was a change of government, even a coup, the euphoria of independence would momentarily return. People would speak extravagantly of a liberation from slavery, of a new dispensation, and tell themselves that things would be better this time around. It reminded me of Karl Marx's penetrating comments on revolution. "Much as we like to believe in renewal," he writes, "the tradition of the dead generations weighs on the minds of the living. And just when they seem engaged in revolutionizing themselves and things, in creating something that has never yet existed, precisely in such periods of revolutionary crisis they anxiously conjure up the spirits of the past to their service and borrow from them names, battle-cries and costumes in order to present the new scene."[1] It occurred to me that the disappointment we feel when we realize that our attempt to create something new is no more than a farcical replay of something old is like the wheel of karma, from which we cannot break free. And I remembered then something I had read about a group of students, protesting the 1997 coup in Freetown, who daubed in big letters on the ground outside the main gate of their college campus, "AFRC = Another Fucking Ruling Council."[2]

If history is doomed to repeat itself, despite our efforts to remember it, what of biography? Can one really create oneself anew? And what is the point of retracing one's steps, as S. B. had done, in memory, recapitulating the past, albeit in a form that makes it more bearable?

I used to think that our lives were broken mosaics. That the longer one lived, the greater the damage done to the original design. Where once was pattern — each tile precisely placed to create a coherent, overall image — now was ruin, fragmentation, and loss. I liked to think of writing as a gathering up of the scattered pieces, recomposing them, recreating the semblance of a picture — the drowned continents of our past lives, the disparate societies where we had felt at home, islands in time, far-flung friends, the dead. But then I asked: "What if the original pattern were an illusion? What if the truth lay not in the composition but in the forces that had fragmented and scattered the very idea of it?"

"Time does not always flow according to a line," Michel Serres observes, "nor according to a plan, but, rather, according to an extraordinarily complex mixture, as though it reflected stopping points, ruptures, deep wells, chimneys or thunderous acceleration, rendings, gaps—all sown at random, at least in a visible disorder. Thus," he continues, "the development of history truly resembles what chaos theory describes."[3]

When one reflects on one's own consciousness, one cannot help but be struck by its chaotic and disconcerted character. Lying on my bed in the Cape Sierra Hotel, I would one moment be overwhelmed by a memory of my first wife, or of the time our daughter was born in Freetown, but the next second my mind would have drifted to something S. B. had said, to an image I wanted to include in my book, or to the stench of the toilet, which for two days had had to be flushed with water brought from the swimming pool. It has always astonished me that human consciousness can be so bewilderingly disconnected—wandering all over the place, as well as shuttling so unrelentingly through time—while outwardly we seem so composed, going about our business, moving steadily in a straight line. But experienced time—as opposed to the concepts of time to which we refer in giving shape, purpose, and order to our collective lives—is not like a white line down the middle of a bitumen road, with a determinate point of departure and a final destination.[4] Time warps and buckles and folds back on itself, bringing the present into intimate contact with the distant past, and making successive moments seem a lifetime apart. If time is a river, it is a river that does not run its course straightforwardly to the sea. There are whirlpools, eddies, oxbows, falls, backwaters, and countercurrents. Periodically the river overflows its banks, obliterating the line between land and water, changing its course entirely. Endings, like beginnings, are misnomers.

Paul Klee painted *Angelus Novus*—the New Angel—in 1920, and exhibited it, with other work, at the Hans Goltz gallery in Munich between May and June. Walter Benjamin saw this small watercolor for the first time in Berlin in 1921, and during a visit to Munich in June bought it for 1,000 marks. Despite the writer's many moves, the painting remained with him until the end of his life, the object of numerous meditations, each one bearing traces of his changing fortunes and preoccupations.[5] His initial view was that the angel embodied the beauty of the fallen angel, Lucifer, whose evanescent form suggested, for Benjamin, the idea of a secret self, an unspoken name, as well as the luminary depths of ordinary appearances. By 1933, however, when living on Ibiza, "his situation . . . that of a refugee who in every sense leads an existence on the brink of desperation," Benjamin saw the angel as the incarnation of patience, in particular the patience of the exile and the unrequited lover. "The angel," he wrote, "resembles all from which I have had to part: persons and above all things. In the things I no longer have he resides. He makes them transparent, and behind all of them there appears to me the one for whom they are intended." In early 1940, after his release from the French camp where refugees from Hitler's Germany had been interned after the outbreak of war, and only a few months before his suicide, Walter Benjamin wrote his famous theses on the philosophy of history, in which the new angel figures once again. In Benjamin's successively poignant and melancholy images of waiting, of the hidden depths of appearances, and of history as a devastating storm in which we are hurled about like leaves, our faces turned toward paradise and the past as we are irresistibly propelled into the future, is it possible to discern a further truth that applies equally to biographical and historical time, and hints at another message this extraworldly visitant has to impart?

When I lived in Sierra Leone I was constantly fascinated by the ways in which Kuranko alluded to birds. The Senegalese fire finches that flitted around the eaves of houses, and contained the souls of children who had died in early infancy. The ungainly and skulking Senegal Coucal, whose call was a descending coo coo coo coo coo, suggestive of water poured from a bottle, and was not eaten because it induced indolence. The long-tailed nightjar, known as the evening bird, which had the power to take the life of one's child if not appeased with gifts. The owl, or witch-bird, associated with the nefarious and clandestine activities of the night. But mostly I was intrigued by the pure white cattle egrets that stalked about under the feet of grazing cows, scavenging for insects. The egrets were the angels of the cows, invisible to them as our angels are invisible to us. But where the Hebrew *malakh* is best translated as messenger, the Arabic word adopted by Kuranko—*malaika*—connoted a guardian or guide. One who is constantly in attendance. A witness who is not himself or herself seen. One whose testimony may confirm, despite the storm of history, that which endures.

Most evenings, I was alone at dinner. If there were others (there were never more than two or three), no one made eye contact, or acknowledged anyone else, isolated in that vaulted, white-painted, poorly lit room where the dolorous waiters stood in the shadows, or awkwardly served food, and took one's plate away the minute one had finished eating. I used to sit down at seven sharp, positioning myself so that I could see the beach and the ocean beyond the frangipanis, the fig trees, and the palms. Five minutes later, the daylight would begin to fade, the trees becoming a massed silhouette, the haze over the distant hills deepening into a watery dark. And then the color would slowly drain out of the beach sand and the sea, so that by 7:10 it was like a moonlit night, everything a shade of deep blue, before, five minutes later, darkness fell.

Because I had been so deeply absorbed in reading and re-reading W. G. Sebald's *Austerlitz* during my weeks in the Cape Sierra Hotel, it was not surprising that this writer should obliquely enter my dreams. In one dream I was visiting, with unknown others, Sebald's home in East Anglia. We found ourselves in a large, dimly lit room. Sebald's widow then appeared—gray-haired, handsome, wearing a dull sea-green dress—and sat opposite me at a large table which was covered with the same seagreen cloth, though latticed, and a sheet of glass. The scene then shifted, and I was in a kind of anteroom or servery, adjacent to the main room, and Sebald's widow was responding to my condolences. "He's dead," she said. "I know he's dead. I'm under no illusions about that. But sometimes I think he's upstairs working, or out on one of his long walks."

When I woke and wrote down this dream, it occurred to me that what I did not altogether like about Sebald's writing was its preoccupation with mortality—with the way things continually decay, falling into ruin, slipping into the darkness, a being-unto-death.[6] Sebald's viewpoint was that of the angels in Wim Wenders's *Wings of Desire*—the viewpoint of someone who has died, yet still hovers in limbo or quarantine, dreamlike above the earth, seeing fragments of history, the work of human hands, a landscape devoid of figures flowing past, and in melancholy wonderment realizes he cannot take his eyes off this stream, though he knows not his own destiny. It was then that I was returned to the theme of natality and renewal with which I had begun, and that nothing in Sierra Leone had destroyed — the smile of the boy standing beside his father at Makeni, small S. B.'s panache, the young war widows in Kabala dancing in a tight circle with their babies asleep on their backs, or, for that matter, the excited voices of my own children on the telephone telling me about their day.

Notes

1 Night Flight to Freetown

1 Hannah Arendt, *The Human Condition* (Chicago: University of Chicago Press, 1958), 33.

2 During the last few months of 2001, before I decided to go to Sierra Leone, I had had recurring dreams that were, in retrospect, aligned along a single thread. In one, I found myself on a cliff path high above the sea, desperately looking for a handhold on the crumbling rock so that I could pull a friend, who had slipped over the edge, to safety. In another, I was in a quagmire of tar pits, entangled lianas, and quicksand, struggling to keep my daughter from being dragged down into the mire. In another I watched as the sea broke through the sand ramparts of a beach castle I had built. In still another, I was thrown from my bicycle onto a hedge that ran along a cliff top, again above the sea. As my daughter tried to clamber up on to the hedge, I struggled for a foothold so that I could push her back to the safety of the street. In all these dreams, I surmised that it *was a part of myself* I was trying to save, and that the images signaled a deep ambivalence about letting go, taking chances, casting myself adrift in the world, and being swept away. Yet I knew that this was precisely what I had to do if I was to revitalize my thinking and my writing.

3 In *On Revolution* (New York: Viking, 1963) Hannah Arendt points out that the violence and radicalism that haunt revolutionary struggle in the twentieth century were not fundamental to the first "modern" revolu-

tions of the seventeenth and eighteenth centuries. The American revolution "did not devour its own children," and was, like the French revolution, conceived as a form of restoration — of freedom by God's blessing restored, of abuses by colonial government redressed, of the old order rescued from the despotism of absolute monarchy (36–37).

4 "And might it not be . . . that we also have appointments to keep in the past, in what has gone before and is for the most part extinguished, and must go there in search of places and people who have some connection with us on the far side of time, so to speak" (W. G. Sebald, *Austerlitz* [London: Hamish Hamilton, 2001], 260).

3 Place of Refuge

1 Kuranko aver that the Marah were the first to migrate into the northeastern districts of present-day northern Sierra Leone, establishing their hegemony around the early seventeenth century. The clan name Marah derives from the verb ka mara: "to keep under control, to command." The long association of the Marah with conquest and power is suggested by the praiseword for Marah rulers, nomor (from no'e, "enforcement," and morgo, "person"). The Marah trace their ancestry to a warrior lord of Mande called Yilkanani — a deformation of the Arabic Dhul-Quarnein, "the two-horned," who was, of course, Alexander the Great (see Michael Jackson, *Paths toward a Clearing: Radical Empiricism and Ethnographic Inquiry* [Bloomington: Indiana University Press, 1969], chapter 10).

2 Yves Person, *Samori: Une Révolution Dyula*, vol. 1 (Ifan-Dakar: Mémoires de l'Institut Fondamental d'Afrique Noire, 1968), 461–63.

3 *Ibid.*, 478–79 n. 51; C. Magbaily Fyle, "Sewa," in *Dictionary of African Biography*, vol. 2, *Sierra Leone-Zaire* (Algonac, Mich.: Reference Publications, 1979), 144.

4 In Sierra Leone, the metaphor of eating is used in an intriguing range of situations. It may connote avarice and greed, capital accumulation, the illicit appropriation of things that belong to others, the consumption of the vital organs of others through witchcraft, and the cannibalizing of a victim's innards in order to gain power (see Mariane Ferme, *The Underneath of Things: Violence, History, and the Everyday in Sierra Leone* [Berkeley: University of California Press, 2001], 180–85; and Jean-François Bayart on "the politics of the belly" in *L'État en Afrique: La Politique du Ventre* [Paris: Fayard, 1989]).

4 In Kabala

1 Hannah Arendt, "Reflections on Violence," *New York Review of Books*, 27 February 1969, 24–26. In remarks that speak directly to the rebellion in Sierra Leone, Hannah Arendt writes elsewhere: "If tyranny can be described as the always abortive attempt to substitute violence for power, ochlocracy, or mob rule, which is its exact counterpart, can be characterized by the much more promising attempt to substitute power with strength" (*The Human Condition* [Chicago: University of Chicago Press, 1958], 203). She adds presciently: "*The vehement yearning for violence . . . is a natural reaction of those whom society has tried to cheat of their strength*" (203–204; emphasis added).

5 The Beef

1 As Rosalind Shaw has so persuasively argued, such fantasies of having one's essence drained, stolen, or "eaten," and access to symbolic capital blocked by men of power, are endemic in Sierra Leone, where inequality is often explained as a result of "economic witchcraft" (*Memories of the Slave Trade: Ritual and the Historical Imagination in Sierra Leone* [Chicago: University of Chicago Press, 2002], 201–24).

2 Milan Kalous, *Cannibals and Tongo Players of Sierra Leone* (Trentham, New Zealand: Wright and Carman, 1974), 94.

3 My thoughts on the relation between human worth and social rank echo Michael Ignatieff's meditation on needs and dues in Shakespeare's *King Lear* (Michael Ignatieff, *The Needs of Strangers* [London: Vintage, 1994], 35–36) — a reminder of the interesting parallels that might be traced between Renaissance Europe and contemporary West Africa.

4 There is ample evidence that status distinctions between Kuranko clans were often blurred, confused, or suspended in the historical past, making for considerable ambiguity when protocols of rank order are observed. This ambiguity is, in practice, resolved by making light of the relationship (i.e., instituting a joking relationship) between the clans concerned, in which verbal and gestural plays on master-slave, senior-junior, and ruler-commoner relationships abound (Michael Jackson, *The Kuranko* [London: Hurst, 1977], 156).

6 Within These Four Walls

1 Lamine Jusugarka, forty-six, was a security guard at Barclays Bank when the rebels entered Freetown on 6 January 1999. Lamine felt sure that he could handle the young men and boys, led by one called Junior, who invaded his neighborhood. But they were many, they were armed, and Lamine became one of their victims (*Scenes and Tales from a Hospital after the Rebel Invasion of Freetown,* http://free.freespeech.org/sierra-leone/civilwar/amputeetales.htm).

7 The Executions

1 Walter Benjamin, "Theses on the Philosophy of History, VI," in *Illuminations,* ed. and with an introduction by Hannah Arendt (New York: Schocken, 1969), 255.

2 A customary joking relationship (*sanakuiye tolon*) exists between the Marah rulers and the cattle-herding Fula in northern Sierra Leone. One day, for example, stopped at a gas station in the city, S. B. summoned the Fula proprietor (whom he knew well) to the car, asking: "Where you bastard pikin?" The derisive wordplay is a way of managing the ambivalent feelings that the Marah traditionally had toward the Fulani, on whom they relied for cattle and to whom they gave grazing rights, but whom they would not tolerate living among them.

3 Max Gluckman, *Custom and Conflict in Africa* (Oxford: Basil Blackwell, 1956), 27–53.

4 Details are from Abdul K. Koroma, *Sierra Leone: The Agony of a Nation* (Freetown: Andromeda, 1996), 9–17, augmented by references to Thomas S. Cox, *Civil-Military Relations in Sierra Leone: A Case Study of African Soldiers in Politics* (Cambridge: Harvard University Press, 1976).

5 Aminatta Forna, *The Devil That Danced on the Water* (London: Harper Collins, 2002), 398, 399–400.

8 Fina Kamara's Story

1 For Hannah Arendt, "action as beginning corresponds to the fact of birth" and is "the actualization of the human condition of natality" (*The Human Condition* [Chicago: University of Chicago Press, 1958], 178). Natality is infused by a "startling unexpectedness" that "is inherent in all beginnings and all origins." The new, she adds, "always happens against the overwhelming odds of statistical laws and their probability, which

for all practical, everyday purposes amounts to certainty; *the new therefore always appears in the guise of a miracle"* (178; emphasis added).

2 James Rupert, "Machete Terror Stalks Sierra Leone," *Guardian Weekly*, 3 January 1999, 12.

3 Hannah Arendt, *The Human Condition* (Chicago: University of Chicago Press, 1958), 237.

4 This conflict between reconciliation and justice was brought sharply into relief on 10 March 2003, when seven former RUF and AFRC junta leaders were indicted by Sierra Leone's war crimes tribunal. Ironically, two of the former RUF commanders had been about to launch projects funded by the government's National Committee for Disarmament, Demobilisation and Reintegration (NCDDR), and other ex–rebel commanders were also reportedly working on community development initiatives. "We actually had already approved four fisheries projects for Issa Sesay, Morris Kallon, Gibril Massaquoi and Eldred Collins," said the NCDDR's executive secretary, Dr. Francis Kai-Kai. Yet another ex–RUF commander, Augustine Gbao, was already at an "advanced stage" in implementing an agricultural project in his home village in Kenema District.

5 In March 2002, after I had left Sierra Leone and was drafting this chapter, news broke of several women in Sierra Leonean refugee camps who had charged UN personnel of rape. Such abuses of power are inevitable, Nietzsche might have argued, for the refugee is condemned to the abject position of a slave or bondsperson in relation to her guardians and caregivers. Not only does she lack the means to provide shelter or food for herself; she has no means to resist the free imaginings of the Other — who sees her only as an object, of compassion, of categorization, or of contempt — and must pay with her body for what she owes those who have given her life.

9 Tina Kome Marah

1 Lieutenant Colonel J. K. Trotter, "An Expedition to the Source of the Niger," *Geographical Journal* 10, no. 3 (1897): 386–401; *The Niger Sources and the Borders of the New Sierra Leone Protectorate* (London: Methuen, 1898).

2 Details are drawn from Tina Kome Marah's letter (22 December 1946) to the commissioner, Northern Province, Makeni, as well as from F. J. Moberly, comp., *Military Operations, Togoland and the Cameroons, 1914–1916* (London: HMSO, 1931); A. H. W. Haywood and F. A. S. Clarke, *The History of the Royal West African Frontier Force* (Aldershot: Gale and

Polden, 1964); M. Crowder, "The 1914–1918 European War and West Africa," in *History of West Africa*, vol. 2, ed. M. Crowder and J. F. A. Ajayi (London: Longmans, 1974); and M. Crowder, *The Story of Nigeria* (London: Faber and Faber, 1978).

3   Details from Tina Kome Marah's letter and from M. Crowder, *West Africa under Colonial Rule* (London: Hutchinson, 1968); and Sir Alan Burns, *History of Nigeria*, 7th ed. (London: Unwin Brothers, 1963).

10 Early Days

1   Claude Lévi-Strauss, *Tristes Tropiques*, trans. John and Doreen Weightman (London: Jonathan Cape, 1973), 57.

2   Friedrich Nietzsche, *Twilight of the Gods* (Harmondsworth: Penguin, 1968), 92.

13 In Government

1   Rugiatu was a niece of the Kabala town chief. At the time he married Rugiatu, S. B. was already married to Nassay Kamara — the mother of his elder daughters, Fatmata and Aisha.

2   It is worth pointing out that though these men were all "northerners" it was neither their ethnic nor their geographical provenance per se that determined their affinities and loyalties, but rather the kinds of personal and peer relationships — school backgrounds, long-established friendships, in-lawship — that tend to underlie political allegiances in all societies.

3   Fore Kande went on to compare belonging to ferensola with belonging to a conspiracy, because both involved intense and clandestine bonds. Not an ordinary conspiracy (*yanfe*), he said, in which only two or maybe three people are involved, but a deep conspiracy (*dede*) in which everyone is embroiled (*Yanfe anbe dede ke l ma na* — Yanfe and dede are not the same).

14 Thinking Back

1   John Berger, *The Sense of Sight* (New York: Pantheon, 1985), 266–67.

2   Friedrich Nietzsche, *Beyond Good and Evil: Prelude to a Philosophy of the Future*, trans. R. J. Hollingdale (Harmondsworth: Penguin, 1973), 173.

15 Seeds of Conflict

1 A paraphrase of Theodor Adorno, from "A Portrait of Walter Benjamin," in *Prisms,* trans. Samuel and Shierry Weber (Cambridge.: MIT Press, 1983), 230. Adorno goes on to say of Benjamin, "The rebus is the model of his philosophy."

2 Pierre Bourdieu, *Pascalian Meditations*, trans. Richard Nice (Cambridge: Polity, 2000), 228.

16 The War

1 References here are to W. H. Auden's famous poem about Brueghel's *Icarus* — "Musée de Beaux Arts."

2 The term *shadow state* is central to William Reno's invaluable commentary on this period: *Corruption and State Politics in Sierra Leone* (Cambridge: Cambridge University Press, 1995).

3 By the mid-1990s, political motives had paled into insignificance, despite the RUF leadership's insistence that the sole reason for waging the war was to liberate the country from oppression and corruption. When I asked small S. B. if he had seen any evidence of political ideology among the RUF who held him captive, he referred to a certain Mr. Lawrence, a high school graduate and slightly older man, who was second in command. But none of the other rebels explained their actions in political terms, he said. My former field assistant, Noah Marah, made the same observation. When he was abducted by rebels at Lunsar in 1996, he asked his captors what they were fighting for. They said, "Pappy [Foday Sankoh] has money for us." They had been promised money if they won the war. However, Noah said, they had no political agenda, no political motives. Noah's son Kaima said the same thing. The ones he knew that joined the RUF saw it as a way of getting money, and they went to Kono where the RUF controlled the diamond mining. "Others," Kaima added, "had grievances," and he mentioned some young men from the north who, cut out of their paternal inheritance, joined the RUF to pillage or destroy the property which, in their view, had been unjustly bequeathed to others. Unisa also mentioned kids he had known at school, with old scores to settle. Such comments make me uneasy about Paul Richards's confident interpretation of the rebellion as a "product of [a] protracted, post-colonial crisis of patrimonialism," triggered by global politico-economic changes in the 1980s that sharply reduced resources available for redistribution (*Fighting for the Rainforest: War, Youth and Resources in Sierra Leone* [London: International African Institute, in association

with James Currey and Heinemann, 1996], xviii). I share Allen Feldman's view that violence cannot be reduced to antecedent conditions, for the simple reason that it always "detaches itself from initial contexts and becomes the condition of its own reproduction" (*Formations of Violence: The Narrative of the Body and Political Terror in Northern Ireland* [Chicago: University of Chicago Press, 1991], 20). Accordingly, chronic violence involves a radical transformation of the sociohistorical conditions under which it emerged and the political rationale with which it began, and rapidly takes on a logic and life of its own — a conclusion, incidentally, that Hannah Arendt reached in her Eichmann book: "Even in the totalitarian book, in the chapter on ideology and terror, I mentioned the curious loss of ideological content that occurs among the elite of the movement. The movement itself becomes all important; the content of anti-semitism for instance gets lost in the extermination policy, for extermination would not have come to an end when no Jew was left to be killed. In other words, extermination per se is more important than anti-semitism or racism" (from a letter to Mary McCarthy, in *Between Friends: The Correspondence of Hannah Arendt and Mary McCarthy, 1949–1975*, ed. Carol Brightman [New York: Harcourt, Brace, 1995], 147–48).

4   On ressentiment, see Friedrich Nietzsche, *On the Genealogy of Morals* (Oxford: Oxford University Press, 1996), 22–37. While Fyodor Dostoevsky's *Notes from Underground* (1864) is surely the exemplary fictional account of ressentiment, the most perceptive ethnographic exploration of this emotion is, in my view, Michael W. Young's *Magicians of Manumanua: Living Myth in Kalauna* (Berkeley: University of California Press, 1983). See pages 72–73 for a succinct account of *unuwewe* (powerful resentment), the folk etymology of which suggests *uwe* as its root ("the term for the wild lawyer cane that tangles, coils, and ensnares with its vicious thorns") and thus implies that "this emotion is largely self-generated, the wounds self-inflicted."

5   Melissa Leach, "New Shapes to Shift: War, Parks and the Hunting Person in Modern West Africa," *Journal of the Royal Anthropological Institute* 6, no. 4 (2000): 577–95; Mariane Ferme, *The Underneath of Things: Violence, History, and the Everyday in Sierra Leone* (Berkeley: University of California Press, 2001), 223; Mariane Ferme, "La Figure du Chasseur et les Chasseurs-Milicens dans le Conflit Sierra-Léonais," *Politique Africaine* 82 (2001): 119–32.

6   Earl Conteh-Morgan and Mac Dixon-Fyle, *Sierra Leone at the End of the Twentieth Century: History, Politics, and Society* (New York: Peter Lang, 1999), 143.

7   Pierre Bourdieu, *Pascalian Meditations*, trans. Richard Nice (Cambridge: Polity, 2000), 223.

8   Hannah Arendt notes that the notion of progress for humanity as a whole, operating as a rule governing all processes in the human species—historical, evolutionary, and social—was unknown in the eighteenth century, but in modern times it has been evoked to justify violence by destroying the old in order to usher in the new, which, by definition, is better, truer, more adaptive, and more just ("Reflections on Violence," *New York Review of Books,* 27 February 1969, 22).

9   Precedents for the rebel trickster-hero and enfant terrible include the epic figures of Mande Sunjata and Gbentoworo (see my *Allegories of the Wilderness: Ethics and Ambiguity in Kuranko Narratives* [Bloomington: Indiana University Press, 1982], 127–32; and *The Politics of Storytelling: Violence, Transgression and Intersubjectivity*, [Copenhagen: Museum Tusculanum Press, 2002], 91–226). One should also remember that in precolonial times, West African societies were often at war with one another (for slaves, land, or plunder) and that many young men, after initiation, fought as warriors. This link between prowess as a fighter and masculinity remains in force, a "quiescent" metaphor, so to speak, that can be quickly realized in action.

10 I am echoing George Devereux's advocacy of a "double discourse" that explains human behavior in wartime from both sociological and psychological points of view, and citing his remarks on the 1956 Hungarian revolution in *Ethnopsychoanalysis: Psychoanalysis and Anthropology as Complementary Frames of Reference* (Berkeley: University of California Press, 1978), 125.

17 Day into Night

1   Milan Kalous, *Cannibals and Tongo Players of Sierra Leone* (Trentham: Wright and Carman, 1974), vii–x.

2   Richard Dooling, *White Man's Grave* (New York: Farrar, Straus, and Giroux, 1994), 174.

3   Wole Soyinka, *The Man Died: Prison Notes of Wole Soyinka* (Harmondsworth: Penguin, 1975), 100.

4   The Kuranko term for retribution or revenge is *tasare,* literally payback.

5   On the connection between paying damages or discharging a debt through inflicting pain and degradation on the body of the culprit or debtor, see Friedrich Nietzsche, *On the Genealogy of Morals* (Oxford: Oxford University Press, 1996), 46. Veena Das has made brilliant use of Nietzsche's comments in her account of the Partition riots of 1949 (*Critical Events* [Delhi: Oxford University Press, 1995], 182–85). Writing of "invisible" forms of symbolic violence in Sierra Leone, Mar-

ianne Ferme observes that getting "satisfaction" through the actual physical punishment of a political opponent is rarer than public ridicule and shaming—"singing in public songs that revealed embarrassing, concealed physical deformities, the infidelity of a spouse, or quirky personal habits" ("The Violence of Numbers: Consensus, Competition, and the Negotiation of Disputes in Sierra Leone," *Cahiers d'Études Africaines* 38 [1998]: 570).

6 Allen Feldman observes that "conditions and relations of antagonism are not identical and are often discontinuous" (*Formations of Violence: The Narrative of the Body and Political Terror in Northern Ireland* [Chicago: Chicago University Press, 1991], 20). That is to say, modal violence characteristically "detaches itself from initial contexts and becomes a condition of its own reproduction" (*ibid.*).

7 One ex–SLA combatant, who had been in Kabala during the 1994 attack (he was sixteen at the time), told Krijn Peters and Paul Richards in an interview, "I liked the army because we could do anything we liked to do. When some civilian had something I liked, I just took it without him doing anything to me. We used to rape women. Anything I wanted to do [I did]. I was free" (Krijn Peters and Paul Richards, "Fighting with Open Eyes; Youth Combatants Talking About War in Sierra Leone," in *Rethinking the Trauma of War,* edited by Patrick J. Bracken and Celia Petty [London: Free Association Books, 1998], 93).

8 Pierre Bourdieu, *Pascalian Meditations,* translated by Richard Nice (Cambridge: Polity Press, 2000), 229.

9 Geneviève Calame-Griaule, *Ethnologie et Langage: la Parole chez les Dogon* (Paris: Gallimard, 1965); and Dominique Zahan, *The Bambara,* (Leiden: E. J. Brill, 1974), 15.

10 See Michael Jackson and Ivan Karp, eds., introduction to *Personhood and Agency: The Experience of Self and Other in African Cultures,* Uppsala Studies in Cultural Anthropology 14 (1990): 15–30

11 In his classic study of peasant insurgency in colonial India, Ranajit Guha notes that forms of resisting or defying politically constituted authority often have precedents in everyday social life (*Elementary Aspects of Peasant Insurgency in Colonial India* [Delhi: Oxford University Press, 1987], 12), and he cites as an example the calendrical rituals of rebellion and role reversal that anthropologists have studied in great detail in India, Africa, and elsewhere. Ritualized, innocuous, simulated, and temporary inversions of the social order—such as the Medieval Feast of Fools and Lord of Misrule, the Shrove Tuesday carnival, the Nomkubulwana ceremonies of the Zulu, the Teyyam festival in Malabar, and the celebration of Holi rite—may, according to Guha's

argument, become models for the permanent violation of social hierarchies, a *"real* turning of things upside down" (36). A similar observation was made by Max Gluckman in one of his talks on the BBC's *Third Programme* in 1955: "The rebellion principle I have outlined for Africa does seem to pull together rules of succession, the law of treason, and other customs, and to explain to some extent the results of civil wars" (Gluckman, *Custom and Conflict in Africa* [Oxford: Blackwell, 1956], 48). Paul Richards has also noted the parallels between initiation and rebellion in his account of the RUF, but I do not agree with his emphasis on the ways in which the RUF sought to "manipulate to its advantage the cultural 'infrastructure' of rural life in Sierra Leone" (*Fighting for the Rainforest: War, Youth & Resources in Sierra Leone* [London: International African Institute, 1995], 30, 81), since cultural models for comprehending disorder and managing misrule are second nature, and do not necessarily have to be orchestrated or consciously mediated to make their appearance. Several trenchant insights on the gendered symbolism of the rebellions in Liberia and Sierra Leone are to be found in Marianne Ferme's essay on the violence of numbers ("The Violence of Numbers: Consensus, Competition, and the Negotiation of Disputes in Sierra Leone," *Cahiers d'Études Africaines* 38 [1998]: 560–61).

12 Paul Richards and Krijn Peters argue that "confusing war and play, child combatants are heedless of danger" ("Why We Fight: Voices of Youth Combatants in Sierra Leone," *Africa* 68, no. 2 [1998]: 183). Though young men often go to war as if it is an adventure or game, combat quickly destroys this illusion. Fear is endemic to all warfare (which is why the rebels devoted to so much effort to combating or masking it), and I agree with Johan Huizinga that combat can only be called play when "it is waged within a sphere whose members regard each other as equals or antagonists with equal rights." This condition changes, Huizinga observes, "as soon as war is waged outside the sphere of equals, against groups not recognized as human beings and thus deprived of human rights — barbarians, devils, heathens, heretics, and 'lesser breeds within the law'" (*Homo Ludens: A Study of the Play Element in Culture* [London: Paladin, 1970], 110–11).

18 The Reversals of Fortune

1 Abdul Koroma, *Sierra Leone: The Agony of a Nation* (Freetown: Andromeda, 1996), 52–53.

2   Salia Jusu-Sheriff was a former colleague of S. B. and a minister in Albert Margai's cabinet, who joined Siaka Stevens's APC government in April 1968 and was appointed first vice president.

3   Amartya Sen, *The Standard of Living*, ed. Geoffrey Hawthorn (Cambridge: Cambridge University Press, 1988), 26–29.

19 The Value of Shade

1   Michel Tournier has explored the differences between initiation and education with great subtlety, showing that postenlightenment modernity involves cleansing from the classroom the kinds of emotional bonds, corporal ordeals, personal relationships, magical techniques, and moral instructions that characterize initiation (*The Wind Spirit*, trans. Arthur Goldhammer [Boston: Beacon, 1988], 42–51). Tournier's insights find an echo in Caroline Bledisloe's observation that in Sierra Leone formal education is never enough to guarantee one's future; blessings must be earned as well. And while knowledge may be learned from books, blessings have to be earned from obedience and respect toward one's teachers and work performed for elders, as well as the endurance of hardship and the cultivation of benefactors ("The Cultural Transformation of Western Education in Sierra Leone," *Africa* 62, no. 2 [1992]: 182–202). The question arises, however, as to what happens when a person's conformity to this ideal brings no rewards. The real issue is then the vexed rationalizations and the vengeful fantasies that arise when the gap between expectation and reward widens, and one receives less than one reckons one deserves.

2   William James, *Essays in Radical Empiricism* (London: Longmans, Green, 1912), 34, 71.

3   Major A. G. Laing, *Travels in the Timanee, Kooranko and Soolima Countries* (London: John Murray, 1825), 186–87.

4   Laing, *Travels*, 433.

5   Michael Jackson, *Minima Ethnographica: Intersubjectivity and the Anthropological Project* (Chicago: Chicago University Press, 1998), 108–24.

6   John Mulgan, *Report on Experience* (London: Oxford University Press, 1947).

7   Odo Marquard, *In Defense of the Accidental: Philosophical Studies*, trans. Jeremy J. Shapiro (London: Allen Lane, 1991), 1–12.

21 In Conakry

1 According to the UNHCR 1998 Statistical Overview there were 192,200 Sierra Leonean refugees in Guinea by the end of 1997. By the end of 1998 there were an estimated 297,200 (Chris Coulter, *Organizing People and Places: Humanitarian Discourse and Sierra Leonean Refugees*, Working Papers in Cultural Anthropology, no. 10 [Dept. of Cultural Anthropology and Ethnology, Uppsala University, 2001], 16).

2 *Ibid.*, 19–20.

22 Trust and Truth

1 This association was particularly important in time of war, when it was imperative to know if strangers were enemy spies. Like Masonic lodges, the Doé had secret handshakes and modes of greeting, a special language, and other codes, to exclude noninitiates (see Michael Jackson, *The Kuranko* [London: Hurst, 1977], 229–30).

2 I am thinking here of Rosalind Shaw's *Memories of the Slave Trade: Ritual and the Historical Imagination in Sierra Leone* (Chicago: University of Chicago Press, 2002) and Mariane Ferme's *The Underneath of Things: Violence, History, and the Everyday in Sierra Leone* (Berkeley: University of California Press, 2001). It is also noteworthy that Denise Paulme should write of the Kissi (who suffered so much from Kuranko slave-raiding during the nineteenth century): "smiles, patience, and generous welcomes dissimulate their deepest feelings. Coming to know them better the observer is struck by the state of tension in which these apparently peaceful people live" ("Formes de Ressentiment et de Suspicion dans une Société Noire," *Journal de Psychologie* 4 [1949]: 969).

23 The Hotel

1 Karl Marx, *The Eighteenth Brumaire of Louis Bonaparte* (Moscow: Progress, 1984), 10–11.

2 Chris Coulter, *Organizing People and Places: Humanitarian Discourse and Sierra Leonean Refugees,* Working Papers in Cultural Anthropology, no. 10 (Dept. of Cultural Anthropology and Ethnology, Uppsala University, 2001), 21.

3 Michel Serres with Bruno Latour, *Conversations on Science, Culture, and Time*, trans. Roxanne Lapidus (Ann Arbor: University of Michigan Press, 1995), 57.

4   Michael Jackson, *The Blind Impress* (Palmerston North: Dunmore, 1997), 188–89.
5   Details concerning Walter Benjamin's reflections on this painting are drawn from Gershom Scholem's "Walter Benjamin and His Angel," in *On Jews and Judaism in Crisis: Selected Essays* (New York: Schocken, 1976), 198–236.
6   The following passage from *Austerlitz*, for example: "the darkness does not lift but becomes heavier as I think how little we can hold in mind, how everything is constantly lapsing into oblivion with every extinguished life, how the world is, as it were, draining itself, in that the history of countless places and objects which themselves have no power of memory is never heard, never described or passed on" (W. G. Sebald, *Austerlitz* [London: Hamish Hamilton, 2001], 30–31).

Index

MICHAEL JACKSON

is a professor of anthropology at the University of Copenhagen. His previous books include *At Home in the World* (Duke University Press, 1995), *Rainshadow: A Novel*, *Barawa and the Way Birds Fly in the Sky: An Ethnographic Novel*, and *The Kuranko: Dimensions of Social Reality in a West African Society*.